TRADE UNIONS AS A PRESSURE GROUP IN THE EUROPEAN COMMUNITY

To my Parents and Joanna

Trade unions as a pressure group in the European community.

EMIL JOSEPH KIRCHNER

SAXON HOUSE

First published in Great Britain 1977 by
SAXON HOUSE, Teakfield Limited,
Westmead, Farnborough, Hants., England

Reprinted 1978

ISBN 0 566 00175 6

Printed in Great Britain by
Ilfadrove Limited Barry, Glamorgan, S. Wales

CONTENTS

Acknowledgements

List of tables and figures

Tables

Figures

Acknowledgements

I wish to acknowledge my gratitude for assistance from several
sources. Above all, I would like to express my sincere appreciation
to Professor Barry Hughes who stimulated my initial interest in the
subject of integration and assisted me to arrange for the present
enterprise. His constant encouragement, advice and criticism has
helped me immensely. I would also like to thank Professor
Kenneth Grundy, whose teaching and advice contributed so much
towards the preparation of this book.

My thanks are also due to the Commission of the European
Communities, which supported the research by a generous grant
(Grants for Research into European Integration) and provided me
with the benefit of a five-month traineeship (*stage*); and to the
Economic and Social Committee of the European Communities for
its financial assistance and office facilities.

The original research necessitated a series of intensive interviews of
interest group officials and European Community administrators in
Brussels, and would not have been possible without a good deal of
generosity and forebearance on their part. I am grateful for their
support. In particular, I am indebted to the following members of
the Commission who assisted me in arranging interviews and advised
me on suitable contacts: Eduard de la Parra, Leo Crijns,
Philipe Van Praag and Detlef Fehrs; and to Helmut Ries,
Konrad Schwaiger, Adriano Graziosi, Otto Kuby and Mr Picco of the
Economic and Social Committee. A special word of thanks to
Leo Crijns, who was instrumental in introducing me to the
Economic and Social Committee and in offering me valuable advice
on a variety of aspects of the European Community which I have
generally tried to keep in mind when carrying out this study. Beyond
this, I should like to extend my thanks to Kaare Sandegren and
Walter Braun of the Secretariat of the European Trade Union
Confederation for their assistance in arranging interviews and making
publications available to me. I should also like to acknowledge the
help given me by all the other officials of the EC institutions and the
Secretariats of the European pressure group organisations to complete

this study.

I would like to extend my gratitude to David Robertson and Anthony Childs for their helpful suggestions.

Finally, my thanks to my wife, who typed the entire manuscript and who helped me greatly in the editing.

In conclusion, I would like to point out that the bulk of the documents which covered the research period between mid-1968 and mid-1974 only existed in French and German and needed translation. I have translated these to the best of my ability but inevitably, in translating idiomatic expressions, the authenticity cannot always be entirely guaranteed. A similar situation arose in interviews.

E.J.K.

1   Trade unions, social policy and the European Community

Introduction

This book is concerned with four independent, though interrelated, facets of research regarding the process of integration in the European Community (EC). These facets are:

1. The co-operative or integrative efforts and achievements among trade unions at the European level;

2. The impact of European trade union organisations on social policy harmonisation of the EC;

3. The Commission's role and effectiveness in the process of EC social policy harmonisation; [1]

4. The trend of social policy harmonisation in the EC.

Although the importance of pressure groups and the Commission in the process of integration has hitherto received a great deal of attention from such scholars as Ernst Haas, Leon Lindberg and Carl Friedrich, only a few systematic attempts have been made to empirically assess their impact on this process. [2] This is even more the case with regard to trade unions as an individual pressure group. [3]

This deficiency, plus the objections raised by Stanley Hoffmann [4] and others, on the relevance of pressure groups in general and trade unions in particular as important actors in the integrative process, as well as the prominent role played by trade unions in policy making in the national context, necessitate European-wide or Community level research and empirical evidence. This would then clarify the strengths, weaknesses or potentials of these particular actors in EC social policy integration. Given the important functions performed by the Commission with regard to initiating Community legislation and aggregating demands of various groups for Community legislation, the study of the role of the Commission, as well as its relationship with the trade unions and other groups, [5] will help to assess the impact which these two actors have, either alone or together, on EC social policy harmonisation.

For the purpose of this study, the term 'pressure group' is based on Robert Lieber's application of the term. [6] It designates those organisations which are occupied, at any time, in trying to influence the policy of public bodies in their own chosen direction. Community or European pressure groups are defined as those associations which consist of representatives of the main national pressure groups in a particular branch, who are concerned with social policy and seek to influence the policy legislation of the central institutions of the EC in the field of social policies.

Finally, social policy as a sector of study was selected because of the logical expectation that integration in the free movement of labour sector (especially after the achievement date of mid-1968) might result in integrative activities in the social policy sector.

Aims of the research

Specifically, this book attempts to analyse:

1.   The rate of formation and level of strength which Community pressure group associations have developed;

2.   The kind of influence which these associations have exerted on the central institutions of the EC [7] with regard to social policy harmonisation [8];

3.   The type of administrative skill or ability practised by the Commission in the preparation of social policy proposals to the Council of Ministers;

4.   The level of harmonisation achieved for certain issues of social policy in the EC, and the extent to which the activities of Community pressure groups and the Commission contributed towards this end.

Going beyond the activities or performances of Community pressure groups and the Commission on the above point, an attempt will be made to analyse conditions or factors which either contributed to or inhibited these activities. In particular, we will examine the extent to which activities of pressure groups and the Commission stemmed from factors arising out of:

1.   Decisions by the Council of Ministers regarding the free

movement of labour, the Customs Union and the Common Agricultural Policy

2.   Proposals prepared by the Commission on industrial policy

3.   Technological changes

4.   International trade changes such as those on tariff and currency exchange rates.

The implications of these factors on the activities of pressure groups and the Commission are further elaborated in figure 1.1. It is further expected that advantages or disadvantages of Community action for the Community pressure groups vary, depending on which factor is involved (Customs Union, free movement of labour, technological changes). Moreover, these factors will affect the employers' organisations and the trade unions in the EC in different ways, so that these two categories of groups will stimulate *each other* into organising their respective activities at Community level.

In addition to the examination of the above factors, we will also consider the position taken by the national governments, and to a lesser extent by national political parties on:

1.   Social policy harmonisation at Community level;

2.   Co-operation among trade unions at European or Community level, as well as consultation and co-operation between trade unions and the Commission.

Such an examination will determine more precisely the conditions under which pressure groups and the Commission are either more or less effective in their efforts and activities at Community level.

The impact made by trade unions and the Commission on social policy harmonisation at Community level, the prevailing trend of social policy harmonisation at Community level, and to a lesser extent at national level, will be measured on five particular social policy issues:

1.   The improvement or extension of social security benefits for migrant workers;

2.   The improvement or extension of the European Social Fund, i.e. in financial resources and types of

3

Figure 1.1   Factors or conditions for pressure group and Commission activities

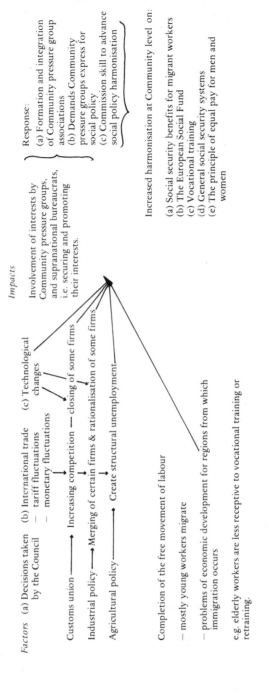

Factors (a) Decisions taken   (b) International trade   (c) Technological
               by the Council   — tariff fluctuations   changes
                                              — monetary fluctuations

Customs union ──────⟶ Increasing competition ── closing of some firms

Industrial policy ──⟶ Merging of certain firms & rationalisation of some firms

Agricultural policy ──⟶ Create structural unemployment

Completion of the free movement of labour

— mostly young workers migrate

— problems of economic development for regions from which
   immigration occurs

e.g. elderly workers are less receptive to vocational training or
retraining.

Impacts

Involvement of interests by
Community pressure groups,
and supranational bureaucrats,
i.e. securing and promoting
their interests.

Increased harmonisation at Community level on:

(a) Social security benefits for migrant workers
(b) The European Social Fund
(c) Vocational training
(d) General social security systems
(e) The principle of equal pay for men and
    women

Response:

(a) Formation and integration
    of Community pressure group
    associations
(b) Demands Community
    pressure groups express for
    social policy
(c) Commission skill to advance
    social policy harmonisation

interventions;

3.   The achievement of a common vocational training policy;

4.   The achievement of equal pay for men and women;

5.   The achievement of harmonisation of social security schemes in general.

There have been four books primarily concerned with trade union movements or structures at European level. One is the book by Michel de Grave entitled *Dimension Européenne du Syndicalisme Ouvrier,* published in 1968. The second is by Colin Beever on *Trade Unions and Free Labour Movement in the EEC,* published in 1969. The third book, by Marguerite Bouvard, is entitled *Labor Movements in the Common Market Countries,* published in 1972; and the fourth is by Norris Willatt on *Multinational Unions,* published in 1974. [9] The main shortcoming of these four books is that in the first three cases they were undertaken before the important changes occurred in the European trade union movement and in social policy at Community level, or, especially in the fourth case, they deal mainly with the structural changes and organisational objectives of European trade union organisations, rather than with their cohesiveness and effectiveness. As far as possible, the findings of these books have been incorporated in this book.

Procedures for the research

This research will involve four basic steps. Chapter 2 will examine whether, in the process of reformulating expectations and demands from the completion of the free movement of labour sector to issues of social policy integration, trade unions have approached one another across national boundaries by formulating either new or 'stronger' associations at Community or European level. This chapter will also examine the main motives for or against the co-operative or integrative efforts of trade union movements at European level. In chapter 3, the prospects of formulating and agreeing to common ETUC policies will be analysed. Chapter 4 will ascertain the extent to which trade unions and employers' organisations are interested in furthering social policy integration at Community level.

In chapter 5, we will look at whether the bureaucrats of the EC central institutions, primarily the Commission, can exercise their skill in such a way as to contribute to the expansion of social policy

5

integration at the EC level. An important part of this research step will be to analyse how skilfully the Commission has:

a)   used the interpretations of the Treaty of Rome in the preparation of proposals concerned with social policy;

b)   channelled the different demands expressed by Community pressure groups;

c)   acted as a broker during bargaining with the Council of Ministers.

In chapter 6 an attempt will be made to ascertain the degree of influence Community pressure groups and the Commission, both individually and collectively, have exercised with respect to the Council of Ministers, regarding legislative and executive action on the five social policy issues. Chapter 7 will report on the final step in the research. It will examine the actual legislation (regulations, directives, decisions and recommendations) passed by the Council of Ministers with regard to the five social policy issues studied in this research. In particular, this chapter will look at the trend of social policy harmonisation in the EC since mid-1968.

Methodology

The data base of this book consisted of a series of approximately one hundred and ten interviews: seventy with Community pressure group officials and forty with administrators of the EC institutions, primarily the Commission and the Economic and Social Committee. For the substantial part of these interviews the interviewing time varied from a minimum of one hour to a maximum of three and a half hours. The interviews were open-ended. The scheme presented in figure 1.2 was usually shown to the interviewee in order to make him (her) aware of the nature of the interview, and this scheme was then used as the general guide-line for the questions. In some interviews emphasis had to be placed on organisational changes rather than on shift in orientations (from the national to the Community level), inter-relationship among different trade union movements, motives for forming new trade union associations at the Community level, and

Figure 1.2   Scheme used to direct interviews with pressure group officials

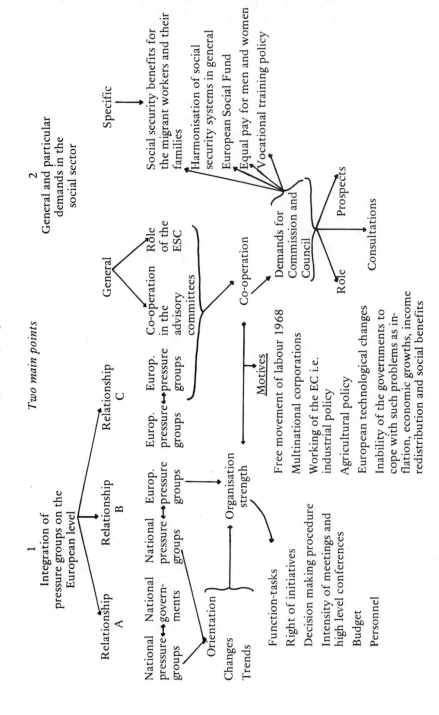

views regarding the central institutions of the EC.

For example, the Secretaries General and Secretaries of the Secretariats of Community pressure groups were much more competent in dealing with the actual organisational changes of personnel, budgetary and decision-making procedures, than with the other issues.

Complementing and supplementing the data base on interviews, a complete and exhaustive survey of publications of Community pressure groups on their organisational structures and their demands on social policy harmonisation in the EC was carried out. In some cases (Dutch, German and British trade unions) certain national publications were surveyed. In addition, a survey was made of the Commission's documents relating to social policy and of the Official Journals of the EC for references to legislative and executive actions in the social policy sector; and of the publications of the Economic and Social Committee on social policy.

By incorporating both interviews and written statements, some of the negative aspects connected with the adoption of one research technique alone can be avoided. [10] The data were mainly collected for the period from mid-1968 (completion of the free movement of labour) to mid-1975; [11] complemented by additional data collection (mainly publication surveys and some follow-up interviews) for the period between mid-1975 to the end of 1976.

Indicators for chapter 2

The following types of data are collected for chapter 2:

a) Changes in the number, size and structure of Community or European trade union organisations;

b) Changes Community or European trade union organisations intended regarding the traditional relationship between trade unions and the national governmental administrations, i.e. changes indicating an increasing orientation of trade unions towards Community concerns and a desire to participate in these concerns;

c) Agreements between Community pressure groups, i.e. collective bargaining agreements between employers' organisations and trade unions;

8

d) Motives or reasons mentioned by Community or European trade unions, either for forming new associations at Community level or for strengthening the organisational structures of the existing associations.

e) Measures introduced by governments to maintain the attention and co-operation of both trade unions and employers' organisations for national considerations.

This analysis of the rate of formation of Community or European trade unions and their relative level of strength will provide information on:

a) Possible changes in the traditional relationship between trade unions and the national governmental administration;

b) Integration at the trade union level, i.e. what are the organisational structures of these Community or European trade union organisations; what is their relative strength with respect to either their national affiliations or to European employers' organisations; and what were the main motives for forming new Community or European trade union associations?

Indicators for chapter 3

Indicators for chapter 3 centre on the ability of the Community or European trade union organisations to formulate common policies with regard to:

a) Industrial democracy: dealing with such issues as works councils, workers' participation, asset formation and collective bargaining;

b) Integration of the European Community: involving such issues as Economic and Monetary Union, majority decision-making in the Council of Ministers, and direct elections to the European Parliament.

These findings will provide an indicator of the extent to which affiliates of the Community or European trade union organisations differ or agree on key policy issues. It will also introduce information on the extent to which cohesion prevails in the

European trade union organisations.

Indicators for chapter 4

To measure the activities of Community pressure groups (both employers' organisations and trade unions) with respect to the central institutions of the EC (primarily the Commission) the following indicators are applied:

a) Demands which certain Community pressure groups make with respect to the Commission regarding: (1) the Treaty provisions in the field of social policy and their realisation; and (2) the expansion of social policy provisions at Community level specified in the Treaty of Rome;

b) Motives or reasons mentioned by Community pressure groups for or against increased social policy harmonisation.

These findings will provide an indicator of:

a) The degree of social policy harmonisation desired by Community pressure groups;

b) Institutional growth, by helping to clarify the degree to which the EC institutions are looked upon as a potential source of rewards.

Indicators for chapter 5

Indicators for chapter 5 centre on the Commission's skill with regard to:

a) The interpretation of Treaty provisions for the expansion of social policy at Community level;

b) The support of Community pressure groups in:

(1) the solution of compromises achieved by the Commission between demands of employers' organisations and trade unions on social policy;

(2) the balance the Commission can maintain in consultations between the employers' organisations and the trade unions;

c) The timing and type of legislation used in proposals as well as the transfer of responsibility and financial resources asked for from the Member States to the central institutions of the EC. Included in this category will be enquiries into the bureaucratic role behaviour of the Commission with respect to the national civil services;

d) Motives or reasons expressed by the Commission for seeking increased social policy harmonisation at Community level.

These findings will provide information on the extent to which the activities of the Commission contributed to the legislative and executive actions of the Council of Ministers in the EC social policy sector.

Indicators for chapter 6

In chapter 6 the following data will be introduced:

a) The extent to which demands by Community or European trade union organisations on the five social policy issues (listed on page 3) were reflected in the legislative and executive actions of the Council of Ministers;

b) The extent to which demands by Community or European employers' groups on the five social policy issues were reflected in the legislative and executive actions of the Council of Ministers.

These findings will provide an indicator of the effectiveness of Community or European trade union organisations as a pressure group in the social policy sector of the EC, i.e. the effectiveness of trade unions in comparison with that of the employers' organisations.

Indicators for chapter 7

At this stage of the research, the following information will be organised:

a) Comparison of EC social policy harmonisation achieved between the period from 1960 to mid-1968 and the period

11

from mid-1968 to 1976; i.e. the extent of legislative and
executive action introduced in each period;

b) Legal judgements passed by the Court of Justice related
to the social policy sector;

c) Changes in social policy legislation of the Member States
of the EC.

Moreover, data will be collected on the share of EC financial
contributions towards vocational training or retraining programmes
and the competences the Commission has in administering EC
financial resources. These findings will provide information on the
trend of social policy harmonisation in the EC; showing the
achievements and prospects of EC social policy and assessing the
extent of convergence or divergence in EC Member States'
legislation or activities on the issues of social security provisions
in general, such as sickness benefits, old age pensions and family
benefits.

Conclusion

To reiterate, the task of this book is to examine the conditions
under which Community or European trade union organisations
contribute to the process of social policy harmonisation in the EC.
The examination of conditions underlying this process has hitherto
received insufficient attention from scholars of integration. [12]
Statements such as: '... interest groups, bureaucratic and technocratic elites, have typically seen European integration as one logical
path towards the maximisation of welfare or profit,' [13] need
precision.
    Thus the conditions under which trade unions and bureaucrats
become active in the EC integrative process and the conditions under
which these activities lead to the expansion of decision-making
capacities of the EC central institutions are the central concerns of
this book.

Notes

[1]   Basically there are two sets of pressure groups concerned with
social policy, distinguished by the importance each set assigns to

social policy harmonisation: (a) trade unions; and (b) employers' organisations of industry, agriculture and crafts. Whereas trade unions assign primary importance to social affairs in the pursuit of their interests, employers' organisations delegate a subordinate role to social policy in comparison to their primary concern with industrial or agricultural policy harmonisation. Whereas trade unions are seemingly more involved in the initiation of social policy with respect to the Commission or the Council, employers' organisations appear to concentrate heavily on expressing the extent to which they can accept the content of what is proposed for initiation. This research will give primary attention to the activities of trade unions, but will also present the stand taken by employers' organisations on social policy harmonisation at Community level.

[2]   Among these attempts are: Leon Lindberg and Stuart Scheingold, *Europe's Would-Be Polity,* Prentice-Hall, Englewood Cliffs, N.J., 1970; Carl J. Friedrich, *Europe: An Emergent Nation?,* Harper & Row, New York 1969; Carl J. Friedrich, (ed.) *Politische Dimensionen der Europäischen Gemeinschaftsbildung* Westdeutscher Verlag, Cologne, 1968; Werner J. Feld, 'National Economic Interest Groups and Policy Formation in the European Economic Community,' *Political Science Quarterly* 81, 1966, pp 392-411; Werner J Feld, *Transnational Business Collaboration among Common Market Countries,* Praeger, New York, 1970; Terkel Nielsen 'Aspects of the EEC Influence of European Groups in the Decision-Making Processes: The Common Agricultural Policy,' *Government and Opposition* 6, Autumn 1971, pp 539-558; and Gerald Braun, *Die Rolle der Wirtschaftsverbände im agrarpolitischen Entscheidungs-prozess der Europäischen Wirtschaftsgemeinschaft,* Duncker & Humblot, Berlin, 1972.

[3]   Some notable exceptions are: Viktor Schierwater, 'Der Arbeitnehmer und Europa-Integrationstendenzen und-Struckturen im Sozialbereich des Gemeinsamen Marktes,' in Carl J. Friedrich (ed.) *Politische Dimensionen der Europäischen Gemeinschaftsbildung,* pp 294-357; Colin Beever, *Trade Unions and Free Labour Movement in the European Economic Community,* Chatham House and Political and Economic Planning, London, 1969; and Marguerite Bouvard, *Labor Movements in the Common Market Countries: The Formation of a European Pressure Group,* Praeger, New York, 1972.

[4]   For example, Hoffmann argues that trade union activities are not enough to bring about greater social policy harmonisation in the EC, and that: 'We may posit as a rule that governments will want to keep the monopoly of distributing benefits to its citizens as long as

13

possible.' See Stanley Hoffmann, Foreword to *Labor Movements in the Common Market Countries* by Bouvard.

[5]   In addition it should be noted that 'influence' is not only exercised by the Community pressure groups on the Commission, but often by the Commission on the Community pressure groups.

[6]   However, Lieber interchanges the terms 'pressure group' and 'interest group'. See Robert Lieber, 'Interest Groups and Political Integration: British Entry into Europe,' in Richard Kimber and J.J. Richardson (eds), *Pressure Groups in Britain,* J.M. Dent & Sons, London, 1974, p.28. For an excellent treatment of the term 'pressure group' and a survey of the various definitions which have been applied in the literature on 'group' studies elsewhere, see the Introduction to Kimber and Richardson's book on *Pressure Groups in Britain.*

[7]   The EC has four principal organs: (a) the Council of Ministers, composed of a Minister (either in Foreign Affairs, Agriculture, Social Affairs, etc.) from each Member Government, which enacts the Community's legislation; (b) the Commission, composed of persons serving without instructions from Member Governments, although chosen by the Member Governments, which formulates policy proposals and administers the legislation adopted; (c) the European Parliament, composed of parliamentarians chosen by national Parliaments, which has the duty to advise the other bodies on Community policy and the power to remove the Commission from office; and (d) the Court of Justice, composed of judges chosen by Member Governments, whose main function is to prevent any action of the institutions that violates a Community regulation or Treaty. For further details, see W.H. Clark, *The Politics of the Common Market,* Prentice Hall, Englewood Cliffs, 1967.

[8]   To a lesser extent, this book will be concerned with the way in which *national pressure groups* try to influence the *EC institutions* via their national governments, or with the influence the central institutions of the EC exert through Community pressure groups on the national governments. Regarding the latter, however, tribute is paid to Feld's belief that: ' ... the maximum interaction between Commission and national interest groups may also serve as 'protractors' in the event of serious conflicts between the Commission and Member Governments.' See Feld, 'National Economic Interest Groups,' p.409.

[9]   Michel de Grave, *Dimension Européenne du Syndicalisme Ouvrier*, Université Catholique de Louvain, Louvain, 1968; Colin Beever, *Trade Unions and Free Labour Movement in the EEC,*

Chatham House and Political and Economic Planning, London, 1969; Marguerite Bouvard, *Labor Movements in the Common Market Countries: The Formation of a European Pressure Group*, Praeger, New York, 1972; Norris Willatt, *Multinational Unions*, Financial Times, London, 1974.

[10]   For example, attitudes expressed in interviews might be belied in practice. On the other hand, many important aspects of integrative activities by pressure groups and administrators of the EC do not find their way into written material.

[11]   The empirical data collection was based in part on the contacts and interviews I had with Commission officials and the material which was made available to me during my traineeship ('stage') at the Commission of the EC during the period from January 1973 to June 1973; in part on the experience I gained while working at the Economic and Social Committee of the EC from July 1973 to Spring 1974; and in part from participation in conferences between the social partners and the Commission during my stay in Brussels from January 1973 to Summer 1974.

[12]   As Stanley Hoffmann points out: 'Until now, in the study of Western European integration, theory has somewhat run ahead of empirical data presentation.' Stanley Hoffmann in a Foreword to Marguerite Bouvard's book *Labor Movements in the Common Market Countries*, Praeger, New York, 1972.

[13]   This statement was made by Lindberg and Scheingold, *Europe's Would-Be Polity*, p.124.

2 Trade union organisation in Europe

Introduction

This chapter deals with the co-operative and integrative attempts by national trade unions at the Community or European level after the EC decisions for the final stage of the free movement of labour and the creation of the Customs Union in July 1968. One of the main aims of this chapter is to examine whether the different trade union movements have, since mid-1968, either formed new associations or strengthened existing ones at the Community or European level, in spite of their technological, religious and political differences.

Specifically, our analysis will be guided along the following questions:

a) What are the organisational structures of European trade union organisations, and what is their relative strength with respect to both their national sub-units and the European employers' organisations?

b) What are the main motives for or against the co-operative or integrative efforts of trade union movements at the European level?

Pressure groups at Community level by mid-1968

In mid-1968 there existed three main trade union movements plus a trade union organisation for white-collar workers at European Community level. The three main trade union movements at this level reflected the formation of trade unions on the international level, namely:

1. *World Federation of Trade Unions (WFTU)*

This Federation was made up of trade unions of the socialist countries, and Communist unions elsewhere from 50 different countries, with a total membership of approximately 150 million, [1] of whom two-thirds were in Russia. Both the Confédération Général du Travail (CGT) from France, with a membership of about

2.4 million, and the Confederazione Generale Italiana del Lavoro (CGIL) with a membership of 3.8 million, were members of this international organisation. No West European regional organisation existed (and still does not exist) but in 1967 the CGT and CGIL set up a Standing Committee with a Secretariat in Brussels.

2. *International Confederation of Free Trade Unions (ICFTU)*

After the withdrawal of the American AFL-CIO in 1969, the ICFTU represented 115 affiliated organisations in 91 countries with a total membership of approximately 48.6 million. Politically, the ICFTU was (and is) broadly Social Democrat. By mid-1968, the European Secretariat of the ICFTU consisted of seven national organisations from the six original Member States of the EC and comprised a membership of about 12 million. There was also in existence a so-called European Regional Organisation of the ICFTU, comprising not only trade unions belonging to the European Secretariat but also those of the other European affiliations to the ICFTU, mainly the EFTA countries.

3. *World Confederation of Labour (WCL)*

This organisation grew out of the International Federation of Christian Trade Unions (IFCTU) which ceased to be officially Christian in 1969, and which had at that time approximately 14 million members in 76 countries. The European Secretariat of the WCL consisted of seven national organisations (including one associated) from the original six EC Member States, plus one organisation from Austria, two from Switzerland and one from Malta by mid-1968; with a total membership of about 3 million.

How these three European Secretariats of the international trade union organisations plus their affiliated industry branch associations compared with the representation of other pressure groups at the Community level is illustrated in table 2.1. This table tries to show the number of so-called Community pressure groups, defined in chapter 1, in different categories, and identifies the central, as well as industry branch organisations [2] that existed in mid-1968 of each category. Note that Appendix A explains the abbreviations used here. An illustration on the distinction between central organisations and specialised industry branch associations, as well as on the relationship between these different organisations, is provided on page 21.

The sources for table 2.1 were two reports produced by the Commission. One lists agricultural organisations: the *Repertoire of Non-Governmental Agricultural Organisations at Community Level;* and the other details non-agricultural economic organisations: *Joint Organisations of Industrial, Craft, Commercial and Service Associations, Associations of Liberal Professionals, Trade Unions and Consumer Groups.* [3]

The table 2.1 total of 321 Community pressure groups was not derived from a simple count of all Community pressure groups listed in the above-mentioned Repertoires. There are approximately one hundred organisations which are listed in both Repertoires. This double listing is in part responsible for conflicting accounts researchers have given on the number of existing Community pressure groups. For example, Lindberg notes that by 1966, 350 groups had formed an organisation at the Community level, whereas Fischer indicates that this number was 273 in 1965. Similarly, while Neunreither and Sidjanski list 350-400 and 350 Community pressure groups, respectively, for 1968, Hammerich mentions 300 for the same year. [4]

Table 2.1 indicates that the number of employers' organisations at the Community level was much higher than that of the trade unions and consumer groups. The central organisation of the Union of Industries of the EC (UNICE) and its associated intermediary groups and branches alone numbered ninety-four, in comparison to the twenty-eight organisations and associations of the trade unions and consumer groups. In addition to the differences in quantity, there were in 1968 also differences in quality between employers' organisations and trade unions. Specifically, the organisational strength of UNICE and the Committee of Professional Agricultural Organisations in the EC (COPA) differed from that of the trade unions in at least three important respects:

a) Both UNICE and COPA had established central organisations which were independent of their respective international organisations. In comparison, the two trade union central organisations, the ICFTU and the WCL, had only established European Secretariats and decisions had to be made by these at the international organisations. Moreover, there were more intermediary or branch associations of UNICE and COPA which had established independent European organisations (independently of their international organisations) than on the trade union side, [5] and the relationship between the central organisation and the

18

Table 2.1
Pressure group organisations
at Community level

1   Industry

Industry in general
Central organisation: UNICE (Union of
Industries of the EC)   1
Intermediary or interprofessional industrial
associations: 19 sectorial industrial branches
with 93 sub-sectorial industrial groups   93

Food processing industries
Central organisation: UNICE (Committee of
Agricultural and Food Industries of UNICE)   1
Intermediary or interprofessional food
processing associations   52

2   Agricultural Producers and Agricultural Co-operatives

Producers
Central organisation: COPA (Committee of
Professional Agricultural Organisations in the
EC)   1
Intermediary or interprofessional agricultural
associations   15

Agricultural co-operatives
Central organisation: COGECA (General
Committee of Agricultural Co-operatives of
the EC)   1
Intermediary or interprofessional agricultural
co-operatives   8

3   Trade/Commerce

Central organisation: COCCEE (Committee of
Commercial Organisations of the EC)   1
Intermediary or interprofessional commercial
associations:
a) agriculture   32
b) others   27
Other commercial associations   5

Table 2.1 (continued)

4   Crafts: small and medium-sized business undertakings

    Central organisation: UACEE (Union of Crafts
of the EC)   1
    Intermediary or interprofessional associations   5

5   Service organisations   12

6   Liberal professions   26

7   Transport   5

8   Trade unions

    Central organisations:

    a) European Secretariat of the ICFTU
(International Confederation of Free
Trade Unions)   1
    b) European Secretariat of the WCL
(World Confederation of Labour)   1

    Intermediary or interprofessional trade union
associations:

    a) associated with the European Secretariat
of the ICFTU   10
    b) associated with the European Secretariat
of the WCL   11

    Other trade union organisations   2

9   Consumer groups

    Liaison committee of the consumers   1

    Other consumer organisations   2

    Miscellaneous   7

                             TOTAL: 321

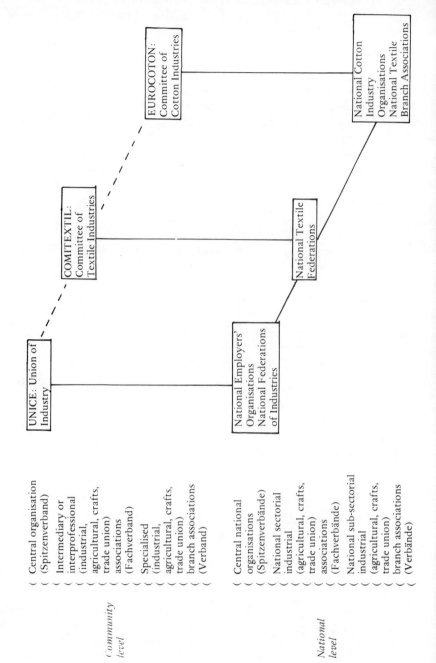

Figure 2.1 An illustration of European pressure group organisations in the textile industry

intermediary branch associations was more formalised, for example, in the case of COPA, [6] than on the trade union side. The latter point was (and still is) particularly important with regard to the flexibility or negotiating strength of a central organisation with respect to the Commission.

b) Both UNICE and COPA (the management organisations) could speak with one voice for their respective sectors. In comparison, the trade unions had at least four different organisations representing the workers' interests in the EC, namely: the ICFTU, the WCL, the CGT and CGIL (Communist) of France and Italy, respectively; and the European Secretariat of the International Confederation of Executive Staffs (white-collar workers). Despite the fact that there was (and still is) some co-operation at the national level between the CGT and CGIL with other unions, Community level relations between the Secretariat of the CGT and CGIL, and the other two main trade union movements of ICFTU and WCL were almost non-existent in mid-1968. In contrast, the European Secretariat of the ICFTU co-operated to a certain extent with the European Secretariat of the WCL in the pursuit of Community social policy interests, but this co-operation was based more on a tacit understanding than on any prescribed rule.

c) Financially, UNICE was better placed than the trade union organisations. [7]

Having examined the relative position of trade union representation at the Community level in mid-1968, we now proceed to examine the major organisational changes of European trade unions made, and the degree of collaboration reached among the different trade union organisations — after the free movement of labour was achieved and after the Customs Union came into being.

Trade union representation at Community level since mid-1968

The interviews and publications surveyed reveal that major co-operative and integrative trends have taken place, both within and between the European affiliates of the three main international trade union organisations (WFTU, ICFTU and WCL) since 1969. They have taken important steps to strengthen their organisations at the European level, to foster inter-trade union co-operation and to seek a unified European trade union movement.

By setting up, first, two European central organisations in 1969 — the European Confederation of Free Trade Unions (ECFTU) [8] and the European Organisation of the World Confederation of Labour (EO/WCL) — which were independent of the international organisations in terms of decision-making rights and budget, the nucleus was established from which a geographic enlargement took place with the joining of ECFTU and the EFTA wing of the ICFTU to form the European Trade Union Confederation (ETUC) in March 1973. The Spanish trade union, UGT, was also a founding member of the ETUC. Since then the ETUC organisation has strengthened its position by being able to integrate the national affiliations of the EO/WCL (January 1974), [9] the Irish TUC, the Finnish SAK and the Spanish STV (all in March 1974), the Italian Communist Trade Union, CGIL, (Summer 1974) and the Greek Confederation of Labour (October 1976). With the exception of the French CGT which, in a letter of Summer 1975, explored the conditions stipulated by the ETUC for membership without, however, applying officially for membership, and the European Trade Union Organisation of Executive Staff, all major Western European trade unions now belong to the ETUC, comprising by December 1976, 31 member organisations from 18 countries and a membership of approximately 38 million. Simultaneously, the ETUC has increased its personnel [10] in the General Secretariat to levels comparable with those of UNICE and COPA, and has narrowed substantially the gap with regard to the annual budget of UNICE and COPA. [11]

Moreover, both the ECFTU and the EO/WCL had adopted two-thirds majority decision-making (except on vital issues such as new members) in their congresses and executive meetings by 1969. This practice not only continued under the ETUC but had, to some extent, been strengthened (voting on new members). By adopting majority decision-making procedures, an important element has been added to the strengthening of European trade union organisations, on the one hand, and to the gradual shift of trade union orientations from the national to the Community level, on the other. Thus, the trade unions have demonstrated that setbacks in the introduction of majority decision-making in the Council of Ministers were not sufficient to deter them from adopting this very practice. They differed in this regard from the employers' organisations, especially UNICE and COCCEE, which still maintain unanimity in their decision-making. COPA has only recently (1973) changed to adopt majority decision-making. More on this later.

Intermediate and branch trade union organisation

The importance of developing a close working relationship between the central trade union organisations and the industry trade union branches was emphasised by most of the trade union officials who were interviewed, and was expressed in various statements by the Secretariats of the ECFTU/ETUC and the EO/WCL. But in spite of the efforts made by the ECFTU, EO/WCL or ETUC, [12] there has been, with a few exceptions, no equal accomplishment in developing close relationships, either between the intermediary or branch associations or between these associations and the central organisations, to that prevailing on the employers' side.

The reason for this deficiency, at least between 1973 to 1975, can be found partially in the lack of 'organisational machinery' on the part of the industry branches, i.e. the failure of most branches, except the European Metal Federation (EMF), the European Federation of Agricultural Workers (EFA) [13] and, to some extent, of the European Federation of Building Workers and Wood Workers in the Community, to set up European organisations independently of the international trade union branch organisation with the necessary finance, personnel and decision-making apparatus. To correct some of these shortcomings and to establish at the sub-trade union movement level the same working atmosphere which has developed at the central level, the ETUC tried to set some standards for the acceptance of industry trade union committees. [14] Some of the industry trade union committees view the ETUC standards with certain reservations. They fear that a too rigid relationship with the ETUC would run counter to their interests, which in part rest on their ties with the international trade union branch federation. They would rather favour a flexible or pragmatic collaboration to meet the European realities.

Other industry trade union committees again view the ETUC standards as an infringement on the autonomy of the industry committees; especially with regard to the geographical factor and the joining with industry committees of international organisations other than their own. Here the claim is made that this is a contradiction to the prevailing constitutions of certain industry committees.

As a compromise solution between the independent or autonomous European organisation desired by the ETUC and the alternative of non-recognition by the ETUC as branch affiliates, some industry committees have founded a number of so-called 'European Committees'. This solution has been adopted by the trade unions in the food, tobacco and catering industries (November 1974), the

24

trade unions of the textile and clothing industries (March 1975), the European Teachers' Trade Union and the transport workers' unions (July 1975). While granting affiliation status for these 'European Committees', the ETUC still urges them to change into independent or autonomous federations. Nevertheless, such important trade unions as those of the chemical industry, have even yet to set up such 'European Committees'.

As a result, the flexibility of the ETUC to deal with the Commission and, more so, to engage in collective bargaining agreements within certain sectors of industry, has been hampered. So far, only one so-called Community level collective agreement has emerged. This was in the agricultural sector in 1968 and concerned agreement on the harmonisation of the length of working time. It proposed a 45-hour, 5-day week and a working year of 2,345 hours for workers in arable farming throughout the original six EC countries. [15]

Thus Beever's conclusion, reached in 1969, still largely holds in 1976: [16]

> As real trade union strength and decisions are felt nationally at the industrial level rather than in the central organisation, so are industrial sub-committees of the ECFTU increasingly becoming the most effective organisation, especially as regards co-ordination of the policies and activities of national affiliations.

Community and national-level organisation relations

The interviews revealed the fact that the national trade unions were taking more and more interest in the activities of the European trade union secretariats, [17] as well as in the affairs of other affiliated trade unions across the national border. Both within the two fore-runners of the ETUC (ECFTU and EO/WCL) and the ETUC, attempts have been made, with varying degrees of success, to establish guidelines for a common trade union action programme. In addition, certain working programmes have been drawn up by the Community trade union organisations serving as recommendatichs for the national affiliations. [18] On various occasions the European trade union organisations have adopted aspects of programmes presented by one of the affiliated trade unions for Community guidelines. [19] Periodically high-level consultations have taken place between different national trade union organisations, especially between the German DGB and the French FO and CFDT.

25

Also noteworthy are the recent inter-regional trade union developments. For example, in May 1976, trade unions from Belgium (Liege and Limburg), Holland (Dutch Limburg) and Germany (Aachen) had a 'joint' meeting. Going a step further in July 1976, trade unions from Germany (Saarland), France (Moselle) and Luxembourg, established the Saar-Lorraine-Luxembourg Inter-Regional Trade Union Council. [20]

However, efforts still need to be made to establish a European trade union organisation which has the same competences for European questions as the national organisations have for national questions. Despite the substantial increases which have been made in personnel and resources for the secretariats of the European trade union organisations, these secretariats, primarily those of the industry committees, need to be strengthened. For example, the secretariat of the ETUC has no efficient research staff to assemble and analyse national and European data, although it is able to entrust national secretariats with European problems. However, if the European trade union organisations are not able to improve this service, they will remain dependent upon their national members, not only for financial resources, but also for the kinds of functions these secretariats can undertake in order to set the stage for Community or European objectives. A similar argument can be made with regard to a possible close reliance on the Commission's services. As stated in the ETUC Objectives 1976-1979: 'The European trade union movement must endeavour to prepare its own expert economic and social surveys in order not to be too dependent on official sources.' [21]

Moreover, greater stability is necessary within the Secretariat of the ETUC. In the three years of its existence, there has been an almost complete turnover of the executive officers of the organisation; including the position of the ETUC Secretary-General. [22]

Factors influencing the organisation of the ETUC

While there had been since 1966 regular consultations and some co-ordination of policies between the ECFTU and the EO/WCL (and between the two European Secretariats of the ICFTU and WCL); and while co-operation increased from 1971 onward when the two organisations agreed to seek closer alignment, relations between the ECFTU and EO/WCL, on the one hand, and the CGT/CGIL, on the other, were nearly non-existent up to 1969. This was in spite of the

26

fact tnat the CGT/CGIL had established a Joint Consultative Committee at Community level in 1967. Up until 1969 both the ECFTU and the EO/WCL had expressed profound reservations about any participation of CGT/CGIL representatives in common consultations between the two sides of industry and the Commission or in Committees such as the ESC. This position changed only slightly with the Commission's recognition of the Joint Consultative Committee of the CGT/CGIL in March 1969 [23] and the latter's participation in the Community Employment Conference in Luxembourg in April 1970. Similarly, the constitutional provisions introduced by the British, Belgian (FGTB) and Scandinavian trade unions in the establishment of the ETUC in 1973, which were favourable to CGT/CGIL membership, [24] and the actual acceptance of CGIL membership in 1974, did not drastically alter the position of some of the former ECFTU and EO/WCL affiliates. Being confronted with the choice of either aligning with the EFTA countries' trade unions under their provisions, or foregoing that alignment altogether, they (particularly the German DGB and the French FO/CGT) agreed to the former. Similarly, in 1974, being pressed into a minority position, [25] they reluctantly accepted the verdict of the Executive Committee majority decision.

It is noteworthy that in 1973 the CGIL had weakened its links with the WFTU by reducing its commitment to that of an associate member. In contrast, the CGT continued as a full member. As mentioned above, the CGT enquired about the possibility of ETUC membership in 1975. The ETUC Executive Committee, following exploratory talks with the CGT in December 1975, decided to send a questionnaire to the CGT apparently seeking clarification on its links with the WFTU and the Communist Party. [26] Depending on the outcome of this questionnaire, and depending on the size of the opposition the two main opponents (the French FO/CGT [27] and the German DGB) can muster, either in the Executive Committee or in the Congress, CGT membership will either come soon or will be delayed for a few years.

There has been little co-operation so far between the five Communist trade union representatives and some of the representatives of the former ECFTU and EO/WCL affiliates in Group II (trade union group) of the ESC.

Having analysed the changes which have taken place in the central and industry trade union organisations, and having pointed out some of the factors which affect the 'strength' or 'weakness' of the ETUC, let us now examine the factors which have either favoured or hindered trade union co-operation and integration at European level.

Motives for community trade union development

Three main factors can be singled out which appear to have favourably influenced inter-trade union co-operation from mid-1968 onward. One was the mergers between business corporations within individual countries and among several countries of the EC, [28] that were encouraged by the operation of the Customs Union, as well as by the Commission's proposals on industrial policy, especially as they related to the promotion of business mergers and the Statute of a European Company. [29] Another factor was Community policies in the agricultural field and the free movement of labour. The third factor concerned the strength the employers' organisations had developed at Community level for the pursuit of their interests and the operation of multinational corporations. An illustration of these three influence factors and their interrelationship, is provided in figure 2.2.

Since these three factors relate both to aspects of trade union co-operation and integration at the Community level, treated in this chapter, and to pressure group involvement in social policy harmonisation, analysed in the next chapter, only a brief analysis of these factors will be given here, and a more elaborate treatment will be provided in the next chapter.

The merger process

With the establishment of the Customs Union, tariff barriers among the Member States of the original six EC countries were abolished almost completely. As a consequence (and in some ways in anticipation of this consequence) some firms were faced with a situation in which they had to merge with others; some firms had to close altogether. In addition, changing technology, the economic recession experienced in some countries (such as Germany in 1967/ 68) and the factor of automation, also had an impact on these changes. Subsequently, a substantial increase in the number of mergers ensued from 1967 on. (See chapter 4, figure 4.2)

The data collected (written records and interviews) indicate that trade unions became increasingly aware by 1968/69 of the potential threat that transnational mergers of firms or the operation of multi-national firms could, in certain circumstances, play off trade unions (and even governments) in different countries against one another. Since multinational companies, and these transnational business collaborations, are able to transfer production units and research

Figure 2.2   Causal linkage

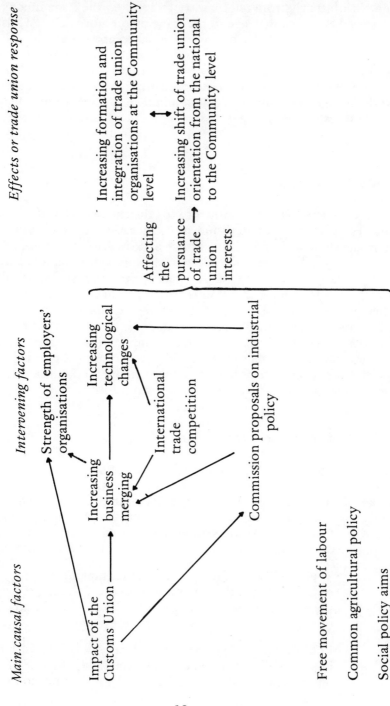

Main causal factors

Intervening factors

Effects or trade union response

Impact of the Customs Union

Strength of employers' organisations

Increasing business merging

Increasing technological changes

International trade competition

Commission proposals on industrial policy

Affecting the pursuance of trade union interests

Increasing formation and integration of trade union organisations at the Community level

Increasing shift of trade union orientation from the national to the Community level

Free movement of labour

Common agricultural policy

Social policy aims

29

centres arbitrarily from one country to another, the trade unions perceived this as a challenge to the trade union movement. Whilst not objecting to the existence of multinational companies as a logical trend in a more and more integrated Community, the trade unions sought control over certain activities of the companies. [30] Their concern for control measures was primarily related to job security, working conditions and participation in management affairs. We shall return shortly to this aspect.

The Common Agricultural Policy and the free movement of labour

In order to exert effective influence for the enactment of the policies directed to counter some of the negative impacts emanating from the Common Agricultural Policy and the free movement of labour, the trade unions, according to the interviews and written statements, felt the need to consolidate their efforts at Community level (through strong Community associations and co-operation). They pointed out that as economic integration proceeds in these two areas, trade unions must utilise their strength to secure and promote the social benefits of economic integration, i.e. to seek appropriate policies and financial aids at the EC level on vocational training, social security benefits or unemployment compensation for both the displaced agricultural force and migrant work force.

Strength of employers' organisations

As pointed out above, the employers' organisations, especially UNICE and COPA were already well organised (numerically, independently and financially) at the Community level by mid-1968. In reconstituting the trade union response to the existing (by 1968) strength of employers' organisations, the following considerations seem to have prevailed:

1. The challenge of the strength of the employers' organisations at the Community level was recognised by the trade unions well before 1968, and so was the challenge of the increasing number of business mergers;

2. Both challenges, however, were greatly increased with the impact of the Customs Union (accelerating the rate of business merging) and the impact of the Commission's

30

proposals on industrial policy;

3.　　As a consequence of point two, trade unions perceived that with the existing strength of the employers' organisations and their urge for increasing the number of business mergers, and with the increasing competence gained by the Commission through the Customs Union, industrial policy, the Common Agricultural Policy and the free movement of labour, a one-sided (employers') interest would prevail at the Community level, if no united effort from the trade union movement was forthcoming. [31]

Another reason for the creation of the ETUC, as well as for inter-trade union co-operation according to the trade unions, although to a lesser extent than the above three, was the integrative attempts between different trade unions at the national level. [32]　For example, attempts were made in Holland between 1969 and 1975 among the three different trade unions (Socialists, Christians and Protestants) to establish a uniform national trade union organisation, culminating in the establishment of the Federatie Nederlandse Vakbeweging (FNV — Federation of Dutch Trade Unions) between the NVV and NKV. The CNV (Protestant) does not form part of the new federation and concertation between the CNV and FNV will not be on a systematic basis. However, twice all three unions have joined efforts to work out a so-called Action Programme on a number of social objectives: one for the period 1971-75 and the other for the period 1976-77. Similar attempts were made in Italy, although considerably less successful, among the different trade unions (Socialists, Social Democrats and Communists).

In 1972 the three respective Italian organisations (CISL, UIL and CGIL) signed a 'Federation Pact'. While they have not agreed upon a full merger except in the case of the metal workers, progress has been made as regards the setting-up of joint structures and the preparation of policies, decisions and joint action, especially in collective bargaining. In both the Dutch and Italian cases, joint statements were issued by the different trade unions urging greater co-ordination and co-operation at the Community level.

In France an effort was made during 1973 to weld together the three main trade union organisations (FO/CGT CFDT, and CGT) into a single national union, but it failed. Collaboration and unification proved difficult to establish, primarily between the FO/CGT and the CGT (Socialists and Communists). Attempts were made between the CFDT and the CGT, such as in drawing up programmes

31

for joint action, and they have been somewhat more successful.

In Belgium, the Christian and Socialist trade unions (CSC and FGTB) have developed a practical working relationship in specific bargaining situations. However, to a large extent because of the language issue (CSC mainly representing the Flemish speaking north of the country and the FGTB the French speaking south), both maintain that the 'common front' is only an ad hoc marriage for practical reasons, but not a step towards trade union unity.

Besides these national integrative attempts among trade unions of different denominational or confessional persuasions, two other successful integrative attempts have taken place within national trade union federations themselves, such as in the case of Denmark and Ireland. [33] On the other hand, attempts to integrate the two federations of blue and white-collar trade unions (DGB and DAG) in Germany since 1974 have not so far brought any positive results.

Finally, three other factors were stressed by trade unions in interviews and written records, although again to a lesser extent than the previous motives mentioned, as having contributed to their integrative activities at the European level. These were:

a)   The geographic enlargement of the EC from six to nine Member States in January 1973;

b)   The desire of the Belgian FGTB and EFTA wing trade unions to seek co-operation between trade unions of Eastern and Western Europe, and thus press for CGIL admittance to the ETUC.

c)   The growing awareness that the national situations were interdependent and that the national governments were not able to deal either sufficiently or effectively with such social and economic issues as economic growth, inflation, unemployment, technological changes, energy and the protection of the environment. For example, the ECFTU stated in 1971 that: [34]

> ... a trade union movement limited to national economical and political activity is no longer capable of securing the interests of its members and pursuing their class-based political aims. These are questions which cannot be solved any longer at the national level.

While the above factors can be seen as attributes to a strengthening of the co-operative and integrative efforts of trade unions at the

Community level, there were (and are) also certain governmental activities which impeded these efforts. For example, the German government increased its efforts by 1968/69 in seeking national solutions to the demands of the social partners by introducing such methods as 'Konzertierte Aktion'. [35] (More on this later.)

However, it appears from the substantial progress trade unions have made in strengthening their Community level engagement since mid-1968, that these governmental attempts could not prevent the co-operative and integrative steps taken by the trade unions.

Conclusion

The main aim of chapter 2 was to discover the integrative attempts trade unions have made at the European level since mid-1968, and the main reasons behind the integrative attempts.

The examination of integrative attempts by trade unions at European level reveals that substantial progress was made between mid-1969 and mid-1974 to establish an organised trade union front at European level. National trade unions have strengthened by a substantial degree the structures (personnel, budget and decision-making procedure) of their European trade union organisations by forming, first, the ECFTU and EO/WCL in 1969, and then the ETUC in 1973, and agreeing, in spite of their ideological, religious and political differences, to merge the organisations of the ETUC and the EO/WCL in the Spring of 1974.

Since the Summer of 1974, there has also been a change in the relationship between the ETUC and the CGIL, indicating that previous hostilities will be transformed into an atmosphere of co-operation, through the joining of the CGIL to the ETUC. In view of the degree of trade union plurality which existed at European level by mid-1968, the achievements reached since then can be viewed as a major breakthrough in the formation of an organised common trade union front.

However, in spite of having narrowed the differences, the ETUC (as it existed by the end of 1976) had not yet the competences or strength of the main employers' organisations at European level, nor in particular, of the national trade union organisations. This relates, in part, to the missing European substructure (industry committees) at the trade union branch level, and in part to the 'insufficient' cohesion in the organisation of the ETUC. The latter point will be elaborated more fully in the next chapter.

Notes

[1]   Most of the figures presented on this and the next page were taken from Leo J. Crijns, 'Collective Bargaining in the EC,' in *Western European Labor and the American Corporation*, Alfred Kamin (ed.), Bureau of National Affairs, Washington 1970, pp 93-8; *Le Monde*, 10 February 1970; *Economist*, 9 September 1972; Willatt, *Multinational Unions.*

[2]   There are some difficulties in translating exactly the German terms: 'Spitzenverband' and 'Fachverband'. The various German-English dictionaries use for 'Spitzenverband' such terms as: central organisation; head organisation; or umbrella organisation. Similarly, the German term of 'Fachverband' has been translated as: sectoral industrial association; professional organisation; intermediary or inter-professional group. For this research the following equivalent terms have been chosen:

German term	English term
Spitzenverband	Central organisation
Fachverband	Intermediary or inter-professional (industrial, agricultural, crafts, trade union, etc.) association
Verband	Specialised (industrial, agricultural, crafts, trade union) branch association

[3]   The two latest editions of these Repertoires are May 1972 for agriculture and January 1973 for industry. The scheme used for the breakdown has been adopted from Fischer who made a similar comparison in 1965. See Fritz Fischer, *Die Institutionalisierte Vertretung der Verbände in der Europäischen Wirtschaftsgemeinschaft*, Hansischer Gildenverlag, Veröffentlichungen des Instituts für Internationales Recht an der Universität Kiel, Hamburg 1965, pp 42-3.

[4]   Lindberg and Scheingold, *Europe's Would-Be Polity*, p.79; Fischer, *Die Institutionalisierte Vertretung der Verbände*, p.43; K.H. Neunreither, 'Wirtschaftsverbände im Prozess der Europäischen Integration,' *Politische Dimensionen der Europäischen Gemeinschaftsbildung*, Carl J. Friedrich (ed.), Westdeutscher Verlag, Cologne 1968, p.401; Dusan Sidjanski, 'Pressure Groups and the EEC,' *The New International Actors in the UN and the EEC*, Carol and Ann Cosgrave and Kenneth Twitchett (eds) Dealings in International Politics, vol.1, J.E. Spence (gen.ed.), Macmillan Wevelback, 1970, p.226; K.E. Hammerich, *L'Union des Industries de la Communauté Européenne dans le Marché Commun*, Sveriges Industriforbund,

Stockholm 1969; Memoire presenté en novembre 1968 au Centre Européen Universitaire de Nancy pour le Diplôme des Etudes Supérieures Européennes, p.11.

[5]   From the 10 intermediary or inter-professional trade union associations of the European Secretariat of the ICFTU, only the European Federation of Trade Unions of Agricultural Workers (EFA) and the Trade Union Group of the Food, Tobacco and Hotel Industries in the EC had an independent status. Similarly, from the 11 intermediary or inter-professional trade union associations, only the Fédération Européenne de Travailleurs Agricoles (EO/CMT)-EUROFEDAG and the Fédération Européenne de Travailleurs de l'Alimentation et Industries Connexes (OE/CMT)-EUROFEDAL, had independent organisations.

[6]   As Fischer points out, the influence of COPA on their associated intermediary or inter-professional groups is very dominant: 'All opinions prepared by the intermediary or inter-professional associations have to be approved by COPA before they can be submitted to the EC institutions.' Fischer, *Die Institutionalisierte Vertretung der Verbände*, p.52.

[7]   In general, exact figures of the available budget are difficult to obtain from the Community pressure group organisations. From data obtained in interviews with officials of these organisations, the annual budget of UNICE and COPA can be estimated as being $200,000 and $100,000, respectively, in 1968. The annual budget of the European Secretariat of the ICFTU was approximately between $125,000 and $150,000 in 1968. The figures given for UNICE and COPA correspond to the estimates presented by Neunreither (between DM 300,000 and DM 600,000). See Neunreither, 'Wirtschaftsverbände im Prozess der Europäischen Integration,' p.407.

[8]   The formation of the ECFTU induced the EFTA countries' trade union organisations of the ICFTU to establish their own trade union committee, leading subsequently to the dissolving of the ICFTU European Regional Organisation in 1970.

[9]   This meant the dissolving of the EO/WCL as an organisation - one of the conditions made by the ETUC for approving membership applications of the EO/WCL national affiliations. On the other hand, the ETUC agreed that these former EO/WCL members could continue to be affiliated to the WCL (their international organisation).

[10]   One administrative secretary, one assistant and three other employees were added, raising the number of staff members in the Secretariat of the ETUC to 28. Prior to the establishment of the

ETUC, there had already been increases in personnel, both in the ECFTU and in the EO/WCL between 1969 and 1972.

[11]   The annual budget is approximately 80 per cent higher than under the ECFTU. The annual budget is between $350,000 and $400,000. However, despite the overall increase in the budget, the subscription share for trade union organisations belonging formerly to the ECFTU decreased. For example, members of the Dutch NVV indicated in interviews that under the ECFTU their sub-scription share for every 1,000 members (trade union members) had been 1.350 BF. Under the ETUC it is only 550 BF for every 1,000 members.

[12]   For example, from 1969 on the ECFTU and the EO/WCL granted proportional representation to their respective associated industrial committees in the decision-making of the Congress. Moreover, the ETUC grants each associated industrial committee one observer (advisory status) in the meetings of the Executive Committee.

[13]   Adopting independent statutes of their international trade union organisations (branches of the ICFTU) in 1971 and 1969, respectively, the EMF and EFA also introduced two-third majority voting procedures. In addition, the EFA increased its membership by approving the Belgian and Dutch Christian trade union organisations and the Italian Communist trade union organisation (CGIL); representing in 1975, 15 national organisations with 1.3 million members. Similarly, between October 1974 and March 1976, the EMF accepted organisations from the Christian Metal Workers' Trade Unions, formerly affiliated to the industry committee of the EO/WCL, as well as organisations from Denmark, Sweden, Norway, Britain, Ireland, Greece and Spain; representing by April 1976, 6.5 million metal workers, who are members of 24 trade unions. See *Report on the Development of the Social Situation in the Community in 1975*, p.66; and *European Communities Trade Union Information*, 7/8, July/August 1976, p.13.

[14]   The standards include the following propositions:
—   The industry committee should have standing bodies, such as a secretariat and an executive committee, and an operating budget at its disposal;
—   There should be a mutual exchange of regular information and the mutual attendance of meetings between the ETUC and the industry committee;
—   The industry committees should, whenever possible, cover the same countries as those covered by the ETUC.

[15]   Although the terms of the agreement are not binding, since

there is no legal basis for a European collective agreement that would be directly applicable in all EC countries, it is hoped that they will be incorporated in binding agreements at the national and local level. Discussions are in progress to extend the agreement to other sectors in agriculture, such as the harmonisation of working hours for workers in cattle-raising.

[16]   Beever, *Trade Unions and Free Labour Movement in the EEC*, p.9.

[17]   Up until 1968/69, as Kulakowski (Secretary General of the EO/WCL) pointed out, national interest groups had not participated fully in the events of the secretariat and often took an opinion such as: 'You are in Brussels, you know what is going on; whatever you think needs to be done in our interest – do it.'

[18]   For example, the European Secretariat of the Metal Trade Union of the ICFTU and the European Secretariat of the Metal Trade Union of the WCL drew up a 'Social Urgency Programme' in 1968. In this programme they called for a production plan, re-adaption and reconversion schemes, and better working conditions and wages for workers in the mines. See Ph. Van Praag, 'Trends and Achievements in the Field of Social Policy in the European Communities,' *Bulletin 1*, Louvain University, Louvain 1971.

[19] For example, the Dutch trade unions (NVV, NKV and CNV) who mostly present a joint Action Programme, are often asked to submit their Action Programmes to the European trade union organisation for consideration and possible adoption of Community guidelines. The preference for the Dutch trade union programmes results from the fact that their Action Programmes consist of two types: those which should be implemented at the national level (Holland), and those which should be carried out at the Community level.

[20]   This Council operates by majority decision-making and has the following organs:

   a) The Joint Conference (held at least every 3 years. One such Conference already took place in January 1977);
   b) The Bureau (consisting of a President and two Vice-Presidents. It meets at least 6 times a year);
   c) The Permanent Secretariat.

[21]   See ETUC *Objectives* 1976-1979. Approved by the Secondary Statutory Congress, London, 22-4 April 1976.

[22]   See B.C. Roberts and Bruno Liebhaberg, 'The European Trade Union Confederation: Influence of Regionalism, Detente and Multinationals,' *British Journal of Industrial Relations*, vol.14, no.3, November 1976, p.267.

[23] For details on the Commission's recognition of the Joint Consultative Committee of the CGT/CGIL, see chapter 3, p.57.

[24] In the Constitution of the ETUC the word 'free' had disappeared - a word which both the ECFTU and the EO/WCL had in their Constitutions. This omission can be viewed as an indication by the ETUC that CGIL and CGT admission was possible in principle.

[25] According to the German DGB's Die Quelle, the decision in the Executive was 21 votes in favour and 7 against. The dissenting votes had come from the DGB, FO/CGT and the Christian trade unions of Switzerland, Belgium and Luxembourg. See Die Quelle, 25 Jahrgang: September 1974, p.355.

[26] See Roberts and Liebhaberg, 'The European Trade Union Confederation', p.264.

[27] The opposition expressed by the FO/CGT to the CGT's membership throws up the question of the electoral alliance and possible government coalition of the French Socialist Party (to which the FO/CGT pays political allegiance) and the French Communist Party (to which the CGT is politically attached). It will be interesting to see whether the Socialist Party can change the intransigent opposition of the FO/CGT towards the CGT, both at European and at national level, which is based on a long-standing dogmatic debate with the CGT over social and economic policies.

[28] In the following, when reference is made to 'increasing number of business mergers', both business merging within individual countries of the EC and transnational (across the borders of the EC Member States) business merging is meant.

[29] The term 'European Company' represents the establishment of joint-stock companies from firms of the EC Member States. The Statute of this European Company concerns the amount of minimum capital; judicial control of incorporation; disclosure requirements; representation of workers on the company's board; the form of shares; taxation; and uniform legal interpretation.

[30] For example, Walter Braum, Secretary of the ETUC, stated in an interview: 'We are not in principle against merging of trans-national firms — what we are concerned with is a control over the activities of these mergers.' For more details, see the ETUC Report on Multinational Companies in the European Communities, Brussels, 24-5 January 1974.

[31] Directly reflecting the concern, Gerritse, in a special report drawn up for the First Congress of the EO/WCL in 1969, stated:

The way in which the employers and bureaucracy begin to

take more European forms must be met by the workers in taking equal European forms. These European forms are not only the addition of national forms. A European trade union organisation is necessary which will have the same prerogatives for the European questions. Such an organisation must be able to carry out policies in a European fashion.

(See 'Die Stellung der Arbeitnehmer in einem sich verändernden Europa,' Berichterstatter: G. Gerritse, EO/WCL First Congress *Activity Report*, Brussels, 7-9 May 1969, p.13.)

[32]   For details, see *Reports on the Development of the Social Situation in the Community* in 1974 and in 1975; *European Communities Trade Union Information*, November 1975, Special Number; and Roberts and Liebhaberg, 'The European Trade Union Confederation,' p.266.

[33]   In Denmark there has been a trend since 1971 towards fewer but larger unions. An example is the merger which occurred in the building industry in 1974; and in Ireland, the Trade Union Act of 1975 facilitates the amalgamation of trade unions and the transfer of engagements between unions.

[34]   See 'Der Europäische Gewerkschaftsbund,' *Europäische Dokumentation*, 1973. See also 'Towards Trade Union Unity on the European Level,' *European Organisation* of the WCL, no.51, Brussels, 18 March 1973.

[35]   *'Konzertierte Aktion'* means greater efforts are to be undertaken by the Government to promote the conclusion of satisfactory collective agreements between the employers' and employees' organisations in Germany. For further details, see Ph. Van Praag, 'Trends and Achievements,' p.169.

Introduction

From the data presented in chapter 2, it became apparent that the existing strength of employers' organisations, together with their transnational operations and involvement in EC policies, were the prime factors in bringing about quantitative and qualitative improvements in European trade union organisations.

Yet it is one thing for the ETUC to demonstrate organisational strength by proclaiming spokesmanship of nearly all the major Western European trade union federations, comprising 38 million members. It is quite another thing for this organisation to formulate uniform policy stands, even with a majority decision-making formula, and to successfully employ the organisational strength with employers' organisations or in negotiations with the EC, EFTA and Nordic Council. Due to different existing national trade union practices, there are many ideas on how best to deal with employers' organisations or multinational corporations, and, to some extent, with internal control over the rank and file of trade union members. While the creation and expansion of the ETUC has brought accompanying signs of convergence on the different ideas, there are also indications that some of the different trade union practices or ideological stands prove difficult to overcome. In order to illuminate these two different aspects, this chapter will elaborate two broad areas of ETUC organisational effectiveness. These are:

a)   ETUC policy formation on industrial democracy;

b)   ETUC policy formation on European integration.

ETUC and industrial democracy

Basically two aims were singled out by the trade unions in interviews and written statements for achieving industrial democracy, also known as democratisation of the economy: [1]

a)   To upgrade the venue of negotiation from the shopfloor to the boardroom, i.e. increase the consultative machinery and

40

effectively allow workers or trade unions to influence management decisions;

b) To expand (broaden and diversify) the subject matter of collective bargaining.

While trade unions experienced (and still experience) difficulties in determining the priorities whereby one or the other aim should be pursued, the appropriate form for pursuing these aims appeared (and still appears) to prove more of a problem; although some progress has been made. It is primarily the first aim which has been the subject of considerable disagreement.

Link between shopfloor and boardroom

Some of the forms which have been suggested for upgrading the venue of negotiation from the shopfloor to the boardroom are:

a) to extend and increase the influence of existing works councils;

b) to adopt and extend the practice of workers' participation on the supervisory board of firms;

c) to adopt and enlarge schemes of asset formation.

Besides the proponents of these suggestions, feelings within the ETUC can be divided into three additional groups: those with sympathetic or lukewarm support; those who oppose; and those who are ambivalent.

Works councils

Before we analyse the pros and cons among trade unions on the importance of works councils, let us briefly consider the nature or original conception up until the late 1960's of these works councils.

Generally speaking, works councils have been established by law in most of the continental West European countries [2] and by national agreements between employers' and workers' organisations in Scandinavia. In some cases, works councils exist in Britain and Ireland, but in contrast to their continental partners, they are established there either informally or, occasionally, under the terms of a collective agreement on a voluntary basis. Works councils in Continental countries are composed equally of workers' and management representatives, with the exception of Germany and Austria, where they are exclusively employee bodies. Works councils represent all the workers employed and not just union members or workers in particular grades or departments. Similarly, representatives of works councils are elected by *all* the workers, unionised or not. In Britain, *only* union members are entitled to vote for the election of shop stewards. While Belgium at least provides that workers' members are elected from lists prepared by the trade unions, in Germany a conscious effort is made in many ways to separate the general stream of trade union influence.

As pointed out by Carew: [3]

> Economic information received by the works councillors is regarded as confidential and must not be passed on to the union. Council members are forbidden to call or lead strikes and in the event a strike does take place, the councillors who are union members usually resign from it to protect themselves.

Partly the events of May 1968 in France and the 'Hot Autumn' of 1969 in Italy, and partly the consequences of the increasing business mergers between 1968 and 1970 (noted above) brought to the fore not only the old issue of the balance of power between workers and management, but also a new issue concerning the balance of power between the rank and file and the leaders of the trade union movement. Consequently, in these two countries, as well as other continental countries, trade union leaders, in an effort to reassert control over their own movement, and to cope more effectively with the changing social and economic situation, called for a strengthening of the system of works councils. They aimed to replace their primarily consultative and advisory role into a decision-taking organ.

Among the measures taken by the trade unions in Germany and Holland, for example, was the introduction of a body of 'confidence men' at the plant level. These are union activists who are given the job of liaising with the works council and trying to cement the link between the membership and the hierarchy. Other measures included, in some countries, the trade union training of councillors, financed by management, which led to an overwhelming proportion of trade union members on the works councils. For example, well over 80 per cent of the members of works councils elected in Germany at the 1975 election belonged to a trade union. [4] A greater trade union influence on councillors' or works councils' policies since 1970/71 has also been noticed in Austria, the Netherlands, Belgium and the Scandinavian countries, and even to a greater extent, in Italy. The developments in the latter indicate a trend towards emulating the status of the British shop stewards. [5]

Furthermore, trade unions were instrumental in the enactment by the governments of 'new' laws aimed to reinforce the power of works councils, such as:

a) In Holland in 1971 concerning plant closure, mergers, manpower and promotion policy, as well as profit-sharing and pension schemes;

b) In Germany in 1971 relating to dismissals and plant closures;

c) In Belgium in 1972 and 1973, covering rights of information;

d) In Luxembourg in 1974, providing for measures over personnel matters.

The powers of works councils have also recently been boosted in Denmark. In some countries works councils have even obtained the formal right to their own auditor examining the economic and financial data of the firm.

Generally, the record of performance with works councils has been different in Germany, Holland, Luxembourg, Austria, Switzerland and the Scandinavian countries from that in Italy and France. The first group is encouraged by the system of works councils and seeks further increases of power and authority, not only for this system but also for other types of participation with management. The latter group feels that because employers' organisations have not responded favourably enough, or the experience with joint management and employee composition of the councils has not been satisfactory, this form, as well as the other forms of management participation, is not advisable for the pursuance of industrial democracy. The two main Belgian trade unions can also be considered as dissatisfied with the experience of works councils. But while the Christian trade union (CSC) mainly takes issue with the representation of management officials in works councils, the Socialist trade union (FGTB) sees them as ineffective instruments for achieving their trade union goal of total control over management.

There seems to be some convergence between the British and Irish system of shopfloor trade union representation (shop stewards) and the European models of in-plant worker representation (primarily works councils). British fears that works councils, being company-based rather than union bodies, would tend to by-pass the organised labour movement or tend to lack the trade union strength in dealing with management, have, at least to some extent, been met with the introduction of 'confidence men' and other more direct forms of trade union participation in works councils in a number of countries given above.

Thus it appears that at the present time there are more trade union affiliations of the ETUC in favour of extending and increasing the influence of works councils, at least in principle, than there are in opposition to it. However, for the principle to become reality, the supporting trade unions must be able to come to terms with such questions as:

—   whether works councils should be statutory or take the form of national agreements between employers' and trade union organisations, as practised in the Scandinavian countries and probably preferred by the British and Irish TUC. The Commission in its Proposal, [6] indicates that existing national laws on works councils would be allowed to continue, but that they be made statutory for European companies. This would mean that Germany and other countries could continue their statutory practice;

—   whether the representatives of works councils should be elected solely by trade unions (Britain and Ireland) as against the prevailing practice in most Continental countries of electing representatives by all employees. Again a compromise could be found, whereby national practices continued, but a uniform method, which seems to favour election by all employees, would be adopted for the European company; [7]

whether the composition of works councils should be based solely on employee representatives (as in Germany and Austria), rather than on half management and half employee, as is the case in most countries with works councils. There are strong indications that the Statute for a

44

European Company will insist on employees' representatives only, but once more prevailing national practices could be maintained.

A solution to these questions is probably also tied up with the prospects of a common ETUC policy on workers' participation on supervisory boards of firms, which is seen by some observers as vitally important for the successful employment of works councils. [8]

Workers' participation

Co-determination or workers' participation exists in various forms in Germany, Holland, Denmark and Luxembourg. [9] Outside the EC it can be found in Austria and Norway. For details of the different forms, see Appendix B. Generally under this system, firms have a two-tier structure: a supervisory board and a management board. The supervisory board is charged with upholding the shareholders' interests, but is also either composed of one-third to one-half of workers' representatives, depending on the industry and size of firm involved, as in Germany; or possesses co-opting functions, such as in the Netherlands, to control in both instances management decisions and the activities of the management board. In the case of Germany, for example, the supervisory board has the ultimate control of investment decisions and of the preparation and presentation of accounts to the annual general meeting. As characterised by Robertson: [10]

> Workers' participation or co-determination places industrial democracy at the company level. So do the works councils. But the supervisory board, by its very structure, puts workers' participation in a totally different context. Whereas the works council links workers and management in discussion of company affairs, the supervisory board brings the owners of capital and the representatives of the labour they employ together in the supervision of major management decisions.

In addition to the above-mentioned countries which practise workers' participation, trade unions in Sweden, Britain and Ireland have indicated tentative support for workers' participation on supervisory boards. But, as in the case of the British and Irish trade unions, this support is subject to conditions, such as 50 per cent of the seats going to union-designated employee representatives and employee representatives being appointed through trade union machinery. Another TUC provision is that these employee representatives would be responsible to trade union members in the firm rather than to shareholders or even the company, and that the supervisory board should have the power of veto on some key matters such as dismissal. However, this tentative support stems primarily from the position taken by some leading TUC officials, such as Jack Jones, head of the British Transport and General Workers' Union. As a matter of fact, at the TUC Congress in 1973 a Resolution to adopt the system of workers' participation in principle was passed only with another resolution rejecting the mandatory imposition of supervisory boards with worker directors, recognising instead the primacy of collective bargaining. [11] As Goodman explains: [12]

> Most British unions are sceptical of becoming involved in management. They rely on collective bargaining to influence management decisions and policies from the outside and preserve an adversary position. Flexibility and voluntarism are preferred to legal enactment.

On the other hand, the announcement by the Labour Government that they would introduce legislation during the Parliamentary session of 1976/77 on workers' participation and set up a committee of enquiry (of which Jack Jones was a participant) to advise on how best to achieve this, seems to indicate that the proponents of workers' participation within the TUC are gaining ground. This committee, presided over by Lord Bullock, submitted its report in January 1977. It confirmed the 1973 TUC General Council's recommendation on industrial democracy to have a unitary management board rather than a two-tier board structure.

The new Swedish system of minority employee representation on supervisory boards is a trial effort to be reassessed with systems in operation in Germany and the Netherlands. [13] While largely sympathetic towards workers' participation, the Swiss trade unions have to accept, for the time being, the verdict of a referendum in which the introduction of such a system was narrowly turned down. [14]

The system of workers' participation is ardently opposed by some of the Italian, French and Belgian trade unions. Part of the reason against this system in the cases of Italy and France has been stated

46

above with the experience of the works councils. Other objections raised were:

a)   The complaint by the Belgian trade union (FGTB) that to share with management the responsibility over management affairs would be tempting trade union leaders to adopt a capitalist mentality, and might thus split them from the rank and file of their movement; and, more seriously, would not enable them to influence really vital decisions of management. Thus total control or self-management is their desire; [15]

b)   The incompatibility for the Communist trade unions of Italy and France of justifying workers' participation with their anti-capitalist outlook.

Partly pressed by the Commission's proposals of June 1970 and 1972 (Fifth Directive) for a Statute for a European Company, with provisions for a supervisory board and one-third workers' representation on this board, and partly pressed by the activities and operations of multinational companies, the ECFTU (the forerunner of the ETUC) tried to respond to these pressures with a common policy stand. With the numerical strength of the German and Dutch trade unions in the ECFTU, the opinion presented by the ECFTU in 1972 on the Commission's proposal reflected not only a favourable attitude towards workers' participation on the supervisory board, but went even further in some respects than foreseen by the Commission. [16]   Similarly, it was the ECFTU's formula of workers' participation rather than that of the Commission which was adopted by the German and Dutch steel firms, Hoesch and Hoogovens, for the supervisory board of the merged company in 1973.

The German and Dutch trade unions have since lost their dominant position in the expanded ETUC, and the minority of trade union affiliates opposed to workers' participation has increased within the ETUC. A further outcome of the ETUC expansion has been that there is a group of trade union affiliates within the ETUC, comprised of such countries as Spain, Greece, Iceland and Malta, which can be seen as taking an ambivalent position on the whole issue of workers' participation. This can mean that, depending on the persuasion used by either the pros or cons of workers' participation, they might join either side.

There appear to be five prevailing dispositions on workers'

participation among affiliates of the ETUC. These dispositions, together with the trade unions which appear to represent them, and their voting strength in the Executive Committee of the ETUC, are shown in table 3.1.

As illustrated in this table, the majority of ETUC affiliates appears to be in favour of either introducing or strengthening the system of workers' participation (exactly two-thirds out of the total of 33 votes). Moreover, at the 1975 ETUC Congress, even less opposition was recorded to a proposal dealing in general terms with the democratisation of the economy which made reference to workers' participation. Only one opposing vote and one abstaining vote were registered for the adoption of this proposal. [17] However, while the majority of ETUC affiliates seem to agree on the principle of workers' participation, the important details of form and method have yet to be settled.

The methods desired among trade unions range from minority trade union representation on the supervisory board of corporations to equal employee representation on these boards (British TUC and German DGB), or variants of this arrangement, such as the Dutch trade unions which prefer increased accountability of the board of directors to employees, rather than direct representation. Similarly, trade unions vary on the method by which an agency should select employee board members, some favouring works councils or employee electorates, as in Austria, Denmark, Germany, the Netherlands, Sweden and Switzerland, and others preferring trade union institutions (exemplified by the system of shop stewards) as in Norway, Sweden, Britain and Ireland.

In addition, in Germany, the country where workers' participation has seen its widest application, recent attempts to expand the system have opened up a thorny problem, namely to determine the breakdown of workers' representatives on the supervisory board into white and blue-collar workers.

Works councils and workers' participation are two of the aims considered in the pursuance of industrial democracy. Another such aim is the acquisition by workers of a financial stake in the enterprise by which they are employed. This aim, known generally as asset formation, is like the other two aims, not without its opponents (although they are in the minority) within the ETUC.

Asset formation

Projects to allow workers to acquire a financial stake in the firm by

Table 3.1

Trade unions' stand on workers' participation

Strengthen existing system of worker participation	No. of votes	Introduce system for the first time	No. of votes	Prepared to participate once the system was enacted either by national or EC law	No. of votes	Ambivalent about the system	No. of votes	Opposed to the system in principle*	No. of votes
German DGB	3	Swedish LO / TCO	1 / 1	Irish TUC	1	Spanish UGT / STV	1 / 1	French CGT / CFDT / CGT/FO	1 / 1 / 1**
Dutch NVV / NKV / CNV	2	British TUC	3	Swiss SGB / CNG / SVEA	2	Icelandic AI	1	Italian CGIL / UIL / CISL	1 / 1 / 1
Danish LO / FTF	1 / 1			Finnish TVK / SAK	1 / 1	Maltese GWU	1	Belgian (Socialist) FGTB	1
Luxembourg CGT-L / LCGB	1 / 1			Belgian (Christian) CSC	1	Greek CGTG	1		
Norwegian LO	1								
Austrian OGB	1								
	11		5		6		5		6

* Opposition includes the CGT of France who is a potential member of the ETUC.

** There are indications that the CGT/FO might change towards a position of acceptance.

which they are employed and thereby to ensure at least a measure of indirect control over management policy, exist in various forms in Germany, France, Holland, Britain, Denmark and Sweden. These schemes are variously known as premium savings, work savings, profit sharing and house saving. [18]   They are either established by the governments or by agreement between management and workers of a firm, according to which all employees can accumulate assets in a firm, and from which employees can receive benefits at a later date. As stated by Barkin: 'Some proponents see in the plan a means of freezing payments to employees in periods of inflation and releasing buying power during periods of slackness.' [19]

This system is not, in its present form, uniformly accepted by the trade unions. Criticisms to the scheme have come from, among others, Roger Louet, formerly National Secretary of the French CGT/FO. According to him, the 1968 French law dealing with asset formation has not brought about any essential change in the matter of participation by wage earners in the functioning of the enterprise. He also condemned it as being motivated by a desire on the part of the employers and the governments to impose enforced savings on working people. [20]

Similar criticisms have come from the Italian, British and Swiss trade unions who maintain that it is not the workers who benefit from such a scheme, but rather the employers, i.e. it tends to be a tax-saving mechanism for the benefit of the employers. Even the Commission in its Green Paper remarks that: ' ... with a very few exceptions, none of the existing systems in practice gives employees any real influence over the decision-making of the enterprise in which they work.' [21]

Recently, proposals have been made in several countries, notably in Denmark, Germany and France, for systems intended to give employees or unions real influence over the conduct of enterprises, but no Member State has put such a system into effect at the present time. None the less, as Willatt rightly observes: [22]

> ... it seems evident that the impetus in the direction of both
> industrial democracy and asset formation is likely to be
> sustained – the more so as the proposed European
> Company Law seems likely to include some provisions along
> these lines.

Moreover, while the Communist and Socialist trade unions of France and Italy remain opposed to asset formation schemes on ideological grounds, it appears that there are some trade unions, such as the British TUC and the Danish LO, which are not opposed in principle, but rather object to the existing techniques. The latter, plus the trade unions in Germany, the Netherlands, Sweden and Austria, which have been in favour of such schemes, have actually pressed for improvements or negotiated plans for improvements.

The adoption by the ETUC Congress in 1975 of a plan covering asset formation schemes seems to bear out the observation made by Willatt. In its adoption of this plan (where apparently no opposing or abstaining votes were recorded) the ETUC Congress remarked that economic democracy should guarantee wage and salary earners greater participation and a fairer share in the growth of a company's assets. [23] However, one can agree with Fogarty, who maintains that asset schemes: '... are not, probably, of the highest priority in the eyes of trade unions.' [24]

Having considered three issues of industrial democracy, namely, works councils, workers' participation and asset formation, let us now move on to the agreements and disagreements among trade unions on the scope and emphasis of collective bargaining.

Collective bargaining

Collective agreements can be broadly defined as any agreement between one or more employers and a group of employees dealing with issues such as renumeration, hours of work, holidays and disputes.

Although with slight variations, the most significant collective agreements have been negotiated at industry level in France, Belgium, Germany, the Netherlands, Luxembourg, Austria, Switzerland and the Scandinavian countries. [25] In contrast, the UK and Ireland have predominantly used the plant level collective agreements, especially in recent years. Similarly, Italy has, since 1969, increasingly substituted plant level collective bargaining agreements.

There has also been a tendency for more collective agreements at plant level outside the UK, Ireland and Italy in the last three to four years. Agreements in these countries, however, differ from those practised in the UK and Ireland in two respects. On the one hand, they have incorporated specific provisions regarding consultations on plant closures which did not prevail in the UK until 1975 and do not exist in Ireland at the present time. [26] On the other hand, these agreements generally lacked the scope, strength and flexibility at plant level on such matters as contract provisions, wage policy and working conditions as exercised in Britain and Ireland. [27]

Generally, collective bargaining in Germany, France, Luxembourg,

Italy and the Netherlands is much more subject to legislation than in Britain and Ireland.

Usually on the Continent, once an agreement has been signed between a union and an employer or group of employers, it is legally binding on both sides. Except in Belgium and Italy, agreements through national negotiation boards, joint industrial councils or similar bodies are relatively rare in the Community.

Collective agreements are not only enforceable in law but may also, in France and Germany, and in a different form in the Netherlands, Luxembourg and Belgium, be extended by government action throughout an industry. For example, the Ministry of Labour or other appropriate authority can make an order whereby the terms of an employer in one industry can, through an extension order, be enforced in all other companies in that industry, whether or not the workers concerned are members of the same or any union.

In Germany, the Netherlands and Luxembourg with regard to the mixed committees, and in Denmark with regard to co-operation committees, [28] the law provides for arbitration machinery or Labour Courts to resolve deadlocks between management and employees' representatives. In Belgium and France, no such provision is made. In Italy, both parties to a collective agreement are under a legal obligation to observe its terms for its duration, which must be at least six months, and to do nothing which may compromise its faithful execution. Generally, industrial disputes between the employer and the works council are prohibited in these countries.

In addition, there are differences with regard to 'right of strike' in the different countries. According to Eric Jacobs: [29]

> In France and Italy the freedom of strike belongs to a
> political tradition ... In Germany, by contrast, there is no
> constitutional right to strike action comparable to that in
> Italy and France. ... Unlike France and Italy, in Britain,
> the freedom has evolved as a series of exemptions from civil
> or criminal liabilities. There is no right to strike as such.

However, the legal conditions under which strikes may take place in each of the above-named countries may be defined in law.

Strikes in breach of a collective bargaining agreement, during the period of contract, can be subject to legal action and financial liability for losses sustained by the employer, especially in France, Germany, Sweden, Denmark and Luxembourg. Once the agreement has expired, freedom to strike is restored.

In contrast to the statutory provisions which are the basis of collective bargaining on the Continent, Britain and Ireland adhere to what is often described as a system of voluntary collective bargaining.

In these two countries, rights of information, consultation and approval either by trade unions or workers from management are *not* generally established by law or by nationally applicable collective agreement; [30] as practised in the Scandinavian countries. Powers of the shop stewards in these two countries have their basis not in law but in the bargaining strength of effective labour organisations.

Although the Industrial Relations Act of 1971 in Britain attempted to give collective bargaining a more legal character, largely due to the boycott by the trade unions, the Act was changed in September 1974 (the Trade Union and Labour Relations Act) to the pre-1971 system. [31] Yet the provisions of the 1975 Employment Protection Bill in the UK point towards legal regulations. [32]

As stated above, while resisting legal or statutory works councils, and while insisting that trade unions are the only channel of representation for workers, [33] the British and Irish trade unions agree that attempts to introduce workers' participation and the existing practice of collective bargaining are complementary. [34] Frustrated by what they conceive as existing legal restrictions stemming from works councils, Italian and French trade unions agree with the British and Irish trade unions on the need to stifle legal provisions and to maintain the single trade union channel, but disagree on the question of complementarity. The latter see the method of collective bargaining as the main method for industrial democracy, providing at plant level the possibility of industrial confrontation, and thus keeping an arm's length stance towards management.

Examining the case for and against the convergence of industrial democracy, a trend towards convergence can be noticed, exemplified by the favourable inclination towards workers' participation in the UK and Ireland, at least as far as the Statute for a European Company is concerned.

On the other hand, Italy, France and Belgium do not show any definite signs of intending to introduce workers' participation.

With regard to the prospects of workers' participation becoming an accepted reality in Italy and France, Sorge offers two interesting arguments. While stipulating that: '... the Fifth Directive [one of the Commission's proposals for the European Company which deals specifically with workers' participation] will be made law only if France and Italy find the way towards board participation of their own volition,' and that: '... the likelihood of this is very small.' He goes on to argue that: '... the long-range possibility of co-determination being introduced and practised in Italy would be at its greatest if the Communist Party comes to power, although it has consistently opposed codetermination.' [35] Irrespective of such future prospects, however, there were indications in the Spring of 1977 that the French CGT/FO was moving from a position of opposition towards a position of acceptance on the principle of workers' participation.

Moreover, while British trade unions have been learning from workers' participation models in Germany and Holland, continental Western European trade unions have paid increasing attention to the British shop steward system. As Fogarty rightly points out: [36]

> In countries such as France, Belgium, and even Germany, where the traditional works council system is particularly deeply entrenched, there has been a strong tendency to supplement it through the activity of the union branch or steward system in each plant.

Against these favourable developments must be held that:

a) the form of workers' participation envisaged by the Bullock Report for Britain differs in two important respects from continental practices;

b) the strength of the opposition within the ETUC towards workers' participation could increase with the joining of the French CGT and the possible joining of the Communist trade unions of Portugal and Spain;

c) the likelihood of the ETUC formulating or advancing specific proposals on workers' participation, especially as it concerns guidelines for national legislation, is still very slim.

Nevertheless, it seems plausible that some common solution on the priority and specific form of works councils, workers' participation, asset formation and collective bargaining will be found within the ETUC, in the not too distant future, to cope with either the growing phenomenon of transnational business mergers, or the proposed legislation on the Statute for a European Company.

Having described some of the difficulties with which trade unions of the ETUC are faced in agreeing on a common approach towards industrial democracy or the democratisation of the economy, let us now consider another thorny issue in the policy formation of the

ETUC, namely, the co-operation with and promotion of the Commission of the EC.

ETUC policy towards the Commission

Throughout the period between mid-1968 and the end of 1972, most of the major trade union declarations contained references which favoured upgrading the institutional role of the Commission and European integration in general. [37] However, between 1973 and 1975, there were indications that the ETUC did not stress the strengthening of the institutional role of the Commission to the same extent as its forerunner, the ECFTU, had done.

On the contrary, there were signs, as the following comparison will show, that the former EFTA wing trade unions of the ICFTU (British, Swiss, Austrian and Scandinavian trade unions) together with the Italian CGIL, differed from the former ECFTU group on the question of 'institutional expansion'.

	Position of former EFTA Group of the ICFTU	Position of the ECFTU
Institutional expansion of the Commission	Opposition	Support
Expansion of the powers of the European Parliament, as well as direct elections for the European Parliament	Opposition	Support
Preservation of the unanimity rule in the Council of Ministers	Support	Opposition
Realisation of the Economic Monetary and Political Union	Opposition	Support
Preference for using the Council, CPR and national governments as the primary channels for advancing social policy demands instead of the Commission	Support	Opposition (preference for the Commission)

The opposition to the institutional expansion of the EC by the EFTA wing trade unions and others stemmed from various causes as the following will show. The Swiss, Swedish, Austrian and Finnish trade unions opposed (and still oppose) because of their stand on neutrality. The Norwegian LO had initially come out in favour of the EC and in favour of Norwegian entry into the EC, [38] but because of the outcome of the Referendum in 1972, turned against it. Similarly, the Danish trade unions had supported Danish entry into the EC in the EC Referendum in 1972, [39] but partly because of the growing discontent among the Danish public about the EC, and partly because of the influence of trade unions from the other Scandinavian countries, they took a view which was not in favour of increasing Community power. While participating in the EC institutions and committees, in contrast to the British trade unions, and while proclaiming that the EC had brought favourable results to Danish workers, [40] the Danish trade unions remained opposed between 1973 and 1976 to attempts to make the EC institutions more supranational.

Both the Irish TUC (1971 and 1972) and the British TUC (1971 to 1975) decided against EC membership in their respective annual congresses, and both had taken steps to organise an anti-EC campaign before the two respective referenda in 1972 and 1975. However, in spite of the decisions of the two congresses, some individual unions in each country had supported membership on the terms negotiated by their respective governments. [41] Initially, leaders of the British TUC had viewed the EC as impeding collaboration between trade unions in Eastern and Western Europe and interfering with programmes calling for the extension of nationalised industries.

No doubt the outcome of the Referendum in 1975 had an important impact on the British TUC policy orientation towards the EC, such as the decision to send representatives to the EC institutions. Still, while recognising that economic benefits can be obtained from participation in these institutions, the majority of the TUC appears to be not fundamentally convinced that there is an advantage to be gained from supporting the growth of Community power.

Finally, the Italian Communist trade union (CGIL), as well as the French CGT, had for a long time denounced the EC as offering benefits to capitalists, but not to workers, and had called for the abolition of the EC. While the CGIL did not seek direct access to the EC institutions, the EC made it clear that it was not in favour of participation in its institutions by members of either the Communist Party or the Communist trade unions from either country. A change, however, took place in 1967 when the CGIL and CGT decided to set up a Co-ordinating Committee in Brussels which was intended to co-ordinate activities with the EC institutions. By February 1969, the Commission of the EC had its first meeting with representatives of the CGT/CGIL Co-ordinating Committee, and on 17 March 1969, the Commission issued a communiqué declaring that contacts had been made with the CGT/CGIL. This communiqué has been generally considered to be the official acceptance by the Commission of the CGT/CGIL Co-ordinating Committee as a Community pressure group. It indicated a willingness to undertake consultations with this Committee, and to offer its representatives the possibility of participating in Advisory Committees and Joint Committees provided for under the framework of the EC, which both accepted.

Influenced in part by national election objectives of the Communist Party, and in part by the economic benefits obtained for Italian workers from the working of the EC, the CGIL has become more co-operative on matters relating to the existence and promotion of the EC in the last two years. While not overtly in favour of the EC, the French CGT also seems to accept its existence and suggests ways of improving it. For example, in June 1974, Georges Seguy, General Secretary of the CGT, stated, during a visit to Brussels, that Europe had become a reality, but that it had no future under domination of the great industrial and financial powers. He stressed that problems arising out of the development of capitalism could not be dealt with at national level, but for measures to be taken there should be real co-ordination of trade union action at European level. [42]

Conclusion

In many ways, the success of forming a large trade union organisation at European level with a number of important structural features, to meet the challenge of transnational business mergers and the working of the European Community, has also been one of the major drawbacks for the effectiveness of the ETUC. The diversity which has been introduced with the numerical strength of 31 member organisations within the ETUC often makes the formation of a common policy or common action programme a formidable task. The diversity stems from a number of factors, the most important of which are the different experiences trade unions have had in dealing with management, especially with regard to:

a) Works councils, workers' participation, asset formation and collective bargaining;

b)   Statutory regulations and legal provisions for settling
     industrial disputes.

Other factors impairing the effectiveness of the ETUC involve the
different states of industrialisation (advanced versus less developed)
of the 18 countries from which the ETUC draws its membership and
the divergent economic policies which these countries have pursued
(inflationary versus deflationary or the preference for fighting
inflation over unemployment). The different trade union strength
(percentage of unionised workers) and more so the extents of
structural cohesion between leaders and the rank and file of the
individual trade union movements have also affected the effectiveness
of the ETUC. [43]   Finally, the political role trade unions have sometimes played in reflecting a certain political line of a national
political party has at times been detrimental to the working of the
ETUC. Related to the latter, but often superimposed on the aforementioned factors, are the different objectives, although less rigid now
than prior to 1973/74, the Socialist, Social Democratic, Liberal,
Christian and Communist trade unions have about the type of
society desired (religiously oriented, mixed economy or a classless
society) and the kind of Europe envisaged (a Europe with Christian
values, a Socialist Europe or a Communist Europe).
    Yet having pointed out the difficulties and weaknesses of the
ETUC it must also be stated that some progress has been made among
the trade union affiliations of the ETUC to come to terms with
crucial issues such as the adoption of workers' participation by about
two-thirds of the ETUC members, recognising, however, that the
envisaged British model will also mean a divergence with regard to the
existing continental forms by which workers' participation is being
practised. Moreover, it appears that the prospects of agreements
within the ETUC on the forms whereby workers' participation should
be practised as it concerns the Statute of the European Company, are
relatively good. In addition, there have also been some improvements
in 1976 on the ETUC stand on matters concerning the EC, such as
direct election to the European Parliament. [44]
    Whether or not the trend towards convergence on trade union
policy will continue, and whether or not more 'flesh' will be put on
the skeleton represented presently by the ETUC, which is still in
many ways an unwieldy organisation, is an empirical question. No
doubt the growing phenomenon of business mergers across national
frontiers, the activities of multinational corporations (transfer of
production sites) in general and the process of European integration,
especially with regard to company legislation and social policy

harmonisation, will have an impact on this trend. To say more on the impact of these pressures and whether or not the trade unions find ways of a suitable response on specific issues of social policy, is the task of the following chapter.

Whereas the emphasis in chapters 2 and 3 has been on the structures and cohesion of the Community pressure groups concerned with social policy (so far mostly in trade unions), chapter 4 will examine the specific demands these Community pressure groups have put forward to the Commission for social policy harmonisation. In chapter 4, we will then examine, for example, whether the re-organisation of European trade union organisations has been accompanied by increasing demands for certain issues of social policy harmonisation, and whether the European trade union organisations have aligned their forces in achieving certain social policy objectives at the Community level. Chapter 5 will assess the role the Commission has played in dealing with the different demands of the Community pressure groups for social policy harmonisation and in combining them with existing provisions of the Rome Treaty on social policy.

Notes

[1]   The following is an extract from a draft opinion the DGB prepared for the (Community) Social Action Programme in April 1973 under the heading of 'Demokratisierung der Wirtschaft' (Democratisation of the Economy). The DGB observes that since the decisions of the large enterprises on investments, marketing and prices influence substantially the economic and social developments, a control is necessary of all economic and social decisions at all levels: at plant level, regional level, national level and European level ... the democratisation of the economy requires primarily a speedy harmonisation of the company law in the EC in order to provide the setting for common rights of the workers and their trade unions. The right to collective bargaining, the collective bargaining autonomy and the participation of the trade unions in the enterprises must be expanded and protected. This also requires the right of the workers' representatives to establish international contacts in the multi-national companies and to establish common (trade union) organs.

[2]   For example, France's Comité d'Entreprise has, since 1945, covered all undertakings with 50 or more employees. Belgium created the Conseil d'Entreprise in 1948 for firms with 150 or more workers. In the Netherlands, the Ondernemingsraad has, since 1950,

catered for firms with 100 or more workers. Germany introduced the Betriebsrat in 1952 for firms with five or more workers. It should be stressed that France and Italy have two additional forms of workers' representation at plant level. These are, in the case of France, the union delegates and personnel delegates, and in the case of Italy, the internal commission and the union delegates. However, there is a great deal of overlapping, both in terms of jurisdiction and of membership between the three forms in each country.

[3]   Anthony Carew, 'Shop Floor Trade Unionism in Western Europe,' *European Studies* 18, 1974.

[4]   See 'Employee Participation and Company Structure,' *Bulletin of the European Communities* (also known as the Green Paper of the Commission on this subject); *Supplement 8/75,*   Office for Official Publications of the European Communities, Luxembourg 1975, p.59. Referred to below as *Supplement 8/75.*

[5]   For further details on the collaboration between trade unions and works councils and on the enactment of 'new' laws concerning works councils, see *Supplement 8/75*; Solomon Barkin, ed. *Worker Militancy and its Consequences 1965-1975: New Directions in Western Industrial Relations*, Praeger Special Studies in International Economics and Development, London 1975, pp 384-6; Willatt, *Multinational Unions,* p.40; Michael P. Fogarty, *Work and Industrial Relations in the European Community,* Chatham House and PEP; European Series 24, London 1975, p.17; Eric Jacobs, *European Trade Unionism,* Croom Helm, London 1973, pp 54-76; and Walter Kendall, *The Labour Movement in Europe,* Allen Lane, Penguin Books Ltd., London 1975.

[6]   This refers to the Commission's proposal of 1972 (Fifth Directive) for a Statute for a European Company, which provides that companies under this Statute should be obliged to have statutory works councils. (More on this in the section on workers' participation.)

[7]   In a document of 1974 the ETUC took the view that the members of the European Works Council (one of the components of the European Company) should be 'elected among people considered as representatives of the workers and/or the representatives of the workers organised in trade unions in the various Member States.' This made allowance for both the British and Continental practices of shopfloor representation. For this point and related matters, see the *ETUC Position* on the Proposal from the European Commission for the Statute of the European Company, Brussels , 9 July 1974; and the enclosure to that Position entitled Proposals for Amendment from the ETUC: Related to European Works' Council.

[8]   For example, the Biedenkopf Report (a document by a group of experts advising the German Government) noted that there appeared to be a relationship in Germany between the participation of employees on the supervisory board, on the one hand, and on the other, the amount of co-operation between the management and the works councils. The scope of the latter appeared to be related to the efficiency of the former. Cited in *Supplement 8/75*, p.26. In addition, it should be pointed out that the German works councils elect workers' representatives to the company board. Similarly, in the Netherlands, works councils nominate candidates to be co-opted by the existing boards and retain veto powers on all new selections.

[9]   Workers' participation also exists in France but in a very limited form. Two workers' representatives with *consultative* powers sit on the Conseil d'Administration.

[10]   John Robinson, 'Giving Workers a Say in Running the Firm,' *European Community*, March 1973, pp 16-18.

[11]   See *Supplement 8/75*, p.98.

[12]   John F.B. Goodman, 'Toward the Social Contract,' Barkin (ed.) *Worker Militancy and its Consequences*, p.75.

[13]   For further details, see Barkin, *Worker Militancy and its Consequences*, p.391.

[14]   See Arndt Sorge, 'The Evolution of Industrial Democracy in the Countries of the European Community,' *British Journal of Industrial Relations*, vol.14, no.3, November 1976, p.290.

[15]   In its 1975 Congress the FGTB confirmed that: 'The long-term objective remains self-management and in the meantime, the line to be taken is that of 'workers' control', which is a complete control of trade union autonomy, as opposed to co-management, while opening the door to concertation, which leads either to the conclusion of agreements or to contestation.' Quoted in *EC Trade Union Information*, Special Number, November 1975. Similar objectives have been expressed by the CGIL and CGT. For further details, see an excellent presentation by Ken Coates and Tony Topham, *The New Unionism: The Case for Workers' Control*, Penguin Books, Harmondsworth, 1974.

[16]   For example, the ECFTU suggested that the new supervisory board should give the shareholders one-third of the seats, like the employees, with the final third filled by neutrals, who would be co-opted according to the wish of the employee and shareholder representatives.

[17]   See *European Communities Trade Union Information*, Special Issue 5, May 1976.

[18]   For details on these schemes, as well as for the prospects of

these schemes, see Barkin, *Worker Militancy and its Consequences*; Willatt, *Multinational Unions*; Fogarty, *Work and Industrial Relations in the European Community*; and *Supplement 8/75*.

[19]   See Barkin, *Worker Militancy and its Consequences*, p.391.

[20]   See Willatt, *Multinational Unions*, p.41.

[21]   See *Supplement 8/75*, p.31.

[22]   See Willatt, *Multinational Unions*, p.41.

[23]   See *European Communities Trade Union Information*, Special Issue 5, May 1975.

[24]   See Fogarty, *Work and Industrial Relations in the European Community*, p.38.

[25]   Centralised collective bargaining, either regional or national, has been preserved to a large extent in the Scandinavian countries and Germany between top level representatives of the employers and trade union organisations. Both general and specific questions are negotiated at this level. This also means that in these countries, including France, collective agreements take precedence as regards basic working conditions, over agreement concluded at works level. For further details, see Jacobs, *European Trade Unionism*, pp 82-4.

[26]   The General Council of the TUC in Britain has acknowledged that, despite the developments (increased scope of collective bargaining agreements and increased plant level agreements) which have taken place in the UK, major decisions such as those on investments, location, closures, takeovers, mergers and the product specialisation of an enterprise, are normally taken unilaterally and are not subjected to collective bargaining. *Industrial Democracy Report* by the TUC General Council to the 1974 Trade Union Congress, July 1974, paragraphs 84 and 85. However, it is important to point out that the Employment Protection Bill, passed by the British Parliament in 1975, alleviates some of these deficiences. For example, it obliges employers not only to disclose to trade union representatives information requested for collective bargaining purposes, but also to inform and consult those representatives in redundancy situations. For more details, see *Supplement 8/75* especially pp 23, 26, 94 and 96.

[27]   Specific references on this point can be found in *Ibid.*, especially p.67; and Barkin, *Worker Militancy and its Consequences*, especially p.399.

[28]   These 'Committees' are comprised of equal numbers of elected employers' and workers' representatives, normally with a lawyer acting as secretary.

[29]   Jacobs, *European Trade Unionism*, pp 50-1. See also Kendall, *The Labour Movement in Europe*, especially p.84.

[30]   See Crijns, 'Collective Bargaining in Nations of the EEC,'
pp 93-8; and Bouvard, *Labor Movements*, p.21.
[31]   As observed by Jacobs: 'The Industrial Relations Act of 1971
attempted to formalise union negotiating rights, give government
powers to suspend strike action in emergencies and make collective
agreements legally binding. ... Few, if any, legally binding collective
agreements were signed as a result of the Act.' Jacobs, *European
Trade Unionism*, p.86.
[32]   See note 26 above.
[33]   As pointed out by Fogarty:

> The British Labour movement accepts that the law can
> play a subsidiary part in facilitating collective bargaining,
> and thus some form of enabling legislation may be useful
> towards developing joint control by unions of firms'
> policies at works level. But it stands firm on the idea that
> it is the union and shop stewards, not any form of
> statutory works council, which must play the key part at
> this level.

Fogarty, *Work and Industrial Relations in the EC*, p.35.
[34]   As quoted by *The Observer*, Bullock states flatly that there
is: ' ... no necessary contradiction between board-level representation
for unions and collective bargaining. Rather we believe they are
similar and complementary processes.' *The Observer*, 23 January
1977.
[35]   Sorge supports his argument with the view that: ' ... the
chances for co-determination improve substantially when a labour
movement experiences a considerable gain in political power.' He
also believes that: ' ... against the background of state repression of
unions in Italy, the logic of the hypothetical situation of the main
forces of the left coming to power is strongly in favour of co-
determination, despite present-day values of the labour movement.'
See Sorge, 'The Evolution of Industrial Democracy,' p.292.
[36]   Fogarty, *Work and Industrial Relations in the EC*, p.17.
[37]   For example, in April 1969, Ludwig Rosenberg, the then
President of the German DGB and retiring President of the EC Trade
Union Secretariat of the ICFTU, made the following comments on
Community membership:

> We trade unionists ... will not tire of reminding people
> that only a politically and economically united Europe
> will allow the achievement of the aims we have set our-
> selves: to assure and increase the material well-being of
> Europeans. ... A Europe made up of different nations

which all act as if they were independent of each other —
but which are not so — this Europe is for us not reality,
but a terrible error, as dangerous as it is reactionary.
... This is why we remain firm in our support of the
spirit of Rome Treaties and of the task which they set out.

Quoted in *Trade Union News from the European Community*, 17,
Spring/Summer 1975, p.26.

[38]   At its special Congress on 2-3 June 1972, the Norwegian
Trade Union (LO) decided, by a vote of 230 to 81, in favour of EC
entry. This large majority in favour is interesting, since the
population in a referendum held thereafter decided narrowly against
the EC entry.

[39]   By a vote of 524 to 406, the Danish Federation of Trade
Unions (LO) decided on 18 May 1972 in favour of Denmark's
membership to the EC on the terms negotiated by the Danish
Government. The Resolution adopted then stated that:

> Congress considers Denmark's participation in enlarged
> co-operation within the EEC and a strengthening of trade
> union co-operation across frontiers to be the basis of a
> solution to these problems, and thereby a further develop-
> ment of society in conformity with the fundamental
> interests of the labour movement.

Quoted in *Trade Union News from the European Community*, 17,
Spring/Summer 1975, p.27.

[40]   For example, in an interview in 1974, Thomas Nielsen,
President of the LO, stated that:

> It must be emphasised that membership of the European
> Community has already brought great benefits to the
> Danish people and to the Danish workers, following a
> sharp rise in earnings from exports, both in agriculture
> and industrial sectors.

Quoted in *Ibid.*, pp 27-8.

[41]   For example, with regard to Britain, the National Union of
Mineworkers and the Industrial Steel Trade Union Consultative
Committee participated in the ECSC Consultative Committee. Both,
however, suspended participation between October 1974 and
October 1975. Other examples of the split in the British TUC ranks
on the EC question were witnessed in: (a) the narrowly defeated
motion for participation at the 1973 Congress, where 4,922,000
voted against and 4,452,000 voted in favour; and (b) the formation
of the Trade Union Alliance for Europe in April 1975, under the

chairmanship of Vic Feather, former General Secretary of the TUC, which claimed support from 50 trade unions and from one-third to one-half of the TUC General Council's 40 members. For more details, see *Trade Union News from the European Community*, 17; and *European Communities Trade Union Information*, Special Issue, August 1975.

[42]   See *Trade Union News from the European Community*, 17, p.28.

[43]   The following are some of the important differences:

a)   The Austrian, Swedish and Belgian trade unions are numerically strong with over 50 per cent of the work force organised;

b)   The British and Danish trade unions have concentrated on individual crafts within an industry rather than on that industry as a whole;

c)   The Danish, Norwegian and, to a lesser extent, the other continental trade unions have a more centralised structure than the British trade unions. Thus the central organisations of the former wield more power over their affiliates, and shopfloor bodies have been more dependent on the upper levels of the union hierarchy than in the case of the latter;

d)   The Scandinavian and German trade unions have a greater financial strength than the British or other continental trade unions, especially the French.

For further details, see Carew, 'Shop Floor Trade Unionism in Western Europe'; and Kendall, *The Labour Movement in Europe*.

[44]   For example, the ETUC made a declaration of solidarity at a demonstration organised by the Union of European Federalists on 12 July 1976; supporting the demand concerning the direct election of the European Parliament. See *European Communities Trade Union Information* 7/8, July/August 1976.

4   Demands of Community pressure groups

Introduction

Chapter 4 examines the demands that Community pressure groups concerned with social policy have put forward to the Community institutions, with regard to the harmonisation of social policy at the Community level between mid-1968 to 1976. Emphasis is placed on the social policy demands of Community pressure groups involving:

1. the expansion of the finance and operation of the European Social Fund (ESF);

2. the establishment of a common vocational training policy at the Community level;

3. the harmonisation of social security provisions for migrant workers;

4. the harmonisation of social security systems in general;

5. the implementation of the principle of equal pay for men and women.

These five social policy issues were selected because of references (some with specific content as to aims and time of implementation, and some with more ambiguous content) in the Treaty of Rome that established the EC. See also chapter 5 on the implications of the Treaty provisions. A major objective of this chapter will be to determine whether the majority of social policy demands expressed by the Community pressure groups in the period between mid-1968 and 1976 called for the expansion of social policy harmonisation at the Community level beyond that specifically mentioned in the Treaty of Rome provisions. In addition, an attempt will be made to ascertain which of such groups, the trade unions, employers' organisations or the ESC, [1] called for the speedy harmonisation of a number of social policy issues at the Community level, and which Community pressure groups had reservations or called for harmonisation steps at a slower pace.

Another purpose of this chapter will be to determine the underlying motives of Community pressure groups for activities in the social policy sector. Attention will be paid to the importance and ranking of these motives in order to ascertain the conditions under which Community pressure groups either exert pressure on the central institutions of the EC for increasing social policy harmonisation, or express reservations about increasing social policy harmonisation.

Extent of harmonisation desired

From the interviews and written data collected for this chapter, it appears that Community pressure groups' demands expressed the following priority preferences (ranked in order of importance) for the harmonisation of the five social policy issues:

a) The European Social Fund (ESF);

b) Social security benefits for migrant workers;

c) Equal pay for men and women;

d) Vocational training provisions;

e) Social security harmonisation, in general.

The ESF was set up in 1962, largely in anticipation of the consequences resulting from the Common Agricultural Policy, in order to facilitate the employment of workers and increase their geographical and occupational mobility within the Community by contributing towards the costs of retraining and resettlement. Both the responses in interviews and the written statements by Community pressure groups indicated the great importance these organisations placed on the improvement of the operation of the ESF and on the expansion of its activities and growth of financial resources. However, there were some disagreements between trade unions and employers' organisations over:

a) The size of the ESF budget and the use of the Community's own resources (rather than the contributions from Member States to the ESF budget);

b) The types or categories of workers benefitting from the ESF;

c) The procedure by which the improved operation should be determined and implemented.

For example, the trade unions initially (1969 to 1971) called for a larger ESF budget and were more in favour of using the Community's own resources for the ESF budget than were the employers' organisations; although the position of the employers' organisations, especially COPA, on these particular issues resembled that of the trade unions from 1972 onward. There were also some differences between the trade unions, on the one hand, and UNICE and the ESC, on the other, over the question of ESF aid for young people and the self-employed. However, the only fundamental difference between trade unions and UNICE concerned ESF assistance for migrant workers. The trade unions, while mainly in favour of ESF inter-vention for migrant workers, started in 1971/72 to express reservations on the application of ESF assistance. They began to fear that ESF assistance could become an instrument for promoting the migration of workers unduly, and stressed that regional transfer of capital should be sought, rather than the movement of labour.

Trade unions pointed out, especially from 1972 onwards, that the ESF aid for migrant workers should be used for:

a) The improvement of vocational training structures, especially in the less developed regions;

b) The improvement of social benefits and services for migrant workers, especially with regard to language, habits or customs, and living conditions. [2] Migrant workers should also be assisted in preparing for new conditions of life and work before departure to a 'new' country and after returning to the country of origin.

c) An interim aid allowance for migrant workers in cases where they had to seek re-employment.

In contrast, the employers' organisations viewed the 'renewed' ESF as an instrument for promoting the migration of workers. Finally, there were also some differences between trade unions and employers' organisations involving the tasks assigned to the Standing Committee on Employment (SCE) and the Advisory Committee of the ESF in the determination and implementation of ESF guidelines. This latter disagreement will be dealt with shortly.

A substantial part of the demands made by the Community pressure groups called for improvements in the payments of social security benefits for migrant workers and their dependants. [3] The trade unions especially maintained that the distortions still existing in the granting of social security benefits between migrant workers and nationals of the host countries deserved priority attention. They also called for progressive adjustments on supplementary social security benefits in order that migrant workers could both acquire and retain all the rights which Article 51 specified. The discrepancies over supplementary benefits stem primarily from the different methods by which companies in the various countries determine extra benefits, such as:

a) The provisions in Germany requiring workers to be in the employment of the company when the risk (sickness, invalidity, retirement, etc.) materialises;

b) The different probationary period requirements insisted upon by firms.

The employers' organisations expressed reservations about the need to harmonise, at least in the short and medium-term, the existing differences on supplementary benefits.

While most groups expressed demands for the implementation of the principle of equal pay for men and women, these were, in the period between mid-1968 to 1972, more in the nature of token expressions than demands. In particular, the statements advanced by the employers' organisations in that period were vague on this issue. In general, the statements made reference to the fact that women were not getting the same opportunities and conditions of employment as men, and that these inadequacies should be eliminated through EC legislation. On several occasions, trade unions also suggested the elimination of any discrimination which existed in certain national laws, directly or indirectly affecting wages.

Trade unions have greatly increased their demands for EC measures and legislation [4] regarding women workers since 1973, calling for:

a) Equality as regards pay;

b) Greater and more secure employment opportunities;

c) Better working conditions and further training aimed at skilled occupations;

d) Equality as regards unemployment benefits.

Trade unions were also keen on the establishment of national committees on women's employment problems. [5] In a statement on International Women's Year in 1975, the ETUC called on the EC to adopt and put into practice all the necessary legal instruments (regulations, directives, recommendations) to promote the upward harmonisation of national laws and practices. [6]

While most Community pressure groups stressed as urgent the expansion of the scope of vocational training throughout the Community, they (especially the employers' organisations) pressed less urgently for the harmonisation of vocational training certificates and the different training levels. In addition, while generally stressing the need for co-operation on research projects in the area of vocational training, there were reservations up until 1973 from the employers' organisations on the establishment of a European Centre for Vocational Training. There were also indications from the employers' groups that harmonisation steps must not be disruptive to the overall economic process in the Community, i.e. they were not to endanger economic growth.

Nevertheless, in spite of the above-cited reservations, the demands of the Community pressure groups, at least from 1973 onwards, called for measures which went beyond the provisions of the Treaty of Rome for vocational training in at least two ways:

a)   The trade unions insisted that Article 128 of the Treaty of Rome, dealing with vocational policy, should be interpreted more broadly, not only with respect to vocational training proper, but also with respect to aspects of permanent education. In addition, the trade unions indicated that Article 128 had not been sufficiently applied;

b)   The establishment of a European Centre for Vocational Training and its finance through Community resources was not foreseen in the Treaty of Rome.

The major European trade union organisations indicated that they were in favour of a gradual harmonisation of the different social security schemes. The position of the trade unions became particularly apparent in a statement delivered by the ETUC in its Opinion of a Social Action Programme in October 1973. The ETUC emphasised that, in principle, they saw no reason why there should be multiple norms of social security for the individual groups in advanced democracies and industrial states. They therefore supported plans for the creation of comparable indices of social security, family allowances and other working conditions in Western Europe. Trade unions also pressed for Community legislation on a forty-hour week and four weeks' annual holiday, to secure that *all* member countries would adopt this principle and to guarantee that most categories of workers, including women and agricultural workers, were covered by such a provision.

In contrast to the trade unions, the ESC and UNICE maintained that because of different historical developments and because social security was composed of a number of complex institutions having such varied social, economic, financial and political repercussions, social security schemes could only be harmonised in the very long-term. Rather than using Community instruments, as preferred by the trade unions, employers' organisations stressed that excessive differences between the various schemes should be met through adequate but not necessarily identical means. By 'adequate' means, the employers' organisations understood that when changes were made in the individual national social security provisions, attention should be paid to developments in the other Member States, and adjustments should be made accordingly by a method of 'natural convergence'. [7] Thus the employers' organisations believed that it would be difficult and useless to aim for complete harmonisation of social security schemes in the medium-term. They were also reluctant to accept the introduction of a forty-hour week. Reservations were particularly expressed by COCCEE in the commerce sector and by COPA in the agricultural sector.

All groups considered an index of social indicators and a European Social Budget (ESB) as indispensable instruments for the progressive harmonisation of social security in the EC, which should be utilised as soon as possible. They felt that these were valuable means of acquiring information about social security, i.e. means for a quantifiable and analytical stocktaking on the basis of common definitions and criteria. However, UNICE had one reservation, namely that the ESB should not specify legally enforceable aims for the Member States.

Having examined the extent to which Community pressure groups desired harmonisation on the above-mentioned five social policy issues, let us now consider the underlying motives of Community pressure groups behind these harmonisation desires.

Motives for Community pressure groups' demands

From the available written data and the interviews conducted (presented in this chapter), three main factors can be singled out which appear to have influenced the Community pressure groups' demands on social policy harmonisation. Two of the factors can be seen as having led to demands calling for increasing harmonisation and one to demands involving reservations on increasing harmon-isation. The first two factors were:

a)   Structural economic changes and employment problems;

b)   The free movement of labour.

These two factors will be referred to as positive factors. The factor causing reservations related to what employers' organisations identified as 'competition interference'. This factor will be known as the negative factor. An illustration of the two positive factors and their inter-relationship with the other main factors, will be provided in figure 4.1.

Structural economic changes and employment problems

Community pressure groups pointed out that a major factor for their increasing demands on social policy harmonisation, primarily regard-ing the ESF and vocational training, with respect to the EC institutions, was the occurrence of great structural economic changes and employment problems in two periods: 1967/68 and 1974/75.

Let us start by examining the causes and implications of the structural changes and employment problems of the 1967/68 period, which coincided with the completion of the free movement of labour sector.

According to the Community pressure groups, the impact of tech-nological changes, [8] together with the occurrence of a slight economic recession in some countries (Germany) of the EC, caused many structural economic changes, and subsequently raised the unemployment level. (See table 4.1). References to technological changes were made especially to the coal mining sector, shipbuilding and textile industries. For example, relevant data indicated that in 1966/67, 36 coal-mining firms were closed in Germany, involving a loss of 53,233 jobs. This trend continued during 1968 to 1970, affecting both Germany and other EC Member States. [9] Similar losses in the number of employees were reported in the shipbuilding (25 per cent between 1967 and 1969) and textile sectors (losing 45,000 jobs in 1968) throughout the EC. [10] In addition, inter-national trade factors (liberalisation of trade and the revaluation and devaluation of currencies) contributed, via increased competition among firms, to the impact of technological changes and economic recession on the unemployment level.

Moreover, Community pressure groups stressed that the impact on

Figure 4.1 *Motives of community pressure groups

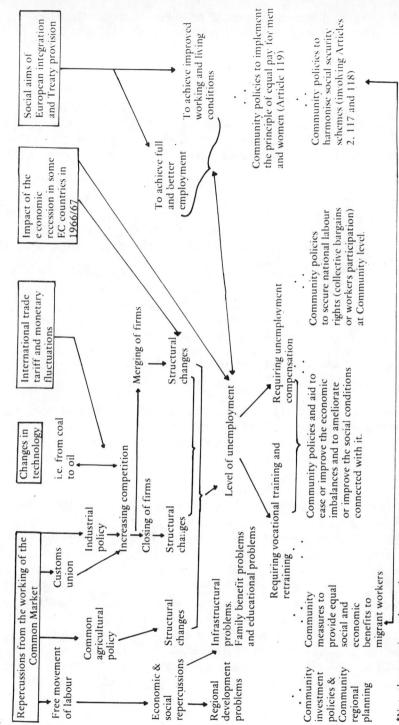

*Note these motives relate only to causes which had a positive result on social policy harmonisation

employment questions and social problems arising both from the technological changes and structural economic changes, was accelerated by:

a)   the anticipation and later the working of the Customs Union, adding, as figure 4.2 shows, to the number of mergers between firms (both within a Member State and between firms of two or more Member States) in order either to safeguard the market share previously held or to capture a share of the expanded 'home market'. (See also chapter 2, p.28.)

b)   the Commission's proposals concerning industrial policy — themselves a consequence of the circumstances described in point (a) and desired by the employers' groups, but in turn provoking trade unions to lobby the Commission for the incorporation of social or labour provisions in these proposals;

c)   the consequences of the Common Agricultural Policy (CAP) which, as table 4.1 shows, had a greater impact on the employment situation from 1967 onward than prior to that date; requiring, for example, financial aids to provide vocational retraining for employment in industry;

d)   the energy crisis of 1973/74, increasing substantially the number of unemployed, as table 4.2 shows.

All Community pressure groups indicated that these above-mentioned factors required improvements in the area of vocational training and retraining, both from a financial point of view [11] (through the expansion of ESF activities) and from a harmonisation point of view (through a gradual harmonisation of the various vocational training standards).

However, while agreeing on the need for improvements in the area of vocational training, the trade unions and employers' organisations differed to some extent on the goals for these improvements. For example, the employers' organisations maintained that conditions existing in the area of vocational training represented an obstacle to the requirements of industry and the development of technology and to economic progress. They also stressed that improvements in vocational training would help the worker to become an integral part of the economic process so that he could contribute to the harmonious development of the economy of the EC.

In contrast, the trade unions saw in the improvements of vocational training a means whereby the extent of negative social

Table 4.1
Persons engaged in agriculture in the
original six EC countries (in 1,000)

	1960	1967	1974	Change (%) $\frac{1960}{1967}$	Change (%) $\frac{1967}{1974}$
Belgium	300	209	140	-33.3	-33.0
France	4, 189	3, 237	2, 452	-22.7	-24.2
Germany	3, 623	2, 742	1, 882	-24.3	-31.4
Italy	6, 567	4, 556	3, 111	-30.6	-31.7
Luxembourg	22	18	10	-18.1	-44.4
Netherlands	465	366	304	-21.3	-16.9
Total	15, 166	11, 128	7, 899	-26.6	-29.0

Persons engaged in agriculture in the
three 'new' EC countries (in 1,000)

	1970	1974	Change (%) $\frac{1970}{1974}$
Denmark	305	227	-25.5
Ireland	320	254	-20.6
UK	792	705	-10.9
Total	1, 417	1, 186	-17.0

Source: Die Arbeitsmarktlage in der Gemeinschaft 1971,
Commission of the EC; and the Agricultural Policy of
the European Community, *European Documentation*,
periodical 1975/6.

Table 4.2
Unemployment in the EC countries (in 1,000)

	1961	1966	1967	1968	1969	1970	1971	1972	1973	1974	1975	1976
G	181	161	459	323	179	149	185	246	273	602	1074	1055
F	203	280	365	427	340	356	446	492	450	498	839	934
I	710	759	679	684	655	609	609	697	668	997	1107	1178
N	36	46	90	84	66	56	69	115	117	135	195	211
B	89	67	92	110	88	76	75	92	96	124	208	267
L	0+	0+	0+	0+	0+	0+	0+	0+	0+	0	0.3	0.4
Total	1219	1313	1685	1628	1328	1246	1384	1642	1604	2356	3430.3	3645.4
UK	287	281	503	542	518	555	724	806	576	615	978	1246
Irl	56	52	56	60	56	65	65	71	66	70	99	111
Dk	..	..	28	26	26	17	27	23	21	53	127	122
									663	738	1204	1479
									1604	2356	3430.3	3645.4
									2267	3094	4634.3	5124.4

Source: *Eurostat: General Statistics* No.1 (1975); No.11 (1976) No.12 (1976). (Statistical office of the European Communities, Luxembourg)

Figure 4.2   Number and types of business mergers

	Subsidiary establishments [1]			Co-operation – Minority shareholding, joint shareholding (participation), common sub-companies, common head-companies [2]			Mergers – shareholding (participation) for the purpose of company control [3]				Total
	Between Member States	From Third Country(ies) to Member States	From Member State(s) to Third Country(ies)	Between firms of one country	Between firms of the Common Market	Between firms of Member State(s) & Third Country(ies)	Of one Member State	Of several Member States	Member State(s) and Third Country(ies)	Third Country(ies) & Member States	
1965	247	409	142	177	140	364	228	17	20	70	1184
1966	320	467	154	205	112	289	221	31	20	93	1912
1967	328	496	196	166	104	292	253	32	36	115	2018
1968	304	381	191	231	160	387	272	35	29	106	2096
1969*	160	239	126	145	83	197	265	50	36	57	1358
	1359	1992	809	924	599	1529	1239	165	141	441	9198

Explanations:
[1] Establishment of a subsidiary company in another Member State or in a Third Country or through a company of a Third Country in a Member State. The national transactions were not recorded.
[2] Operations whereby each participant secures his autonomy
[3] This is the closest form of merging. They involve the domination of a company (in terms of share-holding) by another.

* Only for the first six months of 1969

Source: Opera Mundi (an agency commissioned by the Commission to collect and assimilate analytical data on the merging of firms). Cited in *Die Industriepolitik der Gemeinschaft: Memorandum der Kommission an den Rat* (Kommission der Europaischen Gemeinschaften, Brussel, 1970), p.92.

repercussions from structural economic changes could be minimised. Their desire, therefore, was also to see the ESF providing assistance to workers during unemployment. In addition, trade unions stressed that the harmonisation of vocational training standards was necessary to guarantee that equal chances for workers were being provided in pursuing their occupational career.

While the structural economic changes and unemployment problems were largely responsible for the demands of Community pressure groups on the ESF and vocational training, there was another factor which was also of considerable impact. This factor was the free movement of labour.

The free movement of labour

According to the interviews and written data collected, there were two aspects arising by mid-1968 from the completion of the free movement of labour which influenced Community pressure groups' demands on social policy with respect to the EC institutions.

One aspect was related to the fact that with the completion of the free movement of labour, the number of workers going abroad increased again after it had declined between 1965 and 1967. Table 4.3 provides a general picture of the movements of migrant workers in the EC and shows the increasing number of Italians migrating to Germany [12] (of the EC countries Italy has the highest proportion of workers migrating to other EC countries, and Germany has the highest intake of migrant workers). [13]

An important factor for the increase of Italian workers going to Germany between 1968 and 1970 which reached the 1966 figure, was the abolition of working permits for workers who migrated between Member States of the EC after mid-1968. Moreover, a migrant worker of an EC country becoming unemployed had the right to unemployment compensation from the country in which he worked. This right also meant that a migrant worker could benefit from vocational training or retraining schemes offered in the country where he worked. [14] Subsequently, with the ongoing structural economic changes and employment problems caused by the factors described above, efforts to introduce sufficient vocational training facilities in the highly industrialised countries of the EC, like Germany, proved to be an additional burden. Thus, the need for improvements in the area of vocational training became increasingly pressing in 1969, leading to two specific demands. On the one hand, it was demanded that Community assistance for vocational training

78

purposes should be increased via the ESF, and that the operation of the ESF should be improved to make it more adaptable to the structural economic changes and employment problems. On the other hand, it was recognised that improvements should be made towards a gradual harmonisation of the various vocational training standards or certificates.

The second aspect related to social security benefits for migrant workers and their dependants. Both the employers' organisations and the trade unions stated that after the free movement of labour had been completed, improvements should be made in the payment of social security benefits for migrant workers and their dependants. Furthermore, they stressed that, with the finalisation of the free movement of labour, the need to seek measures at the Community level for granting migrant workers and their dependants the same treatment on social security benefits as nationals of the host country, had become a priority consideration.

However, the Community pressure groups took two views. On the one hand, they recognised that, although with some variations, geographic mobility of workers was necessary for overall economic growth in the EC and the elimination of unemployment in certain areas or in certain economic sectors. On the other hand, Community pressure groups, primarily trade unions, perceived the free movement of labour as ineffective in helping to solve structural problems, especially as they prevailed in certain regions of the EC. Related to the latter perception was the feeling of trade unions that the migration of workers should not be unduly encouraged through ESF assistance because of the social problems which resulted from the free movement of labour. They would rather have seen encouragement in investments, premium allowances for the retraining of workers in the less developed regions, as well as the creation of vocational training centres or facilities in these regions. Somewhat in contrast to the trade unions, the employers' organisations viewed the 'renewed' ESF primarily as an instrument for promoting the migration of workers. [15]

Another issue raised by the trade unions, especially from 1975 onward, was the status of 'frontier workers'; calling for co-ordinated regional policies, collective bargaining provisions and the mutual recognition of diplomas to accommodate 'frontier workers'. [16]

In addition to the two main factors mentioned by Community pressure groups for their demands regarding the ESF, vocational training and social security benefits for migrant workers, as well as, to some extent, social security provisions in general, one other factor deserves noting. This factor relates to social policy provisions of the

Table 4.3
Migrant workers in Germany [1] and other EC countries

Migrants in Germany

Year	1960	1961	1962	1963	1964	1965	1966	1967	1968	1969	1970	1973
No.of Italians	120,000	210,000	275,000	285,000	297,000	365,000	380,000	275,000	300,000	345,000	381,000	409,689
Total	297,000	550,000	697,000	840,000	1,000,000	1,225,000	1,310,000	975,000	1,080,000	1,485,000	1,949,000	2,345,254

Migrant workers
as a percentage of wage and salary earners

		1960	1965	1970	1972	1973
Germany	total	1.4	5.4	8.5	10.6	11.3
	of which EEC a)	0.8	2.1	2.2	2.5	2.7
France	total	7.0	7.7	10.0	10.8	11.0
	of which EEC a)	2.4	1.7	1.7	1.7	1.7
Italy	total	0.0	0.2	0.3	0.3	0.3
	of which EEC a)	0.0	0.1	0.1	0.2	0.2
Netherlands	total	0.8	1.8	2.9	3.0	3.2
	of which EEC a)	0.4	0.7	1.3	1.4	1.3
Belgium	total	6.3	6.2	6.7	7.1	7.1
	of which EEC a)	4.7	4.1	4.1	4.0	4.1
Luxembourg	total	22.1	27.5	30.1	34.4	35.0
	of which EEC a)	19.9	23.4	23.6	23.7	24.0
UK	total	na	na	na	na	3.4 d)
	of which EEC a)	na	na	na	na	1.6 d)
Ireland b)	total	na	na	0.3	0.3	0.3
	of which EEC a)	na	na	(0.2)	(0.2)	0.2
Denmark	total	0.6	0.8	1.3 e)	1.9	1.8
	of which EEC a)	0.3	(0.4)	(0.4)	(0.4)	(0.5)

a) 1960 to 1972: EUR – 6, from 1973: EUR – 9
b) Excluding workers from the United Kingdom and the Commonwealth
c) Excluding workers from the Nordic labour market
d) Provisional (communicated by national experts) - Excluding Commonwealth workers holding UK passport. The 1971 census of population showed that 3% of the labour force were born in the Commonwealth
e) Including non-employee workers; on basis of population census.

Source: System of Structural Indicators, Commission of the European Communities, Directorate-General for Economic and Financial Affairs, Brussels, June 1975, p.19.

[1] Main nationalities of migrant workers in Germany at the end of 1973

Nationality	Number	Percentage
Turks	528,239	22.5
Yugoslavs	466,128	20.0
Italians	409,689	17.4
Greeks	268,096	11.4
Spaniards	179,498	7.3
Dutch	70,000	3.0
Portuguese	69,099	2.9
French	51,000	2.2
British	19,000	0.8
Moroccans	15,317	0.6
Tunisians	11,162	0.4
Belgians	11,000	0.4

[1] Source: Geschäftsbericht 1970, Bundesanstalt fur Arbeit p.23; and Education of Migrant Workers' Children in the European Community European Documentation, School Series Periodical 1975/1 EC Information, Brussels 1975, p.5.

Treaty of Rome.

Impact of social policy provisions

With regard to demands for the improvement of the ESF operation, Community pressure groups stressed in the interviews and written data that these improvements were largely stipulated in the Treaty of Rome (Article 126) and, in fact, provided them with an additional incentive for expressing their demands. Similarly, the Community pressure groups pointed out that with the completion of the free movement of labour in mid-1968, demands for the improvement of social security benefits for migrant workers were largely based on Article 51 of the Treaty of Rome, which contained such improvement provisions. Moreover, in the case of the Community pressure groups' demands on the achievement of equal pay for men and women, the provisions specified in Article 119 of the Treaty of Rome appear to have been the major incentive for these demands. However, with regard to demands on the harmonisation of social security provisions in general, and on the achievement of a common vocational training policy, only the trade unions indicated that the provisions in the Treaty of Rome, Articles 2 and 128, respectively, had increased their demands for harmonisation.

While the factors described so far can be seen as having led to Community pressure groups' demands calling for increasing harmonisation of the five social policy issues, there was one factor which involved reservations on increasing harmonisation. This negative factor related to what employers' organisations noted as 'competition interference'.

Negative factor: competition interference

As pointed out above, the motives of employers' organisations need to be grouped into two categories: those favourable towards harmonisation (primarily regarding the ESF) and those unfavourable towards harmonisation. It is the latter to which we will turn now. For example, while the trade unions stressed the creation of comparable indices of social security provisions at the Community level, the employers' organisations emphasised that, due to different historical developments, and in order to preserve present modes of economic competition in the EC, *no* harmonisation measures, on a large scale, could be implemented in the medium-term. Similarly, the employers' organisations stressed that harmonisation steps on vocational training standards and on social security benefits for migrant workers, especially as they related to supplementary benefits, must not be disruptive to competition rules or to the overall economic process.

Generally, it would appear from the data that the positive factors mentioned above substantially outweighed the negative factor of 'competition interference'. It was only on the issue of social security harmonisation in general that the negative factor appeared to have some inhibiting results.

Conclusion

The main aim in chapter 4 was to discover the extent to which Community pressure groups desired harmonisation at the Community level on five social policy issues and the reasons for these desires.

The interviews and written data collected for chapter 4 indicate that in the majority of cases examined, the trade unions called for the speedy harmonisation of the five social policy issues, followed by similar demands from the ESC. While favouring a speedy harmonisation on the ESF and social security benefits for migrant workers (except supplementary benefits) the employers' organisations indicated reservations on the harmonisation process of social security provisions in general, the principle of equal pay for men and women, and vocational training standards, especially as they related to the mutual recognition of vocational training certificates. Specifically, the following observations can be made:

a) In three out of five social policy issues, the trade unions called for a speedy *expansion* of the respective Treaty provisions. For the two remaining issues, the trade unions called for an immediate or short-term *implementation* of the Treaty provisions in the case of equal pay for men and women, and for a gradual *implementation* in the case of social security provisions in general.

b) In contrast, the employers' organisations called only *once* for an *expansion* of the Treaty provisions, namely in the case of the ESF. On the issues of social security provisions for migrant workers, a common vocational training policy and equal pay for men and women, the employers' organisations desired the gradual *implementation* of the respective Treaty provisions. In the case of the harmonisation of social security provisions in general, the employers' organisations indicated that the relevant Treaty provisions (Articles 2, 117 and 118) could only be implemented in the long-term.

With regard to the main cause(s) for these demands on the five social policy issues with respect to the central institutions of the EC, the following can be noted. Both the trade unions and the employers' organisations indicated that the main causes for their demands on the ESF and vocational training in the period between mid-1968 and 1975 were structural economic problems and employment problems. They further noted that these structural economic problems and employment problems were the result of several factors occurring between 1967 and 1975. These factors were:

a) the economic recession in certain countries of the EC in 1967, as well as large technological changes in 1966/67;

b) the impact of the Customs Union and CAP between 1967 and 1969;

c) the impact of the free movement of labour between 1969 and 1973;

d) the impact of external factors such as trade liberalisation, monetary fluctuations (revaluation and devaluation of currencies), and the energy crisis (late 1974/75) between 1971 and 1975.

Another main cause singled out by both the trade unions and the employers' organisations for their demands on social security provisions for migrant workers and, to a small extent, on social security provisions in general between mid-1968 and 1973, was the completion of the free movement of labour.

Furthermore, both the trade unions and employers' organisations pointed out that the Treaty provisions were a main cause for their demands on the issue of the principle of equal pay for men and women (Article 119). In addition, the trade unions stressed that Articles 117, 118 and especially Article 2 of the Treaty of Rome had been a main cause for their demands on the harmonisation of social security provisions in general.

With regard to the impact of positive and negative factors on increasing social policy harmonisation, it can be maintained that the positive factors, mentioned above, substantially outweighed the negative factor, identified as 'competition interference'. It was only on the social policy issue of social security harmonisation in general that the negative factor appeared to have had some inhibiting results.

Furthermore, the interviews and written data provided in this chapter indicated an increasing orientation of pressure groups, particularly trade unions, towards the central institutions of the EC for the pursuit of interests relating to the five social policy issues between mid-1968 and 1975. This increasing orientation was largely a response to what Community pressure groups perceived as a strengthening of the Commission's competences to deal with problems in a growing number of policy areas, such as in agriculture, industry, the Customs Union and the free movement of labour, and the potential rewards which could be obtained from the Commission's proposals in these areas. However, while the employers' organisations sought to influence the Commission, primarily for economic reasons, [17] the trade unions wanted to be sure that social interests were incorporated by the Commission in proposals concerning the economic and industrial developments in the EC. Thus, while the employers' organisations and the trade unions perceived a similar need for increasing their orientation towards the central institutions of the EC, they did so for different reasons and with different aims.

Finally, in general Community pressure groups, especially trade unions, insisted that they must be given the opportunity to fully participate in the administration and function of such Community instruments as the ESF, the European Centre for Vocational Training and the ESB. Foremost among these demands for participation was the establishment of consultative bodies consisting of representatives of the Commission, governments, employers' organisations and trade unions.

Whether the Commission was able to utilise strengthened European trade union organisations accompanied by certain demands of these groups for the expansion of social policy integration will be examined in the following chapter. There an attempt will be made to analyse the Commission's ability to utilise the existing Treaty provisions in social policy and to gain the support of Community pressure groups in the promotion of social policy legislation.

Notes

[1]   The ESC consists of delegates from economic and social organisations, primarily from the two sides of industry. The national organisations appoint their representatives to the ESC and notify the national governments of their choice. They, in turn, draw up a final

list of the national representatives. Formerly, the total number of delegates of the ESC was 101. With the addition of the three new countries, this number has been raised to 144. Each country has a certain number of representatives. For example, Germany used to have 24 out of 101; now it has 24 out of 144. The ESC divides the delegates into three groups: Group 1 consists of employers' organisations; Group 2 consists of trade unions; and Group 3 consists of agricultural, crafts, transport and consumer organisations. The national governments reflect on this group breakdown by nominating three equally strong numbers of representatives for a period of four years. In other words, in the case of Germany, eight representatives come from employers' organisations, eight come from trade union organisations, and eight from agricultural, crafts, transport and consumer organisations.

[2]   The Dutch trade unions were an exception. They generally indicated in interviews that the issues of housing and other related questions of migrant workers should be dealt with by the national governments and not the ESF.

[3]   No attempt will be made in this section to deal with actions concerning the increasing participation of migrant workers in the economic, social or political life of the host country. Neither will this section deal with housing questions or issues concerning nationals from non-Member States of the EC (so-called Third Countries).

[4]   However, the call for Community legislation was not universal among trade unions. For example, members of the Danish LO indicated in interviews that they opposed the Directive on Equal Pay for Men and Women, submitted by the Commission to the Council in 1973. Paradoxically, as they pointed out, Denmark is a country where equality in pay between men and women is highly advanced, yet it is implemented there without legal codification. Thus they oppose written rules from the EC.

[5]   The trade unions maintained in interviews, however, that they would like to see those committees chaired by trade union members or officials rather than to see them run as independent women's committees.

[6]   See ETUC *Supplement to Report on Activities*, 1973-1975.

[7]   'Natural convergence', as understood by the employers' organisations means basically that there should be co-ordination of measures between Member States, together with efforts to make the national social security systems more transparent. Appropriate studies by the Commission were, therefore, desirable.

[8]   Primarily the changes from coal to oil and the rationalisation measures which were taken in certain industries, such as textile or

shipbuilding.

[9]   See *Die Industriepolitik der Gemeinschaft*, Memorandum from the Commission to the Council, Commission of the European Communities, Brussels 1970, p.86; and *Die Arbeitsmarktlage in der Gemeinschaft 1971*, Commission of the European Communities, n.d., Brussels, p.27.

[10]   See *Zweites Programm für die Mittelfriestige Wirtschafts-politik*, Commission of the European Communities, Luxembourg 1970, pp A1-5; and *Die Industriepolitik der Gemeinschaft*, p.250.

[11]   For example, the number of persons trained or retrained for vocational occupations in Germany increased from 41,485 in 1967 to 263,588 in 1970. See *Die Arbeitsmarktlage in der Gemeinschaft*, p.70.

[12]   No comprehensive account of the number of migrant workers moving between EC countries could be ascertained because with the abolition of working permits in mid-1968, Member States no longer had any effective device whereby these numbers could be traced, and were therefore unable to provide the respective data. It is for this reason, in part, that the data in table 4.3 deal primarily with the situation in Germany, for which some data were available.

[13]   As pointed out, however, in a recent Commission document, there have been dramatic changes in the extent and nature of migration in the EC.

> In 1959 about three quarters of the migrant workers in the Community of the Six came from the Member States, largely Italy, and only one quarter from third countries. By 1975, in the enlarged Community of the Nine, these proportions had been reversed; and moreover, the total numbers involved had greatly increased; over 6 million migrant workers were employed in the Community in 1973, and together with their dependants, comprised a number of 10 million.

(See *Bulletin of the European Communities, Supplement 3/76.*) However, it must also be stressed that in both the Social Reports of 1975 and 1976 the Commission notes (without giving figures) that there has been a fall-off in the sharply rising trend of migration observed during the previous 10 years. See *Reports on the Development of the Social Situation in the Community in 1975*, p.42, and *in 1976*, p.44.

[14]   For example, there were 1,181 migrant workers from Member States who obtained vocational training or retraining in Belgium in 1970. The overall number of trained or retrained persons was 4,916 in Belgium in 1970. See *Die Arbeitsmarktlage in der*

Gemeinschaft, p.67.

[15]   For example, UNICE stated that: ' ... now that legal obstacles have been abolished, the free movement of workers should be encouraged.' See UNICE, *Second Memorandum on Social Policy*, November 1973.

[16]   For example, a meeting was held by the EMF on this issue in Verviers, Belgium, in June 1976, at which 35 trade union delegates from 5 Member States participated. See *European Communities Trade Union Information*, 7/8, July/August 1976.

[17]   Besides the examples provided above on the application of the ESF with regard to migrant workers, a further example of this stress on economic factors was contained in a recent Press Release from the leading employers' organisation, stating that: 'UNICE is in favour of proposals which envisage the alignment of the national economic and social situations which is essential for monetary stability within the Community.' See UNICE *Press Release*, 30 November 1976.

5   Role of the Commission

Introduction

This book has thus far centred on pressure groups concerned with
social policy. The attempts of different national trade unions to
establish a unified structure at European level, the degree of
integration reached within the ETUC and the identification of the
prime motives responsible for the structural changes of European
trade union organisations, were the subjects of chapter 2. The
prospects of formulating and agreeing to common ETUC policies
were analysed in chapter 3. In chapter 4, the specific demands of
Community pressure groups on the harmonisation of five social
policy issues at the Community level were enumerated. Furthermore,
the main motives underlying these demands were outlined.

   In chapter 5, the aim will be to examine the role of the
Commission in the harmonisation of five social policy issues at the
Community level, and its relationship with the Council of Ministers
and Community pressure groups. The five social policy issues
(social security harmonisation in general, social security provisions
for migrant workers, improvements of the European Social Fund
(ESF), a common vocational training policy and equal pay for men
and women) are mentioned in the Treaty of Rome with varying
degrees of specificity as to their goals and times of implementation.
These five social policy issues have served in chapter 4 as reference
for the degree of harmonisation desired in social policy by
Community pressure groups, and are used for a similar purpose
(the Commission's desire for harmonisation) here.

   One of the main reasons for the Commission's interest in the
process of social policy integration is that the Treaty of Rome
assigns the Commission to be the guardian of the Treaty, the
executive arm of the Community, the initiator of Community
policy and the exponent of the Community interests to the Council
of Ministers. The Commission, is, therefore, interested in
introducing initiatives in certain fields in order to ensure that the
aim of the Treaty of Rome, to create an ever more integrated unit,
is being achieved.

There are three important factors which influence the outcome of increased social policy harmonisation at the Community level. These are:

1. The Treaty of Rome provisions referring to social policy harmonisation at the Community level, their precision and achievement dates;

2. The disposition of the governments or Council of Ministers (which is the main decision-making body in the EC institutional framework) towards social policy harmonisation at the Community level;

3. The support or opposition expressed by the Community pressure groups towards social policy harmonisation at the Community level and the degree of either their support or opposition to such harmonisation.

Thus chapter 5 examines whether the Commission's interest is promoted or hindered by the social policy provisions of the Treaty of Rome, the attitudes held by the Council of Ministers towards the Commission's role in promoting social policy harmonisation, and how the activities of the Commission in the initiation and administration of social policy relate to the interests pursued by Community pressure groups on the same subject. Let us first examine the role assigned to the Commission with regard to the harmonisation of the five social policy issues.

The Commission and the social policy Treaty provisions

While for the free movement of labour the Commission had rather explicit Treaty provisions with which to work, the provisions on social policy were not so specific [1] and were even partly ambiguous with regard to the exact role of the Commission, the goals it should pursue and by what time schedule. [2] In fact, only a few direct provisions concerning social policy are specified. These provisions are Articles 51 and 121 on social security benefits for migrant workers, Article 119 on equal pay for men and women, Article 120 on annual and public holidays, and a provision concerning overtime payment. Except for these four cases and provisions for the Social Fund and a vocational training policy, all activities in the field of social policy are based on the very general

Articles 2, 117 and 118 of the Treaty of Rome. Using, for example, a simplified typology of whether a certain social policy issue is either high or low on the goal scale or time scale, according to the specific provisions in the Treat of Rome, the following table 5.1 can be drawn.

The social policy issue of equal pay for men and women can be rated as being high on both scales because the goal and purpose to be achieved, plus the time when it was to be achieved (the end of Phase Three: scheduled for the end of 1969) are adequately stated. A similar rating can be given for the settlement of the issue of social security for migrant workers. [3]

Although it is low in terms of goal and purpose specification, [4] the social policy issue of the ESF ranks high with regard to the achievement specification since the relevant Articles note that 'reviews' of the policy determination of the ESF should take place at the end of 1969. For a common vocational training policy, the goal and purpose are relatively well defined. [5] However, no time sequences have been specified for its implementation.

The issue which must be ranked lowest on both scales relates to social security harmonisation in general. Neither a specific goal nor an exact time have been defined for this issue.

While in the case of equal pay for men and women and social security for migrant workers, the Commission can function according to specific rules on which the governments of the Member States have initially agreed, the role of the Commission is hampered by the lack of specific rules in the case of social security harmonisation in general. It is the latter issue which requires particular ingenuity and skill on the part of the Commission to enhance legislation.

Article 117 of the Treaty indicates in general terms the goals of the Community social policy, and referring to it, Reed and Lawson pointed out its weakness: [6]

> No one is told to get on and do anything. It is unclear
> what the balance between harmonisation as a social
> goal and some process of natural evolution is intended
> to be.

It is Article 118 on which most emphasis has been placed, especially by the Council, as the basis for social security harmonisation in general. According to Article 118: [7]

... the Commission shall have the task of *promoting close co-*

Table 5.1

Specificity of dates set for completion in the Treaty of Rome

	High	Low
Specificity of Goals and Purposes High	Equal pay for men and women (Article 119) Completion date: initially the end of 1962; then postponed to the end of 1969. Social security for migrant workers (Articles 51 and 121) Completion date: largely achieved in 1958; additional measures foreseen after the completion of the free movement of labour (mid-1968)	A common vocational training policy (Articles 57 and 128) Completion date: no specification
Low	The European Social Fund (Articles 123-127) Completion date: a review date was set for the end of 1969.	Social security harmonisation in general (Articles 2, 117 and 118) Completion date: no specification

operation between Member States in the social field ... by
making *studies*, delivering *opinions* and *arranging consultations*
both on problems arising at national level and those of concern
to international organisations.

It is worthwhile to point out that the text of Article 118 does not
entitle the Commission to call for directives or regulations: [8]
something the Commission is entitled to do in other sectors such as
the free movement of labour or agriculture. Instead of providing the
Commission with the right to exercise delegated powers in the fixing
of goals, it has, according to this Article, merely the right to
recommend, to render opinions and propose collaboration among the
Member States in a number of areas related to employment, labour
law and working conditions, vocational training, social security,
safety and health, representation and collective bargaining. Thus, an
initiative by the Commission is not clearly expressed.

As a consequence of the different provisions of Articles 117 and
118, and especially as a consequence of the different interpretations
of Article 118 by the Commission and the Council, a controversy
ensued in the early 1960's over the nature of the role of the
Commission with regard to Article 118. Whereas the Commission
attempted to pursue a 'maximising' role, the Council was only
willing to grant it a 'minimising' role in the social policy harmonisation process under Article 118. [9]

A vital point in the controversy centred on the question of
consultation and co-operation by the Commission with the
employers' and employees' organisations concerned with social
policy. Since neither Articles 117 nor 118 mention the participation
of employers' and employees' organisations, the Council argued that
the Commission, by trying to co-operate with these organisations in
the social field without the consent of the Member Governments,
was violating its assigned role and had thus penetrated the spheres
reserved for national governments.

The Commission, in turn, argued that no uniform Community
social policy could be established without involving the employers'
and employees' organisations in the formulation and, to a lesser
extent, the execution and implementation of such policy. The
Council of Social Affairs, interested in preserving the autonomy of
the Member States in the social field, viewed the co-operation
between the Commission and the pressure groups (especially if it
became more extensive) as:

a)   bringing added pressures to bear on the governments to

92

enact certain social legislation;

b) undermining its traditionally-held role with respect to pressure groups and maybe 'unduly' enhancing the power of the Commission.

In order to emphasise its position and to indicate its disapproval of the Commission's activities, the Council therefore expressly dissociated itself from the activities undertaken by the Commission pursuant to Article 118, by not attending 'officially' (only as observers) a conference called by the Commission on social security on 10-15 December 1962; by not holding any Council meetings on social affairs in the period from 1964 to 1967; and by practising a general reluctance to take any decisions on the proposals the Commission submitted in the social field.

In a counter attack, the Commission accused the Council of not contributing to the harmonisation of social policy [10] and of not allowing the Commission to play its 'assigned role'. The Commission complained that the Council had tried to restrict its function to that of merely a participant in inter-governmental relationships without being able to establish the character of a Community procedure. [11]

Similarly, the European Parliament issued statements in which it regretted the inaction of the Council of Social Affairs. Whereas the employers' organisations had taken a position more in alignment with the national governments, the trade unions sympathised with the cause of the Commission and protested against a claim on the part of some Member States to challenge the Commission's right to consult employers and trade unions, [12] pointing out that consultation was absolutely necessary for a Community social policy to work. [13]

According to his own accounts, Veldkamp, then Minister of Social Affairs in the Netherlands, as soon as he became Acting Chairman of the Council of Ministers or Social Affairs in July 1966, issued a memorandum designed to prepare the ground for a discussion by the Council in order to end 'this unsatisfactory situation' between the Commission and the Council regarding proposed action in the social field. On the basis of this memorandum, the Council of Social Affairs reached a so-called 'Gentlemen's Agreement' [14] in December 1966, by which the Commission would have to be prepared, pursuant to Article 118, to concentrate primarily — and this included consultation with the two sides of industry — on matters which it knew to be of interest to the Member States. Such an agreement would mean that the governments of the Member States would, for their part, be willing to give their full support to the implementation of relevant proposals for co-operation.

Without doubt, the Council agreement did not enhance the role of the Commission in the social field. If anything, it limited the activities of the Commission, especially with regard to its 'maximising' role. Now, in addition, the Commission had to get some sort of consent before it could determine which studies were to be carried out, for which studies it could consult the two sides of industry, and which studies it could publish.

Thus, it can be maintained that the lack of Treaty specification of what the goal should be for social security harmonisation in general, together with the position of the Council of Ministers or Social Affairs throughout the first half of the 1960's, as well as the provisions of the 'Gentlemen's Agreement' of December 1966, were hindering the Commission's activities in the harmonisation of social security in general rather than promoting them.

The Commission's skill and the Council

If we leave aside for the moment the nature of the social policy Treaty provisions and the position held by Community pressure groups on the harmonisation of social policy issues, we can single out three main skill criteria which the Commission could have employed in seeking approval from the Council of Ministers for its proposals. These three criteria related to whether the Commission was:

a)   using the proper timing in introducing proposals;

b)   introducing the proper type of Community legislation; [15]

c)   playing the proper bureaucratic role [16] in the introduction and administration of social policy legislation. [17]

The timing of social policy legislation introduction

The Commission's timing in introducing a certain proposal is often influenced by demands put forward either by a single, several, or all Member Governments, or by a single or several Community pressure group(s). Leaving aside for the moment the balancing act the Commission has to perform in weighing up the pros and cons among Community pressure groups, it is the Commission's task to assess the chances of approval of proposals and to determine whether more

Member Governments will be in favour than opposed at a certain time.

For example, by introducing first a document on the 'Preliminary Guidelines for a Social Policy Programme in the Community in 1971', and a number of studies on social security problems and vocational training throughout 1969 to 1972, the Commission proceeded to issue a catalogue of forty-four social policy actions in the Spring of 1973 and, finally, introduced a Social Action Programme in the Autumn of 1973, consisting, among others, of seven priority actions. [18] The Commission recommended that the Council should decide and seek implementation on these seven actions in the period between 1974 to 1976.

In all these steps the Commission has proceeded pragmatically, preceding action by studies and achieving social policies gradually by a series of measures. [19] Similarly, the Commission proposed not a comprehensive programme on immigration policy, but certain immediate actions on behalf of the migrant workers and their families, in order to solve some of the existing problems in this sector. [20]

Probably the vital element in determining whether a Council decision is made or rejected (let us say 5 months after the Commission has submitted) is the way in which the proposal has been introduced by the Commission, its legal implications (regulation or recommendation), the time foreseen for its implementation, the costs involved and the transfer of jurisdictional and financial authority demanded.

The type of social policy legislation

The Commission must determine the chances of success each type of proposal (regulation, directive, etc.) has for enactment by the Council. For example, in the area of vocational training, the Commission felt that a regulation or directive would have been difficult to implement in those Member States which did not have vocational training or retraining programmes, or lacked the financial or other means to carry them out. Thus the Commission suggested that the Council should make recommendations rather than regulations or directives in those cases where general vocational training or retraining was concerned and asked for a Council regulation on a specific sector of vocational training. This suggests that the Commission's choice of proposal must strike a balance between what the economically advanced Member States can carry out with relative ease and what the less advanced Member States can carry out only with some difficulty (if there is no transfer of resources at the Community level for the less favoured Member States). Similarly, it was the view of the Commission that a proposal for a directive embodying the principle of the 40-hour week and 4 weeks' annual paid holiday would not be acceptable in some Member States in 1973, and it was decided instead to call for recommendations.

In cases in which both the functioning of the Common Market and Community resources are heavily involved, the Commission will usually ask that Council regulations be issued. For example, in the case of the ESF proposals, the Commission decided that regulations were the most appropriate type of proposals since both fundamental issues [21] and Community resources were involved. Thus the method of finance suggested (whether from Community resources or Member States' contributions) is often a crucial choice for the Commission. In addition, the method of describing the benefits to be obtained for the Community or individual countries from certain proposals is essential in influencing Council execution and implementation.

In some cases the Commission has tried to introduce proposals which incorporate components of several sectors such as the agricultural, regional and industrial sectors. Here the Commission attempts both to be more effective, as in the case of an Action Programme for Migrant Workers or the Handicapped, and to ensure that the social aspects are not dissociated from other relevant considerations, such as in the case of a Statute for a European Company and the question of workers' participation on the supervisory boards.

However, this particular approach raises certain difficulties. If the Commission asserts, on the one hand, the independence of Community social policy and, on the other hand, tries to relate it to wider Community programmes, greater clarity is needed in specifying these relationships. This lack of clarity was especially obvious when the Commission put forward the 'Preliminary Guidelines for a Social Policy Programme in the Community in 1971', the forty-four actions outlined in April 1973 and the Social Action Programme of November 1973. This is an aspect which was particularly criticised by the trade unions.

In general, the Commission was careful and cautious in asking for the transfer of responsibility to the central institutions of the EC and for an expansion of its decision-making power in terms of financial resources and jurisdiction. [22] The only exceptions to this were proposals concerning the ESF and social security provisions for migrant workers, where both substantial transfers of financial resources and jurisdiction were proposed. For both of these exceptions, explicit Treaty provisions, as well as Community pressure groups' demands, were of considerable importance.

Bureaucratic role behaviour

Both the timing and method of introducing proposals are important ingredients of the Commission's ability to generate proposals that will emerge as European decisions from the Council and consolidate the integrative process. However, there is a third ingredient which also figures heavily in the Commission's ability to generate such proposals, one which is vital to the very survival of the Commission. Its essence lies in the skill of the Commission in maintaining good relations with the national governments and their administrations. [23]

One of the links the Commission has with the national bureaucracies is provided through the background of most of the officials on its staff, the majority of whom have previously served either in civil service administrations or in government capacities in their own national states. It is not unusual for officials of the Commission to return to their national administration, and thus add to the linkage with state bureaucracy. The Commission also voluntarily solicits the approval of each government for the appointments of Eurocrats to top policy-making offices in the A3 to A1 range. [24]

Another way in which the contacts between the Commission and the national bureaucracies are facilitated is through consultations between the Commission and national civil servants, [25] and through various seminars the Commission conducts for the benefit of national civil servants. [26] These consultations and contacts may instil, via the socialisation process, a European orientation [27] in the national bureaucratic elites. They can also lead to conflicts stemming from what Feld calls 'a tug of war between contending bureaucracies' [28] of the Commission and national civil services. A similar argument is advanced by Bouvard, who maintains that the socialisation process towards the adoption of European values, beliefs and norms of conduct among national civil servants, is strongly resisted by the majority of the national administrative elites. [29] It is the latter negative impact of socialisation described by Feld and Bouvard which seems to gain importance in the Directorate for Social Affairs in the Commission.

The reason for this growing importance seems to be twofold. One is that the national governments and their administrations view the establishment of a strong and efficient Commission bureaucracy in the social policy sector with suspicion and some fear. Naturally social policy issues, especially wage demands, are important concerns for each country's economic policy and thus governments are reluctant to delegate such matters to a supranational bureaucracy. [30] But social policy matters are not an isolated phenomenon in this regard. In general, it appears that the stronger or more efficient the Commission becomes in any particular policy sector, the more distrustful the governments and their administrations become of it and its work. [31]

The second reason concerns bureaucratic ideologies, salary scales [32] and bureaucratic prestige. While the bureaucratic ideologies of the Commission are geared to expand its administrative functions and institutions, the national bureaucratic systems see their functions diminishing. Consequently, in such a situation, as Downs explains, the ideology of the national bureaucracy will define sharply the borders of its traditional activities and also claim that the invading agencies are going beyond the legitimate bounds of their logical functions. [33]

In addition, the 'bureaucratic' role of the Commission was affected by the arrival of a 'new' team of Commission officials in the social affairs sector in 1973, coming from Denmark, Ireland and the United Kingdom. Not only did a new Commissioner and his Cabinet arrive, but also a Director-General and two Directors (who had had no previous experience in the Commission) were included in the Directorate-General for Social Affairs. In the case of the Director-General, there were additional difficulties because his previous post kept him away from Brussels most of the time between January and June 1973. While these new appointees had perhaps good links with the national administrations, they lacked the bureaucratic experience of the Commission. Unfortunately, one must say, this came at a time when the Paris Summit Conference of October 1972 and subsequent Council of Social Affairs sessions had given the Commission a mandate to draft a Social Action Programme. Finally, after only two and a half years, the Director-General resigned from his post, thus creating further upheaval in the administration.

So far, our analysis in chapter 5 has centred on:

a)   The skill of the Commission in utilising the social policy Treaty provisions efficiently;

b)   The skill employed by the Commission in attaining the Council's consent for increased social policy integration;

c) The distinct problems that call into question the Commission's skill in maintaining good relations with the national governments and their administrations.

In the following, we will turn to the position taken by the Community pressure groups. By analysing the position of the Community pressure groups concerned with social policy, we not only get an indication of the support or opposition expressed by them to the Commission's proposals, but we also find out whether or not Community pressure groups can be considered a supportive element for the Commission with respect to the Council.

The Commission's skill and Community pressure group support

Besides the somewhat disadvantageous position the Commission often faces in the execution of proposals, due to the unanimous decision-making modus of the Council of Ministers, it encounters another difficulty in its initiation of policy. This difficulty involves the task of incorporating meaningfully the different demands into proposals which upgrade the Community interest in the social field.

One of the aims of this section is to shed some light on the empirical question of whether the increased integrative attempts of the trade unions on the European level between 1969 and 1974 have helped the Commission to deal more effectively with the position of the trade unions, on the one hand; or whether they have made a compromise solution by the Commission 'more' or 'less' difficult as it stands between the trade unions and the employers.

The following section will examine whether the Community pressure groups:

a) Identified with the major propositions advanced or planned by the Commission for Community legislation concerning the five social policy issues;

b) Felt satisfied with the consultations conducted by the Commission;

c) Intended to support further the institutional role of the Commission, or saw the Commission as the main channel for effectively expressing their demands on the five social policy issues.

The Commission's activities on social policy

The following is a short breakdown of the Community pressure groups' perceptions regarding the Commission's activities in introducing Community legislation on the five social policy issues.

1) With regard to the implementation of the principle of equal pay for men and women, most Community pressure groups indicated satisfaction with the Commission's activities. However, the employers' organisations expressed some reservations on the extent to which the Commission had proposed legislation;

2) With regard to the ESF, more supportive statements than complaints were registered from the Community pressure groups concerning the Commission's activities on this issue. There were some disagreements by the Community pressure groups on the Commission's proposals with regard to recipient categories of workers. The trade unions took a different stand from the propositions introduced by the Commission concerning self-employed workers and the employers' organisations disagreed with some of the Commission's proposals regarding migrant workers.

3) With regard to a common vocational training policy, most groups (ECFTU/ETUC, EO/WCL, CGT/CGIL and the ESC) agreed with the recommendations made by the Commission. However, the trade unions felt that the Commission's Social Action Programme of November 1973 gave inadequate treatment to the establishment of training centres for the backward regions. Both the trade unions and the ESC supported the Commission's proposal for the establishment of a European Centre for Vocational Training. While considering this idea with some scepticism up until 1972, UNICE began to support it in 1973.

4) With regard to the harmonisation of social security provisions for migrant workers, most groups supported the Commission's activities. However, the trade unions indicated that the Commission should do more on the question of 'supplementary benefits' for migrant workers. In contrast, UNICE felt that the Commission should not deal with 'supplementary benefits'.

5)   With regard to the harmonisation of social security systems
       in general, all Community pressure groups indicated that
       they were in favour of the Commission's activities
       regarding a European Social Budget (ESB) and of social
       indicators. However, the trade unions, in contrast to the
       employers' organisations, stressed that the principle of
       'upward harmonisation' should be reflected more in the
       Commission's proposals.

   Thus, from the data gathered, it would appear that both the trade
unions and the employers' organisations were generally satisfied with
the initiation and administration of the Commission on these five
social policy issues.

Extent and method of consultation

Although the Commission does legally have the right, according to
Article 213, [34] to collect the necessary information for the
implementation of its tasks, the Council has taken a rigid stand in
some cases. There are Treaty provisions which explicitly specify
consultation with the social partners (ESF). There are other Treaty
provisions for which the Council has given the Commission a mandate
to consult the social partners, such as to work out progress reports on
the principle of equal pay for men and women since 1964. In
addition, there are Treaty provisions for which the Council was
initially reluctant to grant the Commission the right of consultations
with the social partners (Article 118) but eventually it changed its
position towards a tacit acceptance of such consultations in 1973.
   Thus, the above-listed provisions, to which the Treaty makes
explicit references or for which the Council has granted an explicit
mandate for the Commission's consultations, provide the basis for the
frequent round-table discussions and symposia between the
Commission and the social partners. [35] Presided over by a member
of the Commission (Commissioner or Head of Cabinet, or a high
official of a Directorate-General), the Commission conducts these
meetings:

   a)   to obtain relevant information from the social partners on
        the development of the economic and social problems in the
        Community;

   b)   to pass on information to the social partners on the types of social policy legislation in preparation;

c)   to incorporate the suggestions the social partners express on Commission proposals.

In addition, the President of the Commission or the Commissioner in charge of Social Affairs will occasionally receive delegations both from the trade unions or employers' organisations on an informal basis to discuss current issues in the social policy sector.

When asked to make an evaluation of the Commission's consultation in the social policy field, both the trade unions and the employers' organisations criticised either the lack or method of consultation. Part of these complaints were accusations by either the trade unions or the employers' organisations of being neglected in the consultative process, while the 'other side' received too much attention. Another part of these complaints referred to the increasing consultation of the Commission with national governmental ministries or the CPR, which the Community pressure groups felt often unduly preceded or replaced consultations between themselves and the Commission.

Demands for improving consultations

In 1973, the ETUC began to introduce a variety of demands concerning consultations and participation. These demands aimed at improving consultations, on the one hand, between the social partners and the Commission, and on the other hand, among the social partners at the Community level. They cited the following reasons behind their demands:

a)   The lack of Commission consultation or participation in the introduction of Community legislation concerning the five social policy issues up to September 1972.

b)   The Communiqué of the Paris Summit Conference of October 1972, calling for the participation by representatives of the workers' organisations in the decision-making process of the Community.

Their demands involved primarily the following measures:

a)   The extension of the number of Joint Committees; [36]

b)   The establishment of a European trade union institute.

102

While also calling for increased consultations, the two main employers' organisations (UNICE and COCCEE) took a different position on these two proposed measures. To start with the second measure, the request for EC financial support by the trade unions for the establishment of a European trade union institute was opposed by employers' organisations, who argued that, as both trade unions and employers' organisations were private, it would be unfair to give one group advantage over the other.

With regard to the proposed measures on extending the number of existing Joint Committees, the employers' organisations disagreed with the trade unions' priorities. The employers, in contrast to the trade unions, preferred implementation in the long term, anticipating a causal relationship between an increasing number of Joint Committees and increasing pressure for collective bargaining at European level to which they were opposed. [37]

In contrast, as pointed out in chapter 3, trade unions, while still disagreeing over the form which such collective bargaining should take at European level, had accepted the idea in principle.

The Commission took a position on these two measures which was generally in line with the demands expressed by the trade unions, and called for a short to medium-term implementation of these measures, viewing them as instrumental in:

a) encouraging the active participation of both sides of industry in the decision-making process; recognising, at the same time, however, the stipulation introduced by either trade unions alone or both the trade unions and the employers' organisations, requesting 'administrative autonomy' for themselves in the decision-making of Joint Committees; [38]

b) facilitating the conclusion of European Collective Agreements in which the Commission had taken a keen interest and for which it was drawing up a European Card Index of Collective Agreements.

Accompanying the demands by Community pressure groups for improved consultations was a growing concern in 1973 over what the trade unions in particular perceived as a decline in the institutional role of the Commission, indicating that the Commission had lost its competence, or that it was becoming more and more the administrative secretariat of the Council of Ministers, if it had not already done so.

The following observations were made by various Community pressure groups on what they perceived as the weaknesses of the

Commission in its declining institutional role:

1. The Commission is weak. It hardly consists of a common body which expresses the European political will. The majority of the Commissioners are too involved with the national governments and the CPR. The Commission still submits proposals and memoranda to the Council, but seldom supplies the determination necessary to make them worthwhile. It also appears that the Commission exercises only formal relationships and, thus, does not insist strongly enough on the role assigned to it in the Treaty of Rome.

2. The institutional character of the EC is negatively affected by the increasing technocratic nature of the Commission. The Commission remains the force for technical solutions, but concedes to the Council, and even more to the national governments, the political initiatives. In particular, there are not enough leading personalities in the Commission who sympathise with social policy or the social causes. [39]

There were also a substantial number of favourable statements by Community pressure groups, as well as a number of statements in which Community pressure groups, primarily trade unions, indicated that they themselves had contributed indirectly to the declining role of the Commission. For example, some Community pressure group representatives who were interviewed thought that:

a) The 'new' administration of the Commission (the Commissioner, his Cabinet and the personnel in the Directorate-General for Social Affairs) which began in January 1973, had made an honest attempt to introduce Community legislation;

b) The personnel was pushing harder;

c) The Directorate-General for Social Affairs had some very competent people: Shanks, Rifflet and Crijns;

d) The relationship with the Commission had improved.

Some members of the ETUC pointed out that the trade unions had not always given enough support to the Commission, or had not helped in the work of the Commission by presenting impressive demand lists without setting priorities or by insisting too much on their autonomy with regard to Joint Committees. In addition, so these members have pointed out, discussions have shown that the trade unions frequently disagreed among themselves, even on questions of fundamental importance.

Furthermore, while from mid-1968 to the end of 1972 trade unions, despite various dissatisfactions and complaints over the lack of, or style of, consultation, had ardently expressed support for the cause of the Commission in the initiation and administration of social policy legislation, as well as for a strengthening of the Commission's institutional role, [40] they became more cautious in their support during 1973.

One of the main reasons for this caution stemmed from the composition of the ETUC, which was formed in March 1973 by the joining of trade union organisations from Britain, Denmark and other EFTA countries to the ECFTU. The newly-joined trade union affiliations, as described in chapter 3, often pursued policies which either consisted of anti-EC feeling on their own part or reflected the anti-EC stand taken by certain political parties in their home countries; affecting negatively a number of planned joint meetings and activities between the ETUC and the Commission. They admitted to differ from the former ECFTU group, both with regard to steps which have to be taken in the short term and also the long term to achieve European identity, thus temporarily straining relations between the Commission and the ETUC and leaving the immediate prospects of a Commission-trade union coalition with respect to the Council of Ministers in doubt.

Moreover, defensive explanations were given, both from the Commission and from the trade unions, on the question of sending high-ranking officials to joint conferences. The Commission maintained that often either second or third-string representatives of the trade unions were present in joint conferences and that some individual members' organisations of the ETUC failed completely to send delegates, [41] while the trade unions countered by saying that they were tired of going to conferences after which the Commission would, in any case, make its own decisions.

The revitalisation of the trade union information unit by the Information Directorate-General in 1975 helped to alleviate the strained relationship between trade unions and the Commission. [42] In carrying out its information tasks, under the energetic leadership of Mr Helmut Ries, the Division liaises closely with the ETUC, the European industry trade union committees and the national trade union centres. It produces a monthly publication on Trade Union Information and, more importantly, has taken a leading role in organising meetings among trade unions on such topics as 'Frontier Workers', 'Women at Work' and 'Workers' Participation'.

Meantime, the Commission has repeatedly stated that it will seek to have employers' organisations and trade unions participating more fully in the economic and social decisions of the Community through a more wide-ranging, intensive use of the Tripartite Conference at Community level, the SCE and the Joint Committees. For example, the Commission has emphasised that one of the three-fold aims of the Social Action Programme of December 1973 was the increased involvement of management and labour in the economic and social decisions of the Community.

Against this desire must be held the fact that the ability of the Commission to consult and generate support from Community pressure groups has one important limitation. The Commission is not the decision-making organ of the EC, but rather the recommending body. [43] Thus the Commission can give no full assurance to the Community pressure groups that the objective discussed with them will be executed accordingly. As a result of this, Community pressure groups will always look for additional channels or for improved participation in the decision-making process, especially if there is a widening of the discrepancy between the Commission's initial proposals [44] and the Council decisions thereof.

Demand channels

Almost all Community pressure groups stated that, under normal circumstances, the Commission, in contrast to the Council of Ministers, the European Parliament and the Court of Justice, is the main EC institutional channel used for expressing social policy demands at the Community level. In general, Community pressure groups felt that both the Court of Justice and the European Parliament were not useful channels for expressing demands, due to their limited influence in the policy-making sphere of the EC. Still the record is better with the latter. For example, Community pressure groups noted that they had had some unofficial opinion exchanges with the members of the Social Section of the European Parliament, which often holds its meetings in Brussels. They also stressed that with direct elections to the European Parliament, an increase in consultation with this institution could be expected.

The majority of the Community pressure groups, including the majority of the trade unions, indicated that the influence of labour representatives should be sought at the stage of policy formation, i.e.

in the preparatory stage of the Commission. The belief was that it would be detrimental to let the Commission work out proposals and then ask for major changes. This would definitely be too late. Moreover, due to the position taken by the Council on the application of Article 118 (the 'Gentlemen's Agreement'), many representatives of trade union organisations felt that the same influence or pressure could not be exerted in the Council as in the Commission. Somewhat in contrast, the hope of the British TUC and the Danish LO was that there should be occasional tripartite meetings with the Social or Labour Ministers to discuss problems and, in general, to increase their contacts with the CPR. They stressed that demands should be expressed where decisions were being made and this, they maintained, clearly required that the Council, rather than the Commission, should be approached. However, they also pointed out that various channels should be utilised in the pursuance of Community social policy legislation, such as the Commission, the ESC and the SCE.

Generally, rather than viewing the Council as the primary channel for expressing their social policy demands, the Community pressure groups considered it as a last resort in preventing certain Commission proposals from being accepted by the Council.

Conclusion

The task in this chapter was to examine the Commission's ability to:

a) utilise social policy provisions of the Treaty of Rome;

b) obtain support from Community pressure groups for its proposals;

c) induce Council acceptance for its proposals.

As shown in this chapter, the content of the Treaty provisions on the harmonisation of social security in general and vocational training, and the attitudes of the Council of Ministers towards the harmonisation of these two issues, affected the ability or skill of the Commission to promote harmonisation and to satisfy trade union demands.

On the other hand, while the Treaty provisions on the ESF, social security benefits for migrant workers and equal pay for men and women were much more conducive, the Commission had to employ considerably more ingenuity to work out compromise solutions for its proposals, in order to secure acceptance by both the trade unions and the employers' organisations, rather than one of the two alone. Generally, more satisfaction than dissatisfaction was expressed by both the employers' organisations and the trade unions on the Commission's activities for these three issues. Moreover, most of the trade unions from the EC countries affiliated to the ETUC and the employers' organisations had stressed that because of its role in the decision-making process of the EC, the Commission was the major channel for expressing demands.

However, between 1973 and 1975, both the trade unions and the employers' organisations had complained about the extent and form of Commission consultation. While not perhaps the main factor, the dissatisfaction over the lack of consultation and participation has contributed to the level of criticism advanced by Community pressure groups about the decline of the institutional role of the Commission. However, between 1973 and 1975, there were indications that the ETUC did not stress the strengthening of the institutional role of the Commission to the same extent as its fore-runner, the ECFTU, had done. On the contrary, there were signs that the ETUC, or at least some of its affiliated organisations, tried to diminish this role; thus straining the relationship between the two and making it more difficult for the Commission to obtain support for its proposals on social policy.

The Commission's ability to promote social policy harmonisation appears to have increased since 1972, but its flexibility to effectively employ such ability criteria as: proper timing of a proposal and proper selection of the type of legislation has been brought more and more under the sphere of the CPR since 1972. This is especially the case with regard to social security harmonisation in general and vocational training. To say more on this and on the influence exercised by both the Community pressure groups and the Commission in the executive and legislative actions of the Council of Ministers, will be the task of the following chapter.

Notes

[1]   Specific Treaty provisions indicate prior agreement by the Member States on what can be decided collectively and thus enable the Commission to carry out specific agreed functions or to remind Member States to obey specific rules. A similar observation is made by James A. Caporaso, *Functionalism and Regional Integration: A Logical and Empirical Assessment*, Sage Publications, Beverly Hills,

California 1972.

[2]   Reed comes to a similar conclusion when he states that: 'The European Economic Community came into existence on 1 January 1958, without any specific commitment to a common social policy or to the development of common policies for social and medical care.' For an elaboration of this conclusion, see Roger Lawson and Bruce Reed, *Social Security in the European Community*, Chatham House and PEP, London 1975, especially p.39; and Fogarty, *Work and Industrial Relations in the EC*, especially p.5.

[3]   Articles 51 and 121 and EC Regulation 1612/68 of July 1968 concerning the free movement of labour, specify:

a)   The principle of non-discrimination between nationals of one Member State and nationals of other Member States with regard to work and social security benefits;

b)   The arrangement for transfer of social security benefits received in one Member State to another Member State;

c)   The retention of rights acquired as a result of affiliation to one or more insurance or health protection scheme in two or more Member States.

[4]   The ESF was set up to facilitate the employment of workers and increase their geographical and occupational mobility within the EC by contributing towards the costs of retraining, resettlement or the conversion of plants to new types of work.

[5]   The Treaty of Rome makes reference to the harmonisation of a vocational training policy at the Community level in two Articles. Article 128 specifies that: '... the Council shall ... lay down general principles for implementing a common vocational training policy ...', and Article 57 states that: '... the Council shall ... issue directives for the mutual recognition of diplomas, certificates and other evidence of formal qualifications.'

[6]   See Lawson and Reed, *Social Security in the EC,* p.55.

[7]   *Treaties Establishing the European Communities*, Office for Official Publications of the European Communities, Luxembourg 1973, pp.271-272. (Italics added).

[8]   In implementing the Treaty of Rome, the Council and the Commission issue regulations, directives, decisions, recommendations and opinions. *Regulations* are of general application; they are binding in every respect and have direct force of law in every Member State. *Directives* are binding on the Member States to which they are addressed as regards the result to be achieved, but leave the mode and means to the discretion of the national authorities.

Decisions may be addressed either to a government or to an enterprise or private individual; they are binding in every respect on the party or parties named. *Recommendations* and *Opinions* are not binding. See Emile Noel, 'How the European Economic Community's Institutions Work,' *Community Topics* 39, European Community Information Service, London.

[9]   For more details see G.M.J. Veldkamp, 'Towards Harmonisation of Social Security in the EEC,' *Western European Labor and the American Corporation*, pp 351-73.

[10]   In a rare practice used by the Commission, Levi-Sandri, Commissioner of Social Affairs in 1968, accused the Council publicly of withholding social policy harmonisation. See 'Les Difficultés de la Politique Sociale Européenne,' *Discours* prononcé le 21 mars 1968 à l'Institut d'Etudes Européennes et Association des Diplômes de l'Institut du Travail de l'Université Libre de Bruxelles.

[11]   Here the distinction can be made between mediating or assisting and initiating in the enactment of social policy legislation.

[12]   For example, at its Seventh Congress, the German Trade Union Federation (DGB) stated that it:

> ... rejects with amazement the French Government's opinion according to which all participation in European social measures, provided for under Articles 117 and 118 of the Treaty, should be denied to the trade unions and to employers.

See 'The Trade Unions in Germany,' *European Documentation*, 1969.

[13]   For an excellent account of the trade union response to this event, see Beever, *Trade Unions and Free Labour Movement in the EEC*, pp 22-3.

[14]   For more details of the 'Gentlemen's Agreement', see Veldkamp, 'Towards Harmonisation of Social Security in the EEC'.

[15]   The Commission must, for instance, decide either to call for a binding regulation which the Member States are requested to implement after execution by the Council, or to ask for a mere recommendation of what the Member States should attempt in order to reach certain Community objectives. The Commission's choice of procedure might determine the success or failure of a certain proposal. For a description of the different types of legislation, see note 8 above.

[16]   The Commission may, in conducting its relationship with the national governments and their administrations, especially the CPR, take their advice or it may, on the other hand, try to impose its will upon them by the very preparation of proposals.

[17]   These three skill criteria are interrelated but for analytical

reasons they will be treated separately.

[18]   These seven priority actions were:

1.   Assistance from Article 4 of the Social Fund for migrant and handicapped workers;

2.   An Action Programme for handicapped workers in an open market economy;

3.   The setting up of a European General Industrial Safety Committee and the extension of the competence of the Mines Safety and Health Commission;

4.   A directive providing for the approximation of legislation of Member States concerning the application of the principle of equal pay for men and women;

5.   The designation as an immediate objective of the overall application of the 40-hour working week by 1975 and 4 weeks' annual paid holiday by 1976;

6.   The setting up of a European Foundation for the improvement of the environment and of living and working conditions;

7.   A directive on the approximation of the Member States' legislation on collective dismissals.

[19]   Following similar lines, the Commission stated in its *Social Action Programme* that it did not intend to recommend a uniform social system, or to seek to eliminate the many disparities resulting from different national priorities, needs and values.

[20]   These immediate actions consisted of:

a)   Improving information on job availability.

b)   Increasing the numbers of properly trained social workers.

c)   Securing better treatment on family benefits and maternity allowances.

d)   Improving vocational training facilities for migrant workers.

e)   Improving the education of children of migrant workers.

[21]   Such issues as coping with the growing number of workers which had to be retrained because of the functioning of Community agricultural policies, for instance, and alleviating the chronic unemployment problems which continued to exist despite the economic progress of the Common Market.

[22]   Bouvard comes to a similar conclusion when she states that: '... the Commission has acted more prudently than the high authority

in submitting only those proposals they judged acceptable, thus avoiding the risk of refusal and a consequent loss of prestige.' See Bouvard, *Labor Movements*, p.169.

[23]   Administrations in this context represents the staff members of the permanent diplomatic missions of the Member States in Brussels; the thousands of national civil servants who are called to Brussels on various occasions for expert consultations by the EC Commission, the Council and other EC bodies.

[24]   Of the 6,700 Commission administrative staff, 1,900 were of executive grades which required a completed university degree, and they were thus in the A category. This category, as with the other categories, B, C, or D, is ranked from A7, the lowest A grade, to A1, the highest. Most of the posts of the A3 to A1 categories were held by essentially political appointees who were either sponsored by the national governments or the European organisations of the trade unions or employers' groups. Source: interviews with officials of the Commission of the EC, April/May 1973.

[25]   This takes the form of Commission representatives visiting the capitals of the Member States and/or presiding over a committee of national experts in Brussels. Frequently, these experts are the same as those who advise Ministers in Council discussions.

[26]   For example, the Commission has organised courses for national social security officials to familiarise them with the legislation of each other's countries, or has conducted seminars for the training of vocational training officers.

[27]   For further elaboration of the term 'political orientation' or 'socialisation', see Fred I. Greenstein, 'A Note on the Ambiguity of Political Socialisation: Definitions, Criticisms, and Strategies of Inquiry,' *Journal of Politics* 32, November 1970, pp 969-78.

[28]   See Werner J. Feld, 'Diplomatic Behavior in the European Community: Milieus and Motivations,' *Journal of Common Market Studies* 11, September 1972, p.31.

[29]   See Bouvard, *Labor Movements*, pp 119-120.

[30]   For example, by 1968 the proportion of national income spent on social security alone had reached between 20-23 per cent in the EC countries; it was somewhat lower in Britain. See 'Social Security in the Six,' *European Social Studies* 14, Commission of the European Communities, Brussels 1972, p.1. The high proportion of the national income involved, together with the fact that it is a crucial element for the success or failure of governments in elections, make Hoffmann believe that: '... government will want to keep the monopoly of distributing benefits to its citizens as long as possible.' See Hoffmann, *Foreword to Labor Movements* by Bouvard.

[31]   A discussion of this particular aspect is advanced by
Gerda Zellentin, 'Krisen der Europäischen Integration,' *Integration:
European Studies Review*, Commission of the European Communities,
Brussels 1970, p.32.

[32]   Besides some obvious salary differentials, especially between
the Italian civil service and the Commission, the EC officials benefit
from much lower tax rates and certain diplomatic immunities. These
differences have been seen as giving the EC officials often a feeling of
superiority.

[33]   See Anthony Downs, *Inside Bureaucracy*, Little, Brown & Co.
Boston 1969, pp 242-3.

[34]   Article 213 states:

> The Commission may, within the limits and under the
> conditions laid down by the Council in accordance with
> provisions of this Treaty, collect any information and
> carry out any checks required for the performance of the
> task entrusted to it.

See *Treaties Establishing the European Communities*, p.327.

[35]   In the *Annual Reports on the Development of the Social
Situation in the Communities* (1972-1976), the Commission lists,
under the section on Industrial Relations, a large number of headings
for which the two sides of industry were consulted throughout the
respective years.

[36]   Joint Committees were established in: Coal (1955); Steel
(1955); Salaried Agricultural Workers (1963); Road Transport (1965);
Inland Waterways Transport (1967); Seafishing (1968); and Rail
Transport (1971).

[37]   For example, COCCEE stated in June 1973: 'European
collective bargaining agreements appear to be of considerable concern
in individual branches. COCCEE, together with the Employers'
Liaison Committee, opposes this conception.' See *Ergebnisprotokol
der Generalversammlung von OIC und COCCEE*, 17 and 26 April
1973. Somewhat in contrast, COPA had successfully concluded a
collective agreement with the two agricultural European trade union
branches of the ICFTU and the WCL in 1968. (See chapter 2).

[38]   For further details see *Report on the Development of the
Social Situation in the Communities in 1974*, point 36.

[39]   Many of these criticisms can be found in EO/WVA
Tätigkeitsbericht 1 (1969-72), p.29; EBFG Doc. on *1ter Kongress:
Reden-Beschlüsse-Entschliessungen*, The Hague, 23-25 April 1969;
see also EBFG Doc. *Europa '71*, p.51; Doc. *Für Ein Soziales Europa*,
p.21; CFDT/CMT Doc. *Les Organisations Syndicales et la*

[40]   For example in the *Press Release* No.93, prior to the Summit Conference in Paris in October 1972, the ECFTU stated that: 'The Commission must become again a creative organ and the motor of European integration. It should be assigned with autonomous competences such as in dealing with the ESF.' Both the trade unions and the ESC had demanded that the Council must, following a proposal from the Commission, establish the general criteria necessary to determine the areas and kind of aid for which the ESF is to make contributions. The decision, however, as to which economic sector, region or category of worker should benefit from ESF aid must rest with the Commission, in collaboration with the SCE. Similarly, trade unions had urged the Commission to use an 'extensive' interpretation of Article 118 and had insisted that the Presidency of the SCE should be assigned to the Commission rather than to the Council of Ministers. Trade unions had differed in this regard from the employers' organisation, which were more ambivalent in their support for the Commission.

[41]   For example, the British TUC persistently refused to participate in joint ETUC-Commission meetings for political reasons (position taken by the Labour Party). Similarly, the Danish LO did not in the main attend such meetings either. It is worthwhile to point out in this context that, while the British TUC had not participated (had not sent representatives) up until the Autumn of 1975, in either the working of the ESC or the sessions of the SCE, the Danish LO had participated in both.

[42]   When the European Coal and Steel Community was created in 1951, the High Authority (now the Commission) recognised the importance of keeping trade unions fully informed about its actions. It accordingly set up an Information Unit for this purpose. This concept, although taken over by the EEC in 1958, was neglected for a while until, in 1975, a division was set up in the Directorate-General for Information to revitalise the Unit and its function.

[43]   According to the Treaty of Rome, the Commission can only propose or recommend policies and it is up to the Council to decide upon Commission proposals. However, the Council can only deliberate policies on the basis of a Commission proposal. Furthermore, Article 149 of the Treaty of Rome provides that: 'When, pursuant to this Treaty, the Council acts on a proposal of the Commission, it shall, where the amendment of such proposals is involved, act only by means of a unanimous vote.' Thus, in cases where the majority rule applies in the Treaty of Rome, the position

is that, either the Council adopts the Commission's proposal as it stands by a majority, or it decides against the proposal unanimously, or it fails to come to a decision at all. For more details on this decision-making modus, see Noel, 'How the European Community's Institutions Work.'

[44] The Commission has the right, and often uses this right, to change its proposals during Council deliberations.

6   Impact of pressure groups

Introduction

So far we have examined the activities of pressure groups and the central bureaucracy of the EC. In chapter 2 we traced the structural changes which had occurred in the formation and strengthening of European trade union organisations and assessed the motives behind these changes. The prospects of formulating and agreeing to common ETUC policies were analysed in chapter 3. Chapter 4 was concerned with the degree of harmonisation desired by the Community pressure groups on five social policy issues and the motives behind these desires. Finally, an attempt was made in chapter 5 to examine the Commission's ability to:

    a)   utilise social policy provisions of the Treaty of Rome;

    b)   obtain support from Community pressure groups.

In chapter 6 an attempt will be made to ascertain the degree of influence, both individually and collectively, Community pressure groups and the Commission have exercised with respect to the Council of Ministers or Social Affairs regarding legislative and executive action on five social policy issues.

Impact of Community pressure groups and the Commission

The following presentation aims at showing the extent:

    a)   to which demands by Community pressure groups on the five social policy issues were reflected in the legislative and executive action of the Council of Ministers;

    b)   to which the Commission contributed to the achievement of legislative and executive action by the Council of Ministers.

When examining the demands of Community pressure groups, it should be remembered that the data presented in chapter 5 showed that trade unions and employers' organisations, although differing in their demands, were largely satisfied with the proposals made by the

Commission on the five social policy issues. Thus, the acceptance by the Council of either trade union demands or the demands of employers' organisations also reflects in a way the final position taken by the Commission. This implies that, in certain cases, the Commission may be more in line with one set of groups (let us say trade unions) in its initial proposal concerning the total content of a proposal, but may have to make alterations in line with demands made by another set of groups (let us say employers) once the deliberations of the Council have been concluded. Due to the amendment privilege, the Commission can change its own proposals during Council deliberation, and thus, through slight alteration, might ensure that modified legislative or executive action is taken rather than have a proposal refused in its totality.

Acceptance of Community pressure groups' demands

The following is, therefore, a summary presentation of the extent to which Community pressure groups' demands were reflected in the legislative and executive action of the Council of Ministers. A more comprehensive view of the acceptance of the demands of Community pressure groups by the Council of Ministers on the five social policy issues is provided in table 6.1.

1.   Most of the demands made by Community pressure groups for improving the operation and budget of the ESF were taken into consideration by the Council. However, the Council's decisions, of 1974, 1975 and 1976, to grant ESF aid to young people under twenty-five years of age and to persons engaged in agriculture, and to set an age threshold for women ESF recipients (over 35 years of age), were contrary to demands advanced by the trade unions up until 1973, but reflected the demands of the employers' organisations. From 1974 onward, trade unions also campaigned in favour of ESF assistance for young people under twenty-five years of age. The Council's decision to grant ESF aid for handicapped workers reflected the demands of both employers' organisations and trade unions. Similarly, the Council's decisions in 1975 and 1976 to grant ESF aid for persons employed in the textile sector and clothing industry were in line with demands from both employers' organisations and trade unions. However, a Commission proposal, inspired by trade

union demands, to extend aid under Article 4 (to be described in chapter 7) of the ESF in favour of workers in the sector most affected by the recession, was not approved by the Council at its meeting in December 1975. [1]

The Council's decision of June 1974 to grant ESF aid to help improve migrant workers' living and working conditions through the whole process of migration (from the time they prepare to move to another country to their possible return to their own country) went beyond the desires of the employers' organisations, but covered, to a great extent, the wishes of the trade unions.

Not mentioned in the Council's decisions but demanded by the employers' organisations, was the provision of ESF aid to categories of self-employed persons other than those in agriculture. Similarly not acknowledged by the Council were the demands of the trade unions and the ESC enabling private institutions to apply independently for ESF aid. Nor were the trade union and ESC demands fulfilled with regard to granting the Commission the establishment of criteria for ESF intervention concerning Article 4, i.e. the Council had retained the privilege of deciding each case individually.

2.   While the Council reflected upon many Community pressure group demands on vocational training standards, it did not respond to trade union demands for direct actions on the mutual recognition of vocational training certificates (including apprenticeship certificates for skilled and semi-skilled workers) or the alignment of vocational training levels. (The latter had also been suggested in an ESC Study in 1975). The Council's position was very similar to that of the employers' organisations, which had felt that the latter points were not particularly pressing and only constituted long-range objectives.

However, in a meeting on 16 June 1975, it adopted a directive concerning the mutual recognition of diplomas, certificates and other evidence of formal qualifications in medicine, including measures to facilitate the effective exercise of the right of establishment and freedom to provide services, together with a directive concerning the co-ordination of provisions laid down by law in respect of

Table 6.1
Impact of Community pressure groups

Social policy issues and the relevant Treaty provisions	Position of trade unions	Position of employers' organisations	Position of Council and action level	1968-76 progress
ESF	Convergence of interests on fulfilment and expansion	Some differences over categories of workers to benefit from ESF aid and the rules to govern the implementation of Article 4.	Fulfilment and expansion	Substantial
Social security benefits for migrant workers	Fulfilment and expansion to supplementary benefits	Fulfilment with few exceptions	Fulfilment with few exceptions	Substantial
A common vocational training policy	Attempt gradual fulfilment	Improvements but slight opposition on institutional and legal measures	Small improvements	Small
Social security harmonisation in general	Improvements and gradual harmonisation	Limited improvements and some opposition on actual harmonisation in the short & medium term	Slight improvements	Slight
Equal pay for men and women	Fulfilment and expansion into related areas	Attempt gradual fulfilment	Substantial improvements or near fulfilment	Substantial

119

activities by doctors.

In addition, the Council of Ministers complied with the wishes of the employers' organisations and especially of the trade unions — whose demands went back much further than those of the employers' organisations — by setting up a European Centre for Vocational Training in 1975, to assist the Commission in encouraging, at Community level, the promotion and development of vocational training or in-service training, and to achieve effective implementation of the common vocational training policy.

3. The substantial part of Community pressure groups' demands concerned with social security benefits for migrant workers, found recognition in the Council's position. However, the Council did not respond favourably, except in a very general and roundabout way, [2] to the specific demands of trade unions concerning supplementary social security benefits, such as those arising from company schemes, and thus reflected the position taken by the employers' organisations on this issue.

Nor had the Council adopted a proposal for a regulation relating to the standardisation of the payment of family benefits to workers whose families resided in a Member State other than the country of employment. Trade unions had pressed for the acceptance of this proposal.

Finally, no Council decision had been made regarding the co-ordination of social security systems for the self-employed migrant workers, desired by the employers' organisations.

4. The Council was cautious in responding to the demands of trade unions for the gradual harmonisation of social security schemes, as well as for the harmonisation of these schemes in an 'upward direction', thus adopting a line similar to that of the employers' organisations which had felt that no harmonisation measures on a large scale could be implemented in the medium-term.

A more favourable response from the Council was recorded on related aspects of social security systems, such as:

a)   The Regulation setting up a European Foundation for the improvement of living and working conditions, to stimulate research and foster the exchange of information on social security systems, desired by both trade unions and employers' organisations.

b)   The Recommendation to the Member States on the application of the principle of the 40-hour week and four weeks' annual paid holiday. While satisfying trade union demands in principle, the Council deviated from trade union demands on the priority by which this principle should be implemented — delaying it by two years and thus accommodating to the demands expressed by the employers' organisations.

c)   The Instruction to the Commission to draw up a European Social Budget; desired by both trade unions and employers' organisations.

d)   The Directive calling for the approximation of Member States' legislation concerning collective bargaining dismissals requiring consultations between employers, workers' representatives and public authorities in cases of ten or more impending redundancies; reflecting primarily trade union demands.

e)   The Directive providing that workers' rights will be safeguarded in all Community countries in the event of mergers, transfers or amalgamations involving the firms employing them; fulfilling a trade union demand.

f)   A Programme of Pilot Schemes and Studies to combat poverty in the Community.

g)   The extension of responsibility to the existing Mines Safety and Health Commission to consider preventative action against accident or occupational hazards in all mineral-extraction, whether in mining or not.

Furthermore, the Council of Ministers has asked the Commission to submit proposals:

a)   To extend social security benefits (such as retirement pensions and sickness benefits) to groups without a proper cover or no cover at all (such as some handicapped and self-employed people); employers' organisations had pressed particularly for Community action on the latter category;

b)   To ensure that social security benefits keep pace with

rising prices and wages or that these benefits are not eroded by inflation; trade unions had demanded Community measures on this.

5. The Council's position on the implementation of the principle of equal pay for men and women leaned basically towards the trade unions' position rather than that of the employers' organisations.

   In two meetings in 1975, the Council adopted two directives requiring the abolition of financial discrimination in laws as regards pay, collective agreements and contracts, and aimed at ensuring equality of treatment between men and women as regards access to employment, promotion of vocational training and working conditions. Moreover, at a meeting in 1976, the Council of Ministers encouraged further Commission proposals regarding provisions to ensure progressive implementation of equal treatment in social security matters.

In addition to the Council's reflection of the demands of Community pressure groups on the five social policy issues, there are further aspects which can be considered for such a comparison. These relate to the establishment of: the Standing Committee on Employment (SCE); the Advisory Committee of the ESF: the Advisory Committee on Social Security for Migrant Workers; the Advisory Committee for Safety and Health Protection; the Management Board of the European Centre for Vocational Training; and the Administrative body of the European Foundation for Living and Working Conditions. In all these instances, the employers' organisations and the trade unions had secured representation and participation in the decision-making. While the decision by the Council on the establishment of the SCE [3] largely reflected the demands of the employers' organisations and trade unions, especially those of the latter, and while it corresponded largely with the structural make-up envisaged by the trade unions, there were also several items which the trade unions felt were not sufficiently settled or which had been determined in a way that was contrary to their demands. The latter concerned:

a) The establishment of a Secretariat for the SCE;

b) The equal rights clause of trade unions and employers' organisations with respect to the representatives of Member Governments in determining the affairs of the Committee.

In addition, whereas the trade unions had expressed the wish that the SCE should be presided over by a member of the Commission, the Council decided to assign the Presidency to a representative of the Member Governments. [4] Finally, trade unions had disagreed over the inclusion of representatives from certain 'unaffiliated' (unaffiliated to the ETUC) trade union organisations in the list of representatives for the SCE; leading consequently, after five successful meetings between 1971 and 1972, to a suspension of meetings between 1973 and 1974. However, in December 1974, an agreement was reached between trade unions and the Council, and SCE meetings took place again from February 1975 on.

Without trying to hide the negative aspect of the Council's decision to assign a government representative to the Chairmanship, which is, particularly from the supranational institutional development point of view, a move back rather than a move forward, one should stress that the establishment of the SCE in 1971 was — and is — an important achievement for the Community pressure groups; considering the attitudes certain governments of the Member States had taken up to 1970 with regard to the orientation of, and relations between, pressure groups and the national governments, on the one hand, and pressure groups and the Commission, on the other.

With regard to the establishment of the 'new' Advisory Committee of the ESF, the Council's decision of 8 November 1971 reflected the demands of the Community pressure groups on:

a)   the establishment of the Committee;

b)   the composition or method of selection of the representatives of this Committee. [5]

However, the Council did not rule as favourably with regard to trade unions on the working relationship between this Committee, on the one hand, and the Commission and the Council, on the other. Similarly, the Council was not as forthcoming as the trade unions wished on the numerical expansion of Joint Committees, on which the employers' organisations had expressed reservations. Instead, the Council instructed the Commission in December 1975 to hold more frequent joint meetings at sectoral level. On the other hand, the Council decided in December 1976 to allocate approximately £14,000 to cover the costs of launching the European Trade Union Institute and thus, in spite of employers' objections, fulfilled a trade union demand.

Having presented the reflection of the demands of Community

pressure groups on the Council's decisions on five social policy issues and related aspects, let us now consider the effectiveness of the activities of Community pressure groups and the Commission.

Effectiveness of Community pressure groups and Commission influence

Difficulties have arisen in the attempt to measure influence, as in so many other instances where this has been tried before. There were problems, first of all, in isolating a one-to-one causal relationship between, on the one hand, Community pressure groups' demands and Commission activities and, on the other, the Council's response. Second, the attempt to ascertain the degree of influence exercised by these two actors in persuading the Council either for or against a decision to be taken, proved to be even more complicated.

While there are a number of cases where it appears that Community pressure groups exercised influence, the verification of these cases was not always possible. This relates mainly to the difficulty in locating a particular cause. For example, a particular response by the Council can arise from:

a)   a demand made by Community pressure groups;

b)   a demand made by one or several national pressure groups via their national governments, due to either their own concerns about a certain issue or stimulated through participation in discussion with their colleagues in the European interest group organisations;

c)   a demand made by national governments, largely independent of pressure groups.

Similarly, a particular decision by a national government to align its laws and regulations on social security provisions can either be due to demands expressed by one or several national pressure groups or be the result of its own initiative. Not only is it difficult to separate these possible cases accurately, it is even more difficult to determine the weight of influence each individual case carried if all of the first three, for example, operate. The introduction of the Commission as another source of influence adds still further to the complexity. With these limitations in mind, let us first look at the cases where it appears that the Community pressure groups exercised influence and, second, consider alternative possibilities. This will be followed by still other cases in which the Commission may have had an influence.

Indicators of Community pressure group influence

There are three possible ways in which a measurement of Community pressure group influence can be obtained:

a)   the acceptance of Community pressure groups' proposals in decisions by the Council of Ministers;

b)   the recognition of their demands in communiqués of Summit Meetings of Heads of State or Government;

c)   the views held by Community pressure groups on their success in wielding influence.

With regard to the first, we were able to identify, in the comparison above, a number of cases in which the official Council decision accepted the demands (expressed both in interviews and written statements) of Community pressure groups relating to the five social policy issues, the SCE and the Advisory Committees mentioned above. In addition, such an identification is possible with regard to the first Community Employment Conference held in Luxembourg in 1970, [6] and three subsequent similar conferences in 1974, 1975 and 1976. These conferences are also known as 'Tripartite Conferences' because they are attended by representatives of both sides of industry and Governments of the Member States (represented by their Ministers of Labour and Social Affairs, and sometimes by the Ministers of Economic and Financial Affairs).

There are several items mentioned by Community pressure groups, both in response to interviews and in written statements, which found recognition in communiqués of Summit Meetings of Heads of State or Government. For example, the Summit Meeting at the Hague in December 1969 stressed the need for a reform of the ESF and the importance of social policy in the Community, both having been proposed by Community pressure groups. Similarly, the declaration addressed by the ECFTU to participants of the Paris Summit Meeting in October 1972, [7] carrying both general and specific suggestions on social policy, found recognition in the communiqués. The general suggestions of more forceful initiatives in the field of Community social policy were mentioned in the communiqués, as were references to:

a)   the use of Article 235;

b) the right of initiative of the ESC; [8]

c) the involvement of management and labour in the economic and social decisions of the Community and that of the workers in the operation of firms;

d) the belief that efforts should be made to facilitate the conclusion of collective agreements between trade unions and employers' organisations at the Community level.

In addition, the declarations sent by the EO/WCL and the ETUC to the Summit Meeting in Copenhagen in December 1973, [9] noting that the trade unions expected from the Council the commitment and manifestation that all policies had social aims, found recognition in the communiqués.

Finally, the Paris Summit Conference in December 1974 made reference to a long-standing trade union demand by declaring that: 'The Heads of Government have made it their objective to harmonise the degree of social security afforded by the various Member States, while maintaining progress but without requiring that the social systems obtained in all Member States should be identical.' [10]

Regarding their own views on their success in influencing the legislative and executive action of the Council of Ministers, different ratings were given by employers' organisations and trade unions. The employers' organisations indicated in interviews that they were generally satisfied with their rate of success in influencing the activities of the Council of Ministers on the five social policy issues, the SCE and other Advisory Committees. In contrast, the trade unions thought of themselves as having been successful in their influence on only one social policy issue, namely the ESF, but recognised that progress had been made on their demands, especially from 1974 onward regarding social security benefits for migrant workers, equal pay for men and women, social protection of workers (collective mass dismissals and in cases of business mergers), the 40-hour week and 4 weeks' annual holiday. Trade unions were also generally satisfied with their success in:

a) the granting of the right of initiative for the ESC;

b) the establishment of the SCE and the direct contact it brought with the Council;

c) the establishment of the 'new' Advisory Committees mentioned above;

d) the representation of both sides of industry on the governing bodies of the European Vocational Training Centre and the European Foundation for Living and Working Conditions;

e) the holding of Community Employment Conferences;

f) the establishment of the European Trade Union Institute.

Moreover, while noting that there had been positive results with regard to demands, trade unions also questioned the willingness of the Council to transfer social policy from the planning stage to the implementation stage. [11] According to the trade unions, the Community institutions could only achieve concrete results in social policy in those areas in which the Treaty foresaw obligatory rulings being made, and for which the Commission had been assigned a mandate. Governments were not ready, so some trade unions maintained, to relinquish their powers relating to social policy.

Other sources of influence

While the above presentation indicates cases which suggest that influence was exerted by Community pressure groups on the Council of Ministers, the following examples demonstrate that initiatives which were taken by national governments, either nationally or at the level of the Council of Ministers, cannot be so easily attributed, if at all, to Community, or even to national, pressure groups.

For instance, the Italian Government sent a Memorandum to the Council of Ministers in June 1971 calling for Community measures on:

a) employment policies;

b) social policies for migrant workers;

c) social security harmonisation, in general.

The Italian trade unions claimed in interviews that they had pressed the Italian Government to undertake such an initiative. Yet it is plausible that the Italian Government sought Community measures on its own in view of the severe regional unemployment problems experienced in the South of Italy; or, on the other hand, the trade union pressure added to an already existing concern of the Italian Government and thus resulted in the submission of the Memorandum. Similarly, the representatives of the German Trade Union Congress (DGB) were felt to have been instrumental in the initiatives taken by the German Government between 1968 and 1973 towards:

a)   the co-ordination between economic and social policy or a more independent role of social policy; [12]

b)   the coverage of social security; [13]

c)   the establishment of a European Social Budget (ESB); [14]

d)   the Communiqué of the Paris Summit Conference of October 1972 on social policy.

Again, it is not entirely clear to what extent the Government itself had decided to take these initiatives or had been influenced by national pressure groups. The reasons why the German Government could have taken initiatives of its own are not so different from those the pressure groups cited as having motivated them to seek Community action. These were impacts of:

a)   the economic recession, technological changes and employment problems between 1966 and 1968;

b)   the Common Agricultural Policy (CAP);

c)   the Customs Union, especially with regard to increasing business mergers; [15]

d)   the free movement of labour.

In view of these impacts, as well as other developments in Germany, the German Government might have called either for Community measures or for studies at the Community level in order to find out about trends in social security expenditure and benefits in other countries in order to solve their own problems better, or to deal more effectively with demands of certain groups. Moreover, if, on certain issues dealing with social security, the primary concern of the German Government was to extend social security coverage to those categories like the self-employed, who had so far not obtained coverage, then it would appear that the pressure of trade unions was little, if at all, present.

Furthermore, additional data would be needed to ascertain the following:

a)   Was there a more favourable response to the demands of trade unions by the German Government after the Social Democratic Party (SPD) came to power in October 1969? [16]

b)   What effect did the 'new' Government in Germany (SPD) and the 'new' Government in France have on the reform of the ESF, which they encouraged at the Hague Summit Meeting?

c)   What effect did the general strikes in France in May 1968 have on government concessions in the social policy sector from 1969 on? [17]

d)   How beneficial was the 'European socialisation' of certain trade union members for successfully introducing demands at the national level on social policy? [18] Or, for that matter, how rigid were the ties between trade unions or employers' organisations and national governments to prevent the latter from agreeing to Council decisions?

e)   What impact did the recommendation of the International Labour Organisation (ILO) on equal pay for equal value (ratified by most of the EC Member States) have on the Council decisions concerning Article 119?

Thus, the above presentation has indicated the problems encountered in isolating Community pressure group influence or pressure group influence at the national level from the actions of the Council of Ministers on social policy. The following section attempts to show that the question of influence is further complicated when the role and activities of the Commission are considered.

Indicators of Commission influence

More than in the case of the Community pressure groups, the location of the actual cause of the Commission's influence is a crucial problem. To what extent is the Commission:

a)   taking initiatives of its own;

b)   merely channelling demands of Community pressure groups;

c)   filtering and moulding demands of Community pressure groups;

d)   merely channelling demands of national governments;

e)   filtering and moulding demands of national governments;

f)   using a combination of the first five.

The data presented in chapter 5 suggest that the Commission was not merely channelling Community pressure group demands, but rather attempting skilfully either to take initiatives of its own or to mould the different demands of the trade unions and employers' organisations in order to reach a compromise between the two. A similar observation can be made with regard to the Commission on the handling of demands from national governments.

Generally speaking, as pointed out above, the acceptance of demands from either the trade unions or employers' organisations by the Council on the five social policy issues, also reflects the final position taken by the Commission. Moreover, while it is generally difficult to separate the Commission's own initiatives and contributions from those of Community pressure groups and national governments, there are cases where the Commission's influence, with respect to the Council of Ministers, appeared to be particularly important.

One such case was the promotion of the implementation of Article 119, calling for equal pay for men and women. Neither the trade unions, at least until 1974, nor employers' organisations had pressed very hard on this. Nor does it appear that suggestions were made from national governments. Rather the Commission, being instructed by the Council in 1961 to draw up progress reports on the implementation of this Article, made the principle of equal pay for men and women one of its major promotion causes.

Partly due to the attempt to make an impact on public opinion and promote the image of the Commission held by the public, and partly due to the fact that the Irish Commissioner, Patrick Hillery, had presented himself as the 'champion' of the women's cause, the Commission consistently urged the Council to undertake measures on this issue. [19] The reward for this promotion came in December 1973, when the Council declared that, in principle, it agreed with the October 1973 proposal of the Commission concerning the implementation of Article 119 by the end of 1976. By comparison, however, the Commission appears to have had considerably less influence than Community pressure groups on the holding of the Community Employment Conferences (1970 and 1974) and the establishment of the SCE.

Along with the demands of the Community pressure groups, the Commission's points raised in reports submitted to Summit Meetings, found recognition in their communiqués. The Commission generally indicated satisfaction with its attempts to introduce legislative and executive action on the ESF, social security for migrant workers, and equal pay for men and women, but felt the response could have been better on social security provisions in general and vocational training, especially on the latter.

In the period since 1970, the Council has relaxed the restrictions of the 'Gentlemen's Agreement' and has actually taken some steps to advance social security harmonisation in general by granting a number of mandates to the Commission for the application of Article 118. However, while doing this, the Council also insisted that the Commission should prepare proposals to suit the practical circumstances of current social problems rather than long-range objectives with respect to 'upward harmonisation', and that it should work in close co-operation with the CPR. As one official in the Commission pointed out in an interview, the Legal Department of the Commission is still today very apprehensive and tries to discourage proposals from the Commission's DG for Social Affairs based on Article 118. In general, the Commission has practised a working relationship which can be described as congenial rather than provocative towards the Council of Social Affairs, and increased its consultations with the CPR, both before and during the drafting of proposals. [20]

Thus by adopting a pragmatic approach to problem-solving, and by calling for actions at the Community level which supplement social policy provisions existing at the national level, or by suggesting studies, opinions and recommendations instead of regulations, the Commission has helped to set in motion limited legislation concerning social security harmonisation in general.

Differing views have been expressed over the lack of official Council legislation and the concentration on studies [21] with regard to social security harmonisation in general. By closer examination of the complexities involved in harmonising six or nine different social security systems, which all have their own historical development, both sides of the argument appear to obtain support. Those in favour of limited legislation and extensive studies refer generally to two factors in support of their argument. First, drastic measures in the harmonisation of social security would disturb the competitive factor between the different economies because of the changes in the labour costs. Second, clarity must be established as far as possible on this complex subject and studies are the appropriate means to provide information on the existing differences in the finance, coverage and trends of social security schemes.

Those in favour of speedy legislation point out that further delays augment the differences between the different social security schemes even more, and small steps are not enough to bring about any meaningful correction in the alignment of the different social security standards. Whereas the latter group sees in the emphasis on studies largely a manoeuvre by the governments to delay the actual harmonisation process of social security schemes, the former group claims that once objective studies are available, it would be more difficult for certain governments to take a passive role in the introduction of legislation.

In any case, the numerous studies, reports and working documents provided by the Commission in the field of social policy may make considerable contributions to legislation in the long run, which are not very obvious for immediate or short term consideration as undertaken in this research. For example, the Commission draws up annually a Report on the Social Situation in the Community, allowing governments and pressure groups to see where they stand in relation to others, and keeping them constantly informed of the state of affairs in all Member countries. Similarly, the 'Green Paper', introduced by the Commission in 1975 on workers' participation, was intended to produce a constructive debate which would provide acceptable solutions for the problem of employee participation in the management of firms. In addition, as mentioned earlier, the potential interest in the establishment of such instruments as the European Centre for Vocational Training, the European Foundation for the Environment and Living and Working Conditions, the ESB and the Social Indicators, could very well add to the influence exercised by the Commission with respect to the Council.

Conclusion

An attempt was made in chapter 6 to ascertain the degree of influence, both individually and collectively, that Community pressure groups and the Commission exercised on the Council of Ministers on the harmonisation of the five social policy issues.

While the evidence gathered for this chapter indicated that trade unions were successful in many of their demands on the five social policy issues (such as collective dismissals, the ESF and social security benefits for migrant workers) and their related aspects, there is evidence of equal success on the employers' side. The gains achieved by the employers' organisations can be seen in two ways. On the one hand, they shared with the trade unions the achievement of such issues as the improvement of the ESF, and on the other, they were successful, to some extent, in preventing certain legislative or executive actions taking place (such as 'upward harmonisation' of social security systems or the mutual recognition of vocational training certificates) for which the trade unions had expressed demands. Perhaps it can be said that through the combination of pressing for certain policies and opposing others, the employers' organisations were more successful in achieving their aims than the trade unions. As shown in table 6.1, the demands of the employers' organisations were more in line with the official position taken by the Council of Ministers than those of the trade unions.

The Commission's influence can be seen in many ways as being similar to that of the trade unions. However the Commission's activities, especially concerning studies, reports, seminars, conferences [22] and surveys, while contributing to the diffusion and exchange of information, and thereby helping to stimulate the executive action of the Council, are difficult to evaluate. Generally, the complexity of the decision-making process of the Council of Ministers and the close relationship between the Commission and the CPR do not allow an exact measure for the influence exercised by the Commission on the legislative and executive action of the Council through such influencing factors as timing and type of legislation selected or the role behaviour practised.

In summing up, the data in chapter 6 suggest that progress has been made towards greater social policy harmonisation and that Community pressure groups and the Commission contributed to this increasing harmonisation. However, the data indicate also the important role national governments play in this process and their reluctance to concede to suggestions and demands of trade unions and the Commission on some social policy issues. This will be illustrated further in the next chapter.

Notes

[1]   For more details, see the *Ninth General Report on the Activities of the European Communities*, Brussels-Luxembourg, February 1976, p.121.

[2]   For example, in its resolution of 9 February 1976 on an Action Programme for Migrant Workers and Members of their Families, the Council states:

> ... to seek appropriate solutions with a view to eliminating progressively such unwarranted restrictions on the rights of workers who are nationals of other Member States and members of their families as may still exist under Community Regulations in force.

See 'Action Programme in Favour of Migrant Workers and their

Families' in Bulletin of the European Communities: *Suppiement 3/76*, Commission of the European Communities.

[3]   According to the Council decision of 26 November 1970, the task of the SCE is to continuously secure the concertations and consultations among the Council, the Commission, governments and social partners before the relevant institutions of the EC take a decision, in order to promote the co-ordination of employment policy of the Member States and in accordance with the aims of the EC. The Council also stated that the European organisations of pressure groups should secure that the representation of members to the SCE reflects a proportional composition of the members in their national organisations. In addition, the Council assigned the Chairmanship of the SCE to a representative of the governments (to rotate every six months).

[4]   Under the present set-up, only the currently presiding President of the Council of Social Affairs has the right to call for sessions and to determine the topics for discussion.

[5]   Important from the point of view of the Community pressure groups was the granting by the Council of Ministers that representatives to the 'new' Advisory Committee of the ESF can now be recommended by the respective European organisations of trade unions and employers' groups. This can be seen as a boost to the role and function of Community pressure groups, primarily the secretariats of these organisations with respect to the national affiliations.

[6]   The EO/WCL stated that the Council had initially, in a Council session of 29 July 1968, decided to hold an Employment Conference along the lines of an inter-governmental conference and without supranational characteristics. Consequently, so the EO/WCL noted, the two General Secretariats of the ICFTU and the WCL sent a letter to the President of the Council stating:

> We believe this Conference should have the character of a Community conference where representatives of the Community employers' groups and trade unions are included; and that the selection of themes and organisation of this Conference should be carried out in close co-operation with Community employers' groups and trade unions.

See EO/WCL First Congress *Activity Report*, part 2, 1969, p.18. It is worthwhile to add that it took the Council of Ministers twelve years to agree to such a conference.

[7]   See ECFTU *Pressemitteilung* No.93, 15 September 1972.

[8]   The Communiqué of the Paris Summit Conference of October 1972 notes that:

The Heads of Government asked the Community institutions to accord the Economic and Social Committee the right to issue from now on opinions on its own initiative concerning all questions affecting the Community's work.

See *Seventh General Report on the Activities of the European Communities*, Commission of the European Communities, Brussels, February 1974, p.42.

[9] See EO/WVA *Erklärung im Hinblick auf die Kopenhager Gipfelkonferenz*, December 1973; and the ETUC *Erklärung*, October 1973.

[10] See *Report on the Development of the Social Situation in the Communities in 1974*, p.11.

[11] For example, the EO/WCL issued a declaration aimed at the participants of the Copenhagen Summit Meeting of December 1973, in which it stated that the workers were finally losing patience regarding the repeated failure of the Council to implement decisions adopted by the Heads of State or Government. See EO/WVA *Erklärung im Hinblick auf die Kopenhager Gipfelkonferenz*, December 1973.

[12] According to *Labor*, the German Government introduced a series of initiatives at the Council of Ministers between 1967 and 1969 on this. See *Labor* 4, July/August 15 Jahrgang 1968, pp 17-18. Also in the Council of Ministers on 21 May 1973, the German Government had proposed the adoption of the principle of a 'dynamic concept' (*Dynamisierung*) for social benefits.

[13] The German Government suggested to the Council (adopted by the Council on 26 November 1970) that the Commission should prepare a report on the categories of people eligible for social security to enable the Council to discover what Community action should be undertaken in order to achieve harmonisation. See *General Report*, 1970, p.114.

[14] The German Government introduced a *Note* at a Council Meeting on 9 June 1970, calling for an examination of the possibility of establishing an ESB. *Ibid.*

[15] All three: (a), (b) and (c) require measures to protect workers against unemployment.

[16] The SPD has had traditionally closer ties with the trade unions and appears to be more receptive to their demands than the Christian Democrats (CDU).

[17] There are indications, based primarily on the views of trade unions, that during the May 1968 crisis, Pompidou promised the trade unions to improve wages and other social policy issues, as well as to call for measures at the Community level.

[18]   The question here is whether, and to what extent, national trade union confederations have benefitted in pressing their claims for social policy at the national level from contacts with colleagues in the ETUC.

[19]   The Commission has set up a specialised department, known as the 'think tank', to promote Community action concerning the employment of women. The Commission also made a study on the employment of women in the Member States, held several meetings with women's organisations and made a film designed to inform the public of Community activities relating to the employment of women.

[20]   It is known in Community circles that one of the important changes brought about by the formation of the 'new' Commission under the Presidency of Ortoli, at the beginning of 1973, was to have frequent and intensified contacts with the CPR in order to obtain Council consent and so avoid greater backlogs of Commission proposals.

[21]   For example, Veldkamp, an ardent defender of very small-dosed Community legislation on social security provisions, sees reporting by the Commission as a very valuable practice. He asserts that, if skilfully worded, a report can make it clear where harmonisation has been neglected without good reason or where an existing form of harmonisation has been impaired. See Veldkamp, 'Towards Harmonisation of Social Security in the EEC,' p.368.

[22]   It should be pointed out that in 1976 the Commission obtained the right to be in charge of organising tripartite conferences at Community level. Formerly, this privilege was held by the Council of Ministers.

7 Trend of social policy harmonisation

Introduction

In the following, an attempt will be made to ascertain the trend of social policy harmonisation since mid-1968. We will look at the nature of legislation passed by the Council of Ministers on the five social policy issues since mid-1968 and compare it with the legislation passed in the period prior to mid-1968. The five social policy issues are: the improvement of the European Social Fund (ESF); a common vocational training policy; social security benefits for migrant workers; social security harmonisation in general; and equal pay for men and women.

To carry out this task, we will examine the number of executive actions passed on Community regulations, directives, decisions, recommendations and studies in the two periods under consideration. [1]

Community regulations, whether passed by the Council of Ministers or the Commission, [2] together with judgements delivered by the Court of Justice, are the most legally binding provisions on the Member States. Regulations are thus more demanding on the Member Governments than directives or recommendations. At the same time, the number of regulations passed and the extent of their coverage, followed by the number of directives, indicates Community solidarity and the progress of integration in the respective area or issue. The following table 7.1 provides a comparison of the number of EC legislative actions passed on the five social policy issues in two periods.

Having outlined the criteria for evaluating the legislative and executive action of social policy, and having provided a general comparison on the legislative actions passed, let us now examine the five social policy issues individually, and determine whether a retraction, improvement, fulfilment or expansion has taken place, or whether the situation has remained unchanged since mid-1968. Improvement in this context means progress towards fulfilment of a Treaty provision. An expansion relates to progress after the fulfilment of a Treaty provision.

Table 7.1
Comparison of legislative actions

		Prior to mid-1968	From mid-1968 onwards
Regulations	Council	3 + 8 amending	9 1 implementing
	Commission	2 + 11 implementing	2
Directives	Council	—	6
	Commission	—	—
Decisions	Council	6	17
	Commission	8	5
Recommen-dations	Council	2	1
	Commission	5	—

Equal pay for men and women

The Treaty of Rome had regarded the principle of equal pay for men and women as an obligation to be achieved during the first four years of the Common Market. However, at the end of 1961, the governments observed that this goal was not feasible and passed a resolution calling for equalisation measures by the end of 1969. This resolution widened the content of Article 119, calling for equal pay, not merely for the same work, but for work of similar value, and thus ruling out separate systems of classification for men and women. The Commission, in co-operation with the two sides of industry, was asked to draw up progress reports every two years on the degree of application of this Article.

In spite of specific time references calling for the implementation of Article 119 by 1970, no Community legislation in the form of a regulation or directive had been passed by the end of 1973. As a consequence, the Commission introduced infringement procedures [3] against the six original Member States in 1973 for having failed to comply with the Treaty of Rome timetable. [4]

Starting with the Council declaration of December 1973, and the adoption of two directives by the Council in 1975, substantial improvements have been made towards fulfilment of Article 119.

From February 1976, Member States are required to apply the principle of equal pay, and from mid-1978 they have to assure equality concerning access to employment, promotion, and vocational training, as well as equality in working conditions. These two directives provided minimum standards for women in respect of their right for equal pay; laying down that discrimination still existing in laws, agreements or contracts have to be eliminated, that the right to pursue equal pay for equal work cannot be frustrated by dismissals, and that supervision of the application of these rights has to be ensured by national law. Equally important, the Court of Justice of the EC has, since 1975, delivered judgements ensuring that women are not the object of discrimination based on sex when it comes to pay and social security benefits.

In addition, further legislation can be expected in 1977 regarding provisions to ensure progressive implementation of equal treatment in social security matters (all systems of protection against certain risks such as unemployment, medical care, old age, invalidity and industrial accidents and illnesses); complementing the two directives of 1975. [5]

Although progress towards equal pay was made over the years by the original six members of the Community, it was still far from satisfactory. Following a study conducted by Mrs Sullerot [6] under the auspices of the Commission, on the original six members of the Community, it has become very apparent that there are still numerous differences in treatment, both concerning mandatory schemes (i.e imposed by law) and occupational schemes, which in many cases operate clearly to the disadvantage of women. Some of the points highlighted in Sullerot's Report are:

a) Unemployment is still more marked among young women than among young men, even when the former are better educated;

b) Female workers earn much less than their male counterparts [7] ... [However] the gap between male and female wages has narrowed in Italy, Belgium and Germany, where it was considerable; but in France, where it was smaller, it has not disappeared and follows the fluctuations of short-term economic trends. There is practically no case law and what there is relates to collective bargaining.

c) Overall, the majority of women are in the lower or medium wage categories ... [But] in Germany training has been re-formed to ensure that women receive a sound general education for them to switch to office work and commercial occupations.

d)   Average hourly rates vary more according to industry than according to skills ... A woman will earn more in an industry employing both men and women than she will in an all-female industry.

e)   Some collective bargaining agreements still include discriminations and disadvantages for women. A great number of women workers are not even covered by any sort of collective bargaining agreement, especially in commerce and crafts.

Moreover, a Commission Report in 1974 also noted the continued unsatisfactory position as regards equal pay in Britain, Ireland and Denmark, in spite of steps such as the British Equal Pay Act of 1970.

In spite of these drawbacks in eliminating discrimination between the sexes, one can agree, however, with the Commission that under the impact of the two directives passed and the third planned directive, a very important stage in implementing the principle of equal treatment for women in employment, promotion, vocational training and in matters of social security, has begun.

Social security benefits for migrant workers

Community decisions on social security benefits for migrant workers provide the following comparison of legislative types for the two periods under consideration.

Important regulations concerning social security for migrant workers were passed in the period prior to mid-1968. Already in 1958 two regulations (Regulation no.3 and Regulation no.4) were passed by the Council, based on Article 51 of the Treaty calling for provisions to secure for migrant workers and their dependants the right to social security benefits for all periods which were covered under the laws of the several countries. This meant that:

a)   benefits acquired by any migrant working in more than one EC country would be aggregated;

b)   benefits were exportable to other countries in the EC. [8]

Both the 11 amending regulations issued by the Council and the

13 regulations put forward by the Commission prior to mid-1968, were issued for the purpose of a more 'efficient' implementation of Regulations nos 3 and 4. Similarly, the decisions issued by the Commission prior to mid-1968 were made in order to adjust Regulations nos 3 and 4 to particular circumstances. Moreover, three groups originally not properly covered — seasonal workers, frontier commuters and seamen — were dealt with in these implementing regulations between 1963 and 1967.

Nevertheless, the two Council regulations issued in the period from mid-1968 onward (no.1408/71 in 1971 and no.574/72 in 1972) [9] superseding the two main Regulations nos 3 and 4, were important refinements requiring quicker calculations and prompter transfers of payments, between Member States, of the benefits to migrant workers. [10]

As with the original Regulations nos 3 and 4, Regulations nos 1408/71 and 574/72 supersede most of the bilateral and multi-lateral agreements between Member States that previously governed social security for migrant workers. In addition, Regulation no.1408/71 stipulates that if Member States conclude conventions among themselves, they have to be 'based on the principles and spirit of this Regulation', and the respective governments must notify the Council of Ministers of its content. Finally, the Court of Justice of the EC has been increasingly called upon to enforce, ensure and interpret legal rights arising either out of Regulations nos 3 and 4 or Regulations nos 1408/71 and 574/72. For example, the Court delivered four judgements in 1970 and 1971, followed by five judgements in 1972 and eight judgements each in 1973, 1974, 1975 and 1976. These judgements are binding in the fullest legal sense in the Member States. In 1976 the Commission issued handbooks informing migrant workers of their rights regarding social security benefits.

However, while the principles of Articles 51 and 121 appear to have been substantially achieved, there were three important elements on which actual legislation was missing by the end of 1976, namely:

a) the problem of the so-called supplementary social security benefits as they relate to the transfer of social security payments for migrant workers;

b) social security benefit payments as they relate to independent (self-employed) workers migrating between countries;

c) social security benefits relating to family allowances for those members of the family who have not joined the migrant worker in the country of work.

With regard to the discrepancy on supplementary social security benefits or social assistance benefits, the Commission, in a recent document, [11] lists the following items which are still not extended to migrant workers:

Belgium: guaranteed revenue for old persons and allowances to the handicapped; *France*: allowances for handicapped adults, allowances from the National Solidarity Fund; *Italy*: Social Pension; *Ireland*: non-contributory pension (old-age, widows, orphans, blind persons) unemployment assistance; *Luxembourg*: allowances from the National Solidarity Fund; and the *UK*: supplementary benefits.

Self-employed migrant workers do not have the same rights as are enjoyed by wage earning migrants in equality of treatment, the right of aggregation of periods of insurance and export of benefits. As pointed out by Bruce Reed, this neglect is due to the fact that: 'It is the system of the state in which the worker is residing that is relevant in most cases, and not all allow the self-employed to claim benefits.' [12]

Attempts to adopt a uniform system for the payment of family benefits for Community migrants have been hampered by objections from France, where, in order to stimulate population growth, higher family benefits are paid than in the other Member States. The French Government likes to maintain a system where it only pays family allowances to children left behind at the rate pertaining in their home country. This point and other related examples, such as taxation allowances, means tested benefits in general, maternity grants and distinctions between social security and social assistance in which migrant workers and their dependants are still unequally treated, in comparison to host country workers and their families, are illustrated in a study by Reed. [13] They are also, in part, the subject of Commission proposals, both in the first Action Programme for Migrant Workers (1974) and in follow-up communications to the Council of Ministers, such as in *Supplement 3/76.*

As part of the implementation of the Action Programme for Migrant Workers, the Commission intended to present to the Council of Ministers in the second half of 1977:

a) a draft regulation on the co-ordination of social security systems for self-employed workers moving within the Community;

b) proposals for eliminating certain unjustified restrictions on

142

the rights of migrant workers as regards social security which still exist in Community regulations.

In general, it can be said that the progress towards the achievement of Articles 51 and 121 has reached a stage where harmonisation of social security systems in general between the Member States, at least on some issues, must be pursued and accomplished before further progress, especially on the aforementioned three, can be made.

The European Social Fund

The ESF was established by the EC Treaty in 1958 (Articles 123 to 127) to provide finances for retraining and resettling redundant workers, and it began operating in 1961. It aimed to: 'contribute to raising the standards of living' by 'promoting employment facilities and the geographic and occupational mobility of workers'. It reimbursed the national governments or state agencies 50 per cent for the cost of retraining or resettling workers who lost their jobs. The Fund received its money from the contributions of Member Governments. Member States could ask for refunds of money spent on workers who had been re-employed for at least six months; such expenditure had to be refunded *automatically* by the ESF. However, there were delays of up to two years before expenditures were effectively refunded.

The ESF rules by mid-1968 were very rigid, and its resources were limited (averaging 9 million u.a. per year between 1958 and 1969, but increased to 35 million u.a. in 1968). [14] Its role was passive rather than active, i.e. it was not able to help retrain workers before they lost their jobs.

Following the outline agreement of the 'new' ESF rules at its sessions in July 1970 and November 1970, the Council delivered its main decision on the reform of the ESF on 1 February 1971, and in subsequent decisions on 8 November 1971, finalised the implementing procedures for the decision of 1 February 1971. The main importance of the Council decision of 1 February 1971 lies primarily in the specification of the types of ESF intervention. One type of intervention (A) specified in Article 4 of this decision, states that the ESF can take action when the employment situation:

a)   is affected or is in danger of being affected, either by special measures adopted by the Council in the framework of Community policies, or by jointly agreed operations to

143

further the objectives of the Community;

b) calls for specific joint action to improve the balance between supply and demand for manpower within the Community. [15]

The other type of intervention (B) described in Article 5 of the above-cited decision, stipulates that the ESF can take action: [16]

> Where the employment situation in certain regions, in certain branches of the economy or in certain groups of undertakings is affected by difficulties which do not arise from any particular measure taken by the Council within the framework of a Community policy, but which result indirectly from the working of the Common Market or impede the harmonious development of the Community. In any such cases, assistance shall be granted to eliminate long-term structural unemployment and under-employment, to train a highly skilled labour force and, furthermore, for measures for the absorption and re-absorption into active employment of the disabled, and of older workers, women and young workers.

On 8 November 1971, the Council adopted three Regulations (nos 2396/71; 2397/71; and 2398/71) for the implementation of its Decision of 1 February 1971. These three regulations related to:

a) the reform of the ESF;

b) the aid which may qualify for assistance from the ESF;

c) the assistance from the ESF for persons who are to pursue activities in a self-employed capacity.

The list drawn up by the Council in November 1971 on aid which may qualify for assistance from the ESF only concerns the implementation of Type B (Article 5) intervention of the Council decision of 1 February 1971. This list can be adjusted by the Council (with a qualified majority) following a proposal by the Commission. On the basis of this list, the Commission will be able to take initiatives in deciding where, when and whom to help. In particular, the Commission can propose to the Council which regions, branches of industry or categories of workers shall receive assistance; what form the assistance will take; and how the workers will receive assistance. This new type of aid will also be available to help defray the cost of setting up vocational training centres in backward regions and, under certain conditions, to cover expenditures incurred by workers in their environmental adaptation after having to change their place of residence. The Commission was also given powers, although in a limited fashion, to conduct pilot schemes funded from the ESF.

Thus, under Article 5, the ESF can help to remedy an unsatisfactory employment situation, especially in declining regions, and industries affected by new techniques. It enables the Commission, with the support of the Tripartite Social Fund Committee, to help workers *before* they lose their jobs rather than operating from an *ad hoc* basis as the 'old' ESF did.

For the Type A (Article 4) intervention the Council will, acting on a proposal from the Commission, determine the areas in which the Fund should be able to intervene and define the specific conditions and manner in which it shall intervene. The Commission and Council are now able (under Article 4) to devote a proportion of the ESF budget to helping workers directly affected by the execution of the Community's policies. [17]

With regard to an evaluation of the ESF as a social policy issue the following can be said. The Council Decision of 1 February 1971 cleared the way for an expansion of the Treaty provisions concerning the ESF and provided improvements in the operation (widening the scope of its activities), as well as the budget of the ESF from 56 million u.a. in 1971 to 451 million u.a. in 1976. A summary of aid granted under both the 'old' and the 'new' ESF is provided in table 7.2.

Moreover, the Commission forecasted in 1975 for the next few years as a whole, an average annual increase rate of 20-25 per cent for the present areas of intervention with the aim of stabilising its proportion of the public expenditure of member countries. [18] In accordance with the rules of the reform of the ESF the Commission can reimburse 50 per cent of the cost of retraining schemes financed by a public authority. In the case of schemes carried out by private bodies, the Commission's grant will equal that made by the public authorities. Assistance is in the form of non-repayable grants.

Estimates made by the Commission in 1975 indicate that the ESF accounted for 5-10 per cent of total public spending by the nine Member States on adult vocational training. [19] Although this does not make the ESF a deciding factor, it nevertheless allows it to exercise a considerably stimulating influence, if properly guided. For example, according to Dr Hillery, Commissioner for Social Affairs, in 1973 ESF aid going to Britain represented 40 per cent of direct spending on vocational training by the Department of Employment in Britain. [20]

As the operations of the 'new' ESF are financed by the

Table 7.2
ESF aid granted (in millions of units of account) [1]

	Article 4 Type A Intervention	Article 5 Type B Intervention	Total of Articles 4 and 5	Pilot Schemes	Old ESF	Total
1969	—	—	—	—	36.60	36.60
1970	—	—	—	—	37.00	37.00
1971	—	—	—	—	56.50	56.50
1972	—	50.00	50.00	—	54.00	104.00
1973	28.09	157.96	186.05	—	61.41	247.46
1974	46.70	207.70	254.40	—	52.77	307.17
1975	131.10	245.00	376.10	0.9	4.90	381.90
1976	170.00	270.00	440.00	1.0	10.40	451.40
	375.89	930.66	1,308.45	1.9	313.58	1,622.03

Article 4	1972 to 1974	1975	1976
Agriculture	55.50	*n.a.	66.1
Textiles	9.89	n.a.	20.8
Migrant workers	8.0	n.a.	17.0
Handicapped	1.4	n.a.	66.0
Young people	—	n.a.	

Article 5	1972 to 1974	1975	1976
Assistance to declining regional industries affected by technical progress	334.23	*n.a.	241.1
Handicapped	81.43	n.a.	28.9

[1] For a description of units of account, see note [14], chapter 7.

* Not available

Community's own resources, [21] there is (and will continue to be) less pressure from the Member States to ensure that they receive as much from the ESF as they put in — a method practised up to 1971. [22] Nevertheless, the fact that only the Member States are competent to 'forward to the Commission applications for assistance from the ESF', [23] perpetuates a large control of Member Governments over utilisation of ESF aid.

There are other difficulties associated with the present size and operation of the ESF as seen by the Commission, in spite of the constant increase in the size of the ESF. Demands for vocational training and retraining purposes in the countries of the EC have increased still more. [24] Subsequently the ESF resources are in danger of becoming spread too thinly in their respective interventions. This was a fear expressed by a number of speakers of the European Parliament in a debate on the Commission's Fourth Report on the activities of the ESF in April 1977. While commenting on the valuable contribution of the ESF in retraining the unemployed, they also 'questioned whether the ESF could ever hope to deal in more than a marginal way with the all-embracing problem of joblessness.' [25] In view of this limitation, some speakers recommended the setting-up of an 'Employment Fund'.

Yet the Commission realises that above a certain level aid from the ESF would of necessity influence national aids — which would open up questions of employment policies, priorities, regional preferences and the whole notion of competences between the national administration and the Commission.

More recently, the Commission has recommended:

a)   to group all applications for grants by regions instead of dealing with them on an individual basis, and thus enable the ESF to fit in better with the employment policies that individual countries are applying;

b)   to donate proportionally more aid to those regions with chronic unemployment. In a limited number of regions, the participation level of the ESF should be raised from 50 to 65 per cent. [26]

The Commission began work on an Opinion, based on Article 126, designed to enable the Council to review the Decision of 1 February 1971, concerning the reform of the Fund. The Decision lays down that the review must be carried out by 1 May 1977.

In summing up, therefore, the following can be noted on the Articles concerning the ESF:

147

1. Articles 123 to 125 ('old' ESF) had been fulfilled by 1962, but the budget referring to these Articles almost constantly increased, especially from mid-1968 onward. It seems to have reached its upper limit, however, in 1973;

2. Article 126 ('new' ESF), which specifies that reforms shall be made, has been fulfilled and, to a substantial extent, expanded.

3. Article 127 deals with the implementation of either 'old' or 'new' ESF aid and can be considered as being fulfilled in both instances.

Vocational training policy

Community decisions on vocational training policy provide the following comparison of types of legislation for the two periods under consideration.

In 1963 the Council of Social Affairs laid down the general principles that it considered essential for the common occupational training policy. However, the Council could not agree on the implementing proposal which the Commission had submitted for these general principles, and subsequently no decision was taken by the Council on this issue before mid-1968.

The period from mid-1968 onward indicated a 'greater' willingness of the Council to deal with vocational training at the Community level. The Council forwarded one recommendation to the Member States [27] and two regulations: one concerning vocational training in a specific sector [28] and the other concerning the establishment of a European Centre for Vocational Training (Regulation no.337/75 of 10 February 1975).

The aim of the Centre will be to assist the Commission in encouraging, at Community level, the promotion and development of vocational training and of in-service training. In its Annual Activity Report of 1973, the Council states that this Centre: 'will contribute by its scientific and technical activities to the implementation of a common vocational training policy.' [29] While this might sound more of a desire than a commitment, and because of no time specification might be only a long-term objective, it will certainly, in the immediate future, encourage the exchange of information and the comparison of experience in this area. The Centre was officially opened in Berlin in March 1977. It should also be mentioned that on 9 June 1972 a European Centre for Progress and Training in Agriculture and Rural Areas (CEPFAR) was established through joint efforts by the Commission and the Social Partners.

Moreover, the Council gave an indication in two sessions on the general orientation which should be taken in the area of vocational training. The first indication, delivered in July 1971, provided the general orientation for the Commission to draw up first measures to implement a common policy of vocational training, which the Commission then submitted to the Council in November 1972. The second indication by the Council, made in March 1973, specified a number (thirteen) of measures for priority consideration in the guidelines submitted by the Commission in November 1972. These measures should become the basis for the establishment of a Community Action Programme.

In addition, the Commission has drawn up a draft recommendation in Spring 1977 for governments on the professional training of the unemployed youth or those threatened with losing their jobs.

Thus the measures adopted by the Council on vocational training policy represent primarily Community guidelines rather than Community legislation. While there has been some improvement on the harmonisation of this particular social policy issue, it looks as if there is still a long way to go before a common vocational training policy will be adopted or before vocational training certificates and diplomas will be harmonised.

The extent of harmonisation difficulties encountered in this field is illustrated in the Seventh General Report of the Commission (1973) where it is noted that the Council had failed to adopt 34 proposals for directives involving mutual recognition of diplomas. [30] In the meantime, one breakthrough, after 14 years of work by the Commission, occurred in June 1975 when the Council adopted two Directives to enable doctors and specialists, whether salaried or self-employed, to practise and provide medical services anywhere in the Community; including the mutual recognition of diplomas, certificates and other evidence of formal qualifications in medicine. These two Directives came into force in December 1976. The Council also delivered two Decisions, one establishing a Committee for Public Health which will be concerned with noting and analysing any difficulties which may arise from the implementation of the Directives. The other provided for the formation of an Advisory Committee on Medical Training concerned with the level of training in the Community, both for general practitioners and specialists.

Apart from the doctors, very little progress, in spite of Commission pressure, has so far been made by the Council on the mutual recognition of diplomas for such professions as lawyers, nurses, architects, dentists, opticians, veterinarians and pharmacists.

With regard to the situation in the Member States, the ESC, in a study on vocational training policies in 1976, stressed the great differences still existing [31] between the systems of education and vocational training. Some of the differences outlined in the ESC study related to the different length of compulsory schooling, the age of admission to professional life, the time and place devoted to vocational training and the placement of technical education.

Finally, it is worthwhile to draw attention to the long-term prospects set out in the ESC study for a common vocational training policy. In the conclusion of its study, the ESC states: [32]

> The level of vocational training can be considered and appreciated only in the framework of general education. The demands formulated in the Community concerning free movement of labour, recognition of diplomas, etc., will be intractable as long as the harmonisation of educational content and objectives has not become reality. This is one of the essential conditions of social, economic and political harmonisation.

Social security provisions in general

As to the historical development of social security harmonisation in the EC, it should be noted that no official regulations or directives were passed by the Council up to mid-1968 and that only a small number of recommendations were delivered by the Council on this issue. Neither had substantial progress been made in passing regulations or directives between mid-1968 and the end of 1974. It was only by 1975 that the Council started to adopt a Directive on matters concerned with mass redundancies and a Recommendation related to the principles of a 40-hour week and 4 weeks' annual paid holiday.

In February 1975, the Council adopted a Directive for the approximation of legislation of Member States to ensure that no firm or public authority could dismiss or make redundant ten or more employees without proper consultation between employers, workers' representatives and public authorities. [33] This Directive came into effect in February 1977.

A subject-related Directive was approved by the Council in

December 1976, and adopted by February 1977, providing for the protection of workers' acquired rights in the case of transfer of undertakings, establishments or parts of establishments, i.e. assuring workers their rights from existing contracts of employment. [34] Furthermore, it forbade dismissal in the event of transfer of undertakings and it laid down the procedures for informing and consulting the representatives of the workers affected by the merger.

In July 1975, the Council adopted a Recommendation on the principle of the 40-hour week and the principle of four weeks' annual paid holiday, which recommended Member States to take appropriate measures, either by means of legislation, by encouraging employers and labour to conclude collective agreements or by any other means, to secure that these principles are applied throughout the Community in all sectors by 31 December 1978 at the latest. In its most recent Social Report (1976) the Commission points out that both principles have largely been achieved or are within sight of achievement in most Member Countries. [35]

Having noted that there has been no substantial progress in the application of Articles 117 and 118 towards Community legislation, let us now look more fully at that component of Article 117 which makes reference to the beneficial contribution of the Common Market operation towards social policy. Specifically, we will explore:

a)   whether changes have taken place in the interpretation practised by the Council up to mid-1968 regarding this 'beneficial contribution' towards general social security harmonisation;

b)   whether Member States have made progress in aligning their national laws and regulations on social security more closely since mid-1968.

The Council's position on the automatic levelling-off of social policy

In response to the Commission's Action Programme of 1966, in which stress was laid on 'corrective thinking' with regard to the provision of Article 117 and the inauguration of an independent programme [36] to harmonise social security schemes, the Council adopted a resolution on 29 February 1968. This Resolution provided that the social policy tasks arising both for the Community and for the Member States from the various common policies, should be examined. Further to this Resolution, and on the basis of a Commission report, the Council noted in its session of March 1969 that all Community measures must be subservient to social and economic targets. [37]

An even more important step towards a more independent social policy at the Community level was taken at the Summit Conference of the Heads of State or Government in the Hague in December 1969. At this Conference the desire was expressed to bring about a close concentration between the policies necessary for the establishment of an Economic and Monetary Union and social policy. This desire represented a break with the past: for the first time an official decision indicated that social policy depended on 'more' than the free market interplay of economic co-operation in the Community. The Hague Conference also stressed the necessity of reforming the ESF. [38]

However, a real turning point, with regard to the importance of social policy at the Community level as an individual consideration, came at the Paris Summit Conference on 19-20 October 1972. At this Conference the Heads of State or Government declared that they attached as much importance to vigorous action in the social field as to the achievement of the Economic and Monetary Union, and that vigorous action in the social field could not be dissociated from achievement of the Economic and Monetary Union. They invited the Community institutions to draw up an Action Programme by 1 January 1974. This programme should aim, in particular, at carrying out a co-ordinated policy for employment and vocational training, and improving working and living conditions. In October 1973 the Commission submitted this Social Action Programme to the Council of Ministers and on 21 January 1974, the Council expressed the 'political will' to adopt the measures necessary to achieve the main objectives contained in this Programme over a defined period of time. As noted above, several of these objectives have since been achieved.

Moreover, the Communiqué of the Paris Summit Conference of October 1972 contained an important statement with regard to the provisions of the Treaty of Rome, namely that it was advisable to use as widely as possible all the provisions of the Treaties, including Article 235 of the EC Treaty. [39]

On 9 November 1972 the Council provided the Commission with a mandate to draw up in successive stages a European Social Budget (ESB), [40] which the Commission subsequently submitted to the Council in December 1974. This first ESB covered the period 1970 to 1975. Its main purpose, according to the Commission's Social Report, was 'to give a greater knowledge of the present trends in the

Member States ... in the development of expenditures (and the financing of them) for several sectors of social policy, and especially social security.' [41]   In the meantime, at its meeting in April 1976, the Council agreed that the Commission should draw up the second ESB on the basis of its guidelines, updating the first collection of evidence and providing projections on the expenditure on social protection and its finance up to 1980.

By establishing comparable data collection on expenditures and receipts in certain sectors (social security, social assistance) and by illuminating the social problems encountered by such groups as the elderly, the disabled, the young and the migrant workers in periods of high unemployment, inflation and economic recessions, the ESB could make an important contribution towards harmonisation of social security systems. [42]   In many ways, the European Foundation for the Improvement of Living and Working Conditions, established in 1975, will be a useful instrument for achieving the objectives of the ESB.   The aims of the latter are to foster the exchange of information and experiences in such areas as: organisation at work and job design; problems peculiar to certain categories of workers (such as the handicapped); long-term aspects of improvement of the environment.

Moreover, on 22 July 1975, the Council approved a programme of pilot schemes and studies to combat poverty.   This decision enables the Commission to promote and provide up to 50 per cent of the cost of pilot schemes which test and develop new methods of helping the poor and those threatened with poverty in the Community.   In November 1975, the Commission was able to approve assistance for such schemes for over 40 million u.a. by the end of the year; contributing to 23 projects covering all the Community countries.

As the above shows, the Council changed its position on the 'automatic levelling-off' of social security harmonisation since mid-1968 by assigning a more 'independent' role to its harmonisation, but it remains to be seen to what extent work on the ESB and the operation of the European Foundation for the Improvement of Living and Working Conditions will provide the basis for future Community legislation.

National legislation on social security provisions

Comparing national legislation on social security provisions and especially the changes which have occurred since mid-1968, seems, as table 7.3 shows, to lead to both positive and negative findings.

Table 7.3
Comparison of national social security systems

Social benefits per function as % of the net disposable income				Sickness				Old age pensions				Family benefits			
	1970	1975	% increase 1970-75		1970	1975	% increase 1970-75		1970	1975	% increase 1970-75		1970	1975	% increase 1970-75
WG	23.2	30.6	+7.4	NL	6.5	9.5	+3.0	L	10.8	14.3	+3.5	F	3.9	3.7	-0.2
NL	21.8	31.0	+9.2	WG	6.3	9.2	+2.9	WG	10.4	12.3	+1.9	B	3.5	3.5	—
Dk	21.3	28.8	+7.5	Dk	6.1	8.6	+2.5	NL	8.9	11.2	+2.3	Dk	3.2	4.0	+0.8
F	20.1	22.9	+2.8	F	5.1	6.2	+1.1	UK	8.0	9.5	+1.5	NL	2.9	3.3	+0.4
L	20.0	25.9	+5.9	It	4.9	6.0	+1.1	Dk	7.7	10.1	+2.4	L	2.2	2.3	+0.1
B	19.3	24.2	+4.9	UK	4.6	4.8	+0.2	F	7.6	9.1	+1.5	WG	2.0	2.9	+0.9
It	18.7	24.1	+5.4	B	4.2	5.6	+1.4	B	7.2	9.5	+2.3	It	2.0	2.4	+0.4
UK	17.1	20.1	+3.0	Ir	3.8	4.9	+1.1	It	6.5	8.7	+2.2	Ir	2.0	2.8	+0.8
Ir	13.3	17.7	+4.4	L	3.4	5.7	+2.3	Ir	4.9	6.4	+1.5	UK	1.4	1.5	+0.1
Average	19.3	25.0	+5.7	Average	5.0	6.4	+1.4	Average	8.0	10.1	+2.1	Average	2.6	2.9	+0.3

Difference between extreme NINE countries:

Social benefits				Sickness				Old age pensions				Family benefits			
	23.2	31.0			6.5	9.5			10.8	14.3			3.9	4.0	
	-13.3	-17.7			-3.4	-4.8			-4.9	-6.4			-1.4	-1.5	
	9.9	13.3	+3.4		3.1	4.7	+1.6		5.9	7.9	+2.0		2.5	2.5	—

Difference between extreme SIX countries:

Social benefits				Sickness				Old age pensions				Family benefits			
	23.2	31.0			6.5	9.5			10.8	14.3			3.9	3.7	
	-18.7	-22.9			-3.4	-5.6			-6.5	-8.7			-2.0	-2.3	
	4.5	8.1	+3.6		3.1	3.9	+0.8		4.3	5.6	+1.3		1.9	1.4	-0.5

Source: Extracted from Statistical Survey of *Report on the Development of the Social Situation in the Communities in 1976*, pp 224-5

On the positive side, we can note that Member States have become closer on family benefits. While the two extreme cases did not vary in percentage terms for the 'nine' between 1970 and 1975, the totalled growth rates recorded by the 3 countries at the bottom were twice as high as those of the 3 top countries. A greater convergence still is involved when the six 'old' EC countries are considered, where the difference between the country with the highest family benefits and that with the lowest decreased from 1.9 per cent to 1.4 per cent from 1970 to 1975, and where the total growth rates of the three bottom-ranked countries are seven times the percentage size of the top-listed countries.

On the negative side, we find that total social benefits as percentage of disposable income, sickness expenditures and old age pensions have greatly widened between the country with the lowest percentage and that with the highest of the EC countries; widening respectively from 9.9 per cent to 13.3 per cent, 3.1 per cent to 4.7 per cent and 5.9 per cent to 7.9 per cent. Expressed in another way, table 7.3 shows that the 3 countries which ranked top in columns one and two totalled growth rate increases between 1970 and 1975 which were nearly double the totalled growth rates of the bottom listed countries. Higher growth rates were also recorded in column three between the 3 countries at the top and those 3 at the bottom. The respective totalled percentage figures are: 24.1 per cent as against 12.8 per cent; 8.4 per cent as against 4.8 per cent; and 7.7 per cent as against 6 per cent; thus indicating a trend towards greater divergences rather than towards convergence.

In contrast, the figures for the 'old' six EC countries between the 3 top and the 3 bottom-ranking countries over the same period, while still manifesting divergence, represent smaller differentials. The respective figures for the first two columns are: 19.4 per cent as against 16.2 per cent; and 7.0 per cent as against 4.8 per cent. For the third column, the figures between the 'nine ' and the 'six' are the same. This is also reflected in the figures pertaining to the difference between the top and bottom-ranking country in both columns two and three; revealing 0.8 per cent instead of 1.6 per cent and 1.3 per cent instead of 2.0 per cent in divergence. In contrast, the figure in column one shows a slight increase in the divergence between the 'six' and the 'nine': 3.6 per cent to 3.4 per cent. Moreover, looking at the existing social security schemes of the original 'six', we find the following differences. [43]

Although France, Luxembourg and Belgium do not have a statutory unemployment insurance programme and provide a flat-rate benefit to the unemployed, Germany, Holland and Italy have a statutory unemployment scheme which is based on earnings-related allowances. With regard to family allowances, Germany and Holland do not automatically pay an allowance for the first child, as is the case in France, Italy, Belgium and Luxembourg. In addition, France differs from the other five in that it pays the greatest number of additional benefits (handicapped children, housing, parental allowances, welfare services, etc.).

With regard to old age pensions, the benefits in most countries (of the original six) are related to the number of years insured and the earnings obtained during work. However, in Italy and France, a minimum of fifteen years' contribution is required before any benefit (other than a small flat rate one in France) may be granted. In addition, the size of the pension varies very much between the countries. In Germany, it can reach two-thirds of previous earnings. In France, the maximum is 20 per cent. Some countries have no guaranteed minimum pension.

However, the six original EC countries share certain features not found in Britain (one of the three 'new' EC Member States). Foremost among these British differences is the large share and direct role of the contributions of the Government and the smaller employer's share in the finance and administration of social security benefits. [44] Table 7.4 singles out these differences more accurately.

Another contrast between the original six EC countries and the UK is the earnings-related nature of the benefits and contributions paid by the 'six'. In these countries a straight percentage of earnings up to a specified maximum is paid into the social security scheme and there is no 'flat rate' element involved. In contrast, under the UK system, a 'flat rate' contribution is paid by everyone. Above that, an earnings-related supplement is paid by all except the lowest wage earners. However, there are also certain similarities between the former 'six' and the U K. For example, in both the benefits of medical care are the same and in neither does the injured person contribute towards it. In addition, there are indications that Britain is adopting certain of the earnings-related features.

Furthermore, while Britain has one national health scheme which covers virtually the entire population, the continental countries have a wide scope of different insurance funds (2,000 in the case of Germany) and individuals can choose with whom they are to insure. Membership in a particular fund depends on one's occupation, which can mean, and it does in fact happen, that certain groups (such as the handicapped, temporary workers and the self-employed) can be excluded from some kinds of benefits.

Finally, in response to the economic difficulties experienced

Table 7.4
Social security: sources of finance in 1970 and 1975

Country	Employer		Employee		State		Others	
	1970	1975	1970	1975	1970	1975	1970	1975
Belgium	46.6	45.5	21.1	21.3	27.3	30.0	5.0	3.2
Denmark	10.1	10.4	6.8	2.8	80.1	84.1	3.0	2.7
France	65.5	65.5	20.0	20.3	12.8	11.6	1.8	2.6
Germany	45.4	44.9	24.6	24.3	25.8	26.8	4.2	4.0
Ireland	19.3	22.0	12.5	13.7	67.5	63.6	0.7	0.7
Italy	55.0	59.7	15.7	15.2	23.7	19.8	5.6	5.3
Luxem- bourg	36.4	38.7	24.8	24.3	29.9	30.0	8.9	7.0
Netherlands	43.9	41.6	35.8	33.6	11.9	15.9	8.4	8.9
UK	34.1	35.0	18.4	16.3	38.7	42.1	8.8	6.5
Average	39.4	40.3	19.9	19.8	35.3	35.9	5.1	4.5

Source: *Report on the Development of the Social Situation in
the Communities in 1976*, pp 224-5

between 1974 and 1976, different measures were taken in most EC
countries to increase or improve the economic security of workers
who were victims of unemployment. These related to unemployment
benefits, pensions for the elderly, handicapped persons, women
workers, students, family support and extension of social security.
[45]   As observed by Dr Hillery, these differences, while difficult to
ascertain in the short-term, reflect: [46]

> ... genuinely distinct socio-economic priorities, needs and
> values within the Community and explain why the European
> Commission has never proposed centralisation at Community
> level as the solution to all socio-economic problems. Nor
> could or should such problems be treated in a uniform manner
> throughout the Community.

No doubt these differences in national social security laws and
regulations have developed over a long period of time in which these
countries tried to meet their own particular needs. These differences
appear to be deeply ingrained and not easily changeable, quite apart
from the cost involved. Thus, any substantial increase in similarity
between the services of the different countries seems unlikely in the

157

near future.

Conclusion

An attempt was made in this chapter to examine the trend of social
policy harmonisation in the EC since mid-1968. The data introduced
suggest that progress has been made towards greater harmonisation
since mid-1968, varying from slight progress in the case of social
security provisions in general and vocational training, to substantial
progress in the case of the ESF, social security benefits for migrant
workers and equal pay for men and women. There were no cases
where either a retraction took place or where the situation remained
unchanged. Furthermore, four other items are worth mentioning in
the harmonisation trend of the five social policy issues:

1. More legislation, involving either regulations or
   directives, was either passed or had been agreed upon in
   principle, in the period since mid-1968 than the period
   prior to mid-1968. However, no substantial progress in
   passing regulations or directives in either period was made
   on vocational training standards or social security
   provisions in general.

2. No important bilateral or multi-lateral agreements were
   passed by the Member States of the EC since mid-1968.
   Rather, as in the case of the regulations concerning social
   security for migrant workers, previously existing bilateral
   and multi-lateral agreements had been superseded. In
   addition, on the latter, Community approval rules were
   set for the conclusion of new agreements.

3. More emphasis was placed on an 'independent' social
   policy in the period since mid-1968, especially with regard
   to the harmonisation of social security provisions in
   general. Previously, it had been assumed that under
   Article 117 there would be an 'automatic levelling-off' of
   social policy stemming from the operation of the
   Common Market.

4. However, as table 7.3 showed, while some of the
   differences between national laws or social security
   provisions have been narrowed, there are also a number
   of cases in which the differences between Member States

have actually widened since mid-1968.

Notes

[1]   For a description of the different types of EC legislation, see chapter 5, note 8.
[2]   The Treaty of Rome gives the right to both the Council of Ministers and the Commission to issue regulations and directives. However, the Commission's right relates primarily to 'implementing regulations and directives', i.e. after an initial regulation or directive has been passed by the Council.
[3]   This Decision was based on Article 169, which gives the Commission, as the guardian of the Treaty of Rome, the right to issue infringement procedures in cases of Treaty violations.
[4]   Another Decision by the Commission against the three new Member States was issued in 1974.
[5]   A draft Directive to this effect has been submitted to the Council by the Commission in December 1976. This Directive will cover social security schemes established by law, occupational schemes and social assistance arrangements so far as they relate to the risks described above. In these areas, all discriminations based on sex will no longer be allowed and conditions for receiving benefits, the rates, the duration, etc. must be the same for men and women.
[6]   See *The Employment of Women and the Problems it Raises in the Member States of the European Community* (abridged version of Mrs E. Sullerot's Report). Published by the Commission of the EC. No date.
[7]   The difference is slightly smaller in the case of white-collar women (mainly because of the moderating influence of public authority rates). *Ibid.*
[8]   Not included in Regulations nos 3 and 4 were family allowances for those members of migrant workers' families who had not yet joined them in the country of work.
[9]   Both Regulations came into force on 10 January 1972 in the original six EC countries and on 4 January 1973 in the three 'new' ones. For more details, see *Official Journal*, nos OJ L 149 (5 July 1971) and OJ L 74 (27 March 1972).
[10]   Matters covered according to Article 4 of Regulation no. 1408/71 consist of: (a) sickness and maternity benefits; (b) invalidity benefits; (c) old age benefits; (d) suvivor's benefits; (e) benefits in respect of accidents at work and occupational diseases; (f) death

grants; (g) unemployment benefits; and (h) family benefits.

[11]   See Action Programme in favour of Migrant Workers and their Families in *Bulletin of the European Communities: Supplement 3/76*, p.16.

[12]   Lawson and Reed, *Social Security in the European Community*, pp 51-4.

[13]   *Ibid.*, p.51.

[14]   'Units of account' (u.a.) is the term used by the EC to specify a uniform currency measurement. One u.a. equals one US dollar prior to the 1971 devaluation of the US dollar.

[15]   Quoted from *The New European Social Fund*, Commission of the European Communities, Brussels 1973, p.4. See also *Official Journal* no. OJ L 28 (4 February 1971), p.15; and Special Edition (December 1972, 1971 I), p.52.

[16]   See *The New European Social Fund*.

[17]   The Council of Ministers has thus far designated ESF aid under Article 4 for the retraining of workers who leave agriculture or the textile industry, or who need to acquire a new skill in textiles; to retrain migrant workers and to help them and their families integrate into the host country; to retrain handicapped workers and to help train young people under 25 years, the unemployed or those in search of first-time employment.

[18]   Taken from 'Third Report on the Activities of the New European Social Fund,' *Information Memo* P-44, Commission of the European Communities, Brussels, July 1975.

[19]   *Ibid.*

[20]   Dr P.J. Hillery, Opening Address of a Seminar held in the University of Manchester on *The Evaluation of Vocational Training*, January 1975; Office for Official Publications of the European Communities, Luxembourg 1975, pp 7-10.

[21]   The Community's own resources consist largely of import duties imposed under the common external tariff and levies on imported farm produce.

[22]   The 'old' ESF was more or less a passive clearing house, with the Member States receiving as much from the Fund as they had put in (the famous principle of *'juste retour'*).

[23]   Private institutions applying for ESF aid must obtain the prior approval from their respective Governments.

[24]   Dr Hillery, Commissioner for Social Affairs, gave the following figures: in Britain, direct public expenditure on training has gone up from £30 million in 1968 to £85 million in 1974, with the number of Government Training Centres rising from 13 in 1963 to over 50 in 1974. In France, the number of trainees helped by

public expenditure has almost doubled from 500,000 in 1969 to 920,000 in 1974. Finally, a recent Press Release from the German Government shows that it has provided vocational training for 30,000 young people as compared with 9,000 in 1972. See Dr P.J. Hillery, Opening Address of a Seminar at Manchester, January 1975; and *Latest from Germany: Facts, Figures Background no. 45/76*; issued by the Embassy of the Federal Republic of Germany, 13 December 1976.

[25]   See *The Week*: Strasbourg, 18-22 April 1977, European Parliament, Directorate-General for Information and Public Relations, Luxembourg, pp 32-3.

[26]   See *Euroforum*, no.12/77, 22 March 1977.

[27]   This Council Recommendation is based on the Commission's drafts concerning a European career brief for the training of skilled machine operators. According to the Commission, this proto-type will determine the method used for alignment of training levels and also for reciprocal recognition of diplomas and certificates. See *General Report*, 1970, p.117.

[28]   Council Regulation no. 543/69 of 25 March 1969, concerning road haulage, determined driving time and rest periods, laid down the composition of crews and made provisions for means of control. See *Official Journal* no. L77, 29 March 1969, p.49. It should be mentioned that this Regulation has not yet been implemented. The Commission Decision of October 1972, addressed to the Member States, intended to obtain information from the Member States on its implementation. In 1976, the Commission put forward new proposals designed to simplify, replace and supplement legislation based on Regulation 543/69. The Commission also expressed the wish that all the provisions of the new Regulation should come into force in the first half of 1977.

[29]   See *Twenty-third Review of the Council's Work: 1 January– 31 December 1975*, General Secretariat of the Council of the European Communities; Office for Official Publications of the European Communities, Luxembourg, p.41.

[30]   See *Seventh General Report on the Activities of the European Communities 1973*, Brussels-Luxembourg, February 1974, p.137.

[31]   For details on these differences, plus related aspects of educational and vocational training policies in the nine Member States, see the excellent study of the ESC on Systems of Education and Vocational Training in the Member Countries of the European Community, Office for Official Publications of the European Communities, Luxembourg, 1976. See also *The Evaluation of*

Vocational Training, Report of a Seminar held at the University of Manchester, January 1975.

[32] *Ibid.*, p.54.

[33] The Directive specifies that: 'Dismissals affected by an employer for one or more reasons not related to the individual workers concerned where, according to the choice of the Member States, the number of redundancies is either, over a period of 30 days, at least 10 in establishments normally employing more than 20 and less than 100 workers, at least 10 per cent of the number of workers in establishments normally employing at least 100 but less than 300 workers, and at least 30 in establishments normally employing 300 workers or more; or, over a period of 90 days, at least 20, whatever the number of workers normally employed in the establishments in question.' Quoted from the *Twenty-third Review of the Council's Work*, 1 January-31 December 1975, p.45.

[34] Collective agreements will remain in force in their original form until at least one year after the change of ownership. For more details, see *Report on the Development of the Social Situation in the Communities in 1976*, p.9.

[35] *Ibid.*, p.90.

[36] That is, independent of the provision text of Article 117 or the result of economic progress of the Common Market.

[37] For more details, see Van Praag, 'Trends and Achievements'.

[38] Largely as a consequence of the reference made to social policy at the Hague, one important supplementary step was taken by both the Council and the Commission, when the Commission drafted a report on *Preliminary Guidelines for a Social Policy Programme in the Community*, which was submitted to the Council in March 1971.

[39] This Article can be seen as an additional source of strength in the application of Article 117. As Fischer points out, Article 235 carried 'implied powers' and thus increases the decision-making capacity of the Commission. See Fischer, *Die Institutionalisierte Vertretung der Verbände*, p.23. One such instance where Article 235 was used involved the Council Decision concerning a Programme of Pilot Schemes and Studies to Combat Poverty.

[40] Already on 26 November 1970 the Council had indicated the need for the establishment of an ESB. See *Fourth General Report*, 1970, p.114.

[41] See *Report on the Development of the Social Situation in the Communities in 1974*, p.12.

[42] This is a point well made by Reed in Lawson and Reed, *Social Security in the European Community*, p.60.

[43] Unless otherwise stated, the figures cited in this section were

extracted from *Information*: Social Policy (Social Security Finance in the Six Countries: 1965-1970-1975) no. 24/72, Commission of the European Communities, Brussels, July 1972; 'Social Security in the Six,' *European Studies* 14, 1972; and *Comparative Tables of the Social Security Systems in the Member States of the European Communities*: Eighth edition, Commission of the European Communities, Brussels 1976. It should be pointed out that these figures (and those which follow) give an indication of the size of contributions, but they should not be taken to be strictly comparable, since the costs and standards of living are not the same.

[44]   In Britain the social security system is administered entirely by a Government Ministry. Britain also differs in that the State finances the entire cost of family benefits. In the original six countries, employers and employees either pay substantial contributions in family benefits or, as in the case of France and Holland, pay it entirely.

[45]   The different measures taken by the Member States and, to some extent, their implications, are covered in greater depth in the Commission's *Reports on the Development of the Social Situation in the Communities in 1974*, p.177; and *in 1975*, pp 152-5.

[46]   See *Information*: Social Policy no. 98/75. Text of a speech by Dr P.J. Hillery to the Royal Irish Academy, Dublin, on 28 April 1975. Published by the Commission of the European Communities.

8   Performance and prospects of the ETUC

Introduction

The striking features of the European Trade Union Confederation
(ETUC) are, on the one hand, its numerical strength, its declared
objective to fight multinational companies and its decision-making
style; and, on the other, its lack of central authority, its insufficient
substructure, its inability to adopt specific methods in pursuit of
common objectives and its inability to co-ordinate economic interests
with political aims. A prime factor for the existence of the first
three characteristics stems from the operation of multinational
corporations in Western Europe and the existing strength of the
European employers' organisations (UNICE, COPA, COCCEE).
Perhaps the major explanations for the four latter characteristics
relate to the different historical experiences of various national trade
unions, either with governments or public administrations, and to
different social and economic developments, both past and current.
[1]
   In response, primarily, to the activities of multinational
corporations and European employers' organisations, major
integrative trends (both in co-operation and association) took place
among trade unions at European level between 1969 and 1974,
resulting in one organisation to which nearly all the major national
trade union federations in Western Europe are affiliated; comprising
31 affiliations from 18 countries with 38 million members by the
end of 1976. Besides improving its budget and personnel to levels
comparable with those of the European employers' organisations,
the ETUC (and its forerunners, the ECFTU and EO/WCL) allowed
majority decision-making to take place in the Executive Committee,
and thus went further in its integrative attempts than UNICE, or, for
that matter, the Council of Ministers of the EC, which still largely
practise unanimity.
   At first sight, the co-operative and integrative attempts made by
trade unions at European level over the 1969 to 1974 period appear
to be considerably far reaching. However, a closer examination
reveals that the mere numerical expansion of European trade union
organisations and their perception of common interests, although
creating some bonds, did not necessarily erase all the existing

ideological or political differences among trade unions in the ETUC. The following will, therefore, centre on the internal unity of the ETUC as an organisation; its ability to co-ordinate the different policy proposals or interests of its affiliations and to formulate common policy stands; and its effectiveness as a pressure group in successfully employing its organisational strength with respect to employers' organisations or in negotiations with the EC institutions.

The strength and effectiveness of the ETUC

In spite of improvements, the ETUC is still lacking sufficient resources and expert personnel similar to those in the national trade union federations to assemble and analyse national and European data. For example, the TUC, with one quarter of the membership of the ETUC, has a budget of around £800,000 for its headquarters' activities; the ETUC has a budget of around £300,000.

With few exceptions, there has been no development of close relationships, either between the ETUC and the industry trade union branch committees, or among the industry committees themselves, such as that on the employers' side. This is primarily because of the refusal of many industry trade union committees to set up independent European organisations (independent of their international organisations). This factor considerably affects the organisational strength of the ETUC in negotiations both with the employers' organisations and the EC institutions, as we shall see shortly.

Attention should also be drawn to the fact that even in the national context where the relationship between the leadership of the trade union organisations and the rank and file membership is a close one, there have been occasions when the legitimacy of the leaders has been severely questioned and put to the test. The events of May 1968 in France and of Autumn 1969 in Italy were two such examples where spontaneous direct action by the workers at least temporarily displaced the authority of the trade union leadership. As a consequence of these two events, some experts have argued that in France and Italy a shift of power from the leadership to the rank and file membership has taken place. [2] Developments of this kind brought Dr Hillery, the Commissioner for Social Affairs, to the following conclusion: [3]

> Interest groups are less and less able to bind their members in the pursuit of compromises with other interest groups. Any interest group has, in speaking for itself, an obligation to

ensure that it is speaking for all the subgroups within it. Recognition of this obligation becomes vital as small subgroups become more adept at pursuing their own sectoral interests. This suggests the need for an increase in the degree of sophistication with which interest groups are organised and led. It also suggests the possibility that the level at which different interest groups can reach detailed agreements may have to be nearer to the 'rank and file' membership of such groups.

If Hillery is right, and the events of May 1968 and Autumn 1969, mentioned above, tend to support his view, then the need for more industry trade unions to establish European organisations with the necessary budgets and personnel, and for closer collaboration between industry committees and the ETUC, becomes not only more prominent but more imminent.

In addition, the ETUC affiliates have not yet found a cohesive relationship. Not only has the CGIL membership left some unhealed scars in what was already a tenuous web after the merger of the EFTA and the ECFTU trade unions, but there are also only lukewarm relations between the British TUC and the German DGB, the two biggest national federations of the ETUC. There are also such minor problems as the integration of the EO/WCL national federations with their Christian outlook, and the participation of trade unions from Greece, Spain and Ireland, who had no former international affiliations.

With regard to ETUC authority, a great deal of effort still needs to be made to establish a European trade union organisation which has the same competences for European questions as the national organisations do for national questions. This does not deny the fact that, in general, the mutual understanding and willingness to compromise have increased greatly among trade unions since 1969. Nor does it overlook the fact that trade unions are becoming more and more involved in the activities of the ETUC and increasingly feel the impact of ETUC decisions or guidelines. Some of these impacts even impinge upon national trade union interests. The ETUC majority decision on the admittance of the Italian CGIL is a case in point. Both the German DGB and the French FO/CGT had expressed dissenting votes against this admittance. The British TUC, the Belgian FGTB and the Scandinavian trade unions had comprised the majority of ETUC affiliates in favour of CGIL membership.

However, rather than insisting on 'binding' decisions, the ETUC has concentrated mainly on guidelines and recommendations when advising its affiliates on what policy stands should be taken. Yet in spite of this, officials in the Secretariats of the European trade union organisations thought that there was a gap between what was recommended in the organisations in Brussels and the willingness of the national organisations to implement these guidelines or recommendations, or to exert pressure on their national governments to ensure compliance. Although the gap also exists between the European employers' organisations and their national affiliations, it does not seem to be as marked as in the case of the ETUC.

A substantial part of trade union powers (what we might call trade union sovereignty) still remains in the hands of the national organisations. The delay in transferring this 'sovereignty' from the national trade union level to the European level is largely due to different historical circumstances in the countries of the EC, particularly with regard to the special ties which developed between certain trade unions and political parties, which often reflect political rather than economic interests. [4]

The recent adverse economic situations and the deterioration in employment levels have also renewed the traditional bonds between trade unions and governments. For example, there has been a trend recently for governments in many of the EC Member States to lay down national rules for general wage agreements, either as guidelines or as enforceable regulations. Examples range from wage guidelines in the case of Germany ('Konzertierte Aktion') to regulations on minimum wage rates in France and maximum wage increases in Great Britain (Social Contracts) and Denmark. [5] In this context, it is also important to note Feld's findings that national civil servants are on the whole unwilling to relinquish their power of decision over pressure group demands on the shaping of Community policy in general; thereby providing additional backing to the preference of pressure groups for the national governmental route. He refers to this as the 'gatekeeping function.' [6]

While both trade unions and employers' organisations are somewhat reluctant at present about a complete transfer of their nationally-held autonomous bargaining position to the European level, there appears to be more reluctance on the employers' side. Trade unions, in many ways justifiably, pointed out that the employers refused to engage with them in any serious discussions on the establishment of collective bargaining agreements at European level. Indicative of this reluctance was the opposition expressed by employers' organisations on the numerical expansion of Joint Committees at the Community level. But if the employers would agree to such discussions there can be no doubt that the trade unions, as shown above, would encounter difficulties in settling for the aims, and more so for the means, to be employed in such agreements. Most serious, perhaps, on the trade union side, is the lack of the necessary organisation and co-ordination at the level of industry committees, which could provide both the information and expertise needed for drawing up such agreements and lend the muscle necessary for implementation. While some work on gathering information and expertise on European collective bargaining can be provided by the offices of the Commission, the latter lacks the political power to bring about such agreements.

ETUC policy formation

The ETUC has largely been unable to formulate a common policy on key issues mainly because there appears to be disharmony between economic interests and the political or ideological outlook [7] among its members. For example, political rather than economic interests divide ETUC affiliates into four possible camps on the question of EC integration:

a) those ardently in favour of the speedy construction of a political union - exemplified by the former ECFTU and EO/WCL trade unions;

b) those drawn into the integrative process because of referenda outcomes and which try to adapt to the EC environment, but which, as yet, show no real commitment to such aspects as Economic and Monetary Union, direct elections to the EP or the abolition of the unanimity rule in the Council of Ministers — desired by the trade unions mentioned in a). The British TUC and Irish TUC comprise this group to which, for different reasons, the Danish trade unions and Italian CGIL can be added; [8]

c) those which are interested but as yet undecided on policies of EC institutional expansion because they are unable to weigh up the potential rewards to be obtained from such an expansion. These are the trade unions from Greece, Spain and Malta;

d) those which are opposed or disinclined to an increasing supranationality of the EC, primarily for reasons of neutrality, such as the Swiss, Swedish, Austrian and Finnish trade unions. The Norweigan LO also fall into this category.

Thus no clear stand on the issue of EC institutional expansion or the process of integration in Western Europe has emerged from the ETUC. The anti-EC (or better the supranational EC) feelings of some of the EFTA trade unions might change into a more committed role once the respective Member States (UK and Denmark) have become fully-fledged participants in the EC policy-making process. Judging from the experience of other trade unions, it seems that initial negative feelings towards the EC usually changed into either co-operation with the Commission or support after a certain time. This was certainly the case with the German Trade Union Congress (DGB) and also, to some extent, with the Communist trade unions of France and Italy.

In the meantime, the TUC has also recognised that the EC is not such a major obstacle to the extension of nationalised industries as initially assumed. Equally, the former ECFTU and EO/WCL, while still relentless in their pressure and commitment to an integrated Europe, have realised that there are limits to that pursuit, and that it is still better to convince others like the CGIL or TUC than to go it alone.

Closely related to the issue of EC supranationality have been differences within the ETUC over its role in co-operation between trade unions from Western and Eastern Europe. Initially, leaders of the British TUC had viewed the EC as impeding collaboration between trade unions in Western and Eastern Europe. [9] So far the ETUC has found it difficult to develop a common view on this subject or to reconcile the more far-reaching conceptions of co-operation held by the former EFTA trade unions, the Belgian FGTB and the Italian CGIL, with the apprehensions expressed by the German DGB, the French FO/CGT and some of the former affiliates of the EO/WCL.

Similarly, different practices or ideological considerations, arising from different historical experiences in dealing with management, [10] interfere in the formation of a common ETUC policy on industrial democracy. For example, there seem to be five prevailing dispositions on workers' participation among affiliates of the ETUC, ranging from outright support and readiness to accept the system in principle, to ambivalence or outright opposition. The latter opinion is held primarily by most of the trade unions in France and Italy and the Belgian FGTB. While approximately two-thirds of the ETUC members appear to be in favour of workers' participation in principle, no clear policy stand has yet been taken by the ETUC due in part to the remaining differences over the forms and methods proposed for implementing the system. [11] Yet there are indications that the notion of socialism, as seen by the British and some of the EFTA trade unions, can be stretched to incorporate participation with management. We can even expect that some common solution on the priority and specific form of workers' participation will be found within the ETUC in the not too distant future to cope with either the phenomenon of transnational business mergers or the proposed legislation on the Statute of a European Company.

In many ways the two forerunners of the ETUC, the ECFTU and the EO/WCL, while also without sufficient resources, personnel or substructure, appeared to be more integrated and cohesive than the ETUC. For example, the ECFTU had a common stand on the EC, was in agreement, with one exception (FGTB) on their relationship with Communist trade unions both in Western and Eastern Europe, and was able to take a decision on both the principle and form of workers' participation, in spite of opposition from Italian and Belgian trade unions.

Yet it would be unwise to attribute the lack of cohesiveness among the ETUC affiliates entirely to the size of its membership. Certainly, the existence of 31 member organisations, themselves conglomerates of often widely spread interests in the national environment, [12] has made it more difficult to overcome the ideological or political differences, outlined above, within the ETUC; nor do the current different economic developments (strong and weak economies) make this task any easier. But the task is not insurmountable and there are factors where a larger organisation can be more beneficial than a smaller one. If, for example, the ETUC should be able to adopt specific policies with respect to industrial democracy, or better yet, in dealing with multinational firms, and if these policies were implemented by the national organisations, either through the help of EC legislation, EFTA guidelines or governmental action, then it would be much more difficult for multinational firms to change plants, shift production capacities or alter investment strategies for countries with low wage policies or 'less developed' labour laws.

Another aspect which should be considered when assessing the ETUC's effectiveness is its decision-making style. By practising majority decision-making, the ETUC does not have to co-ordinate policies until all members consent — a situation described as the lowest common denominator. It is usually the case, for example, that opinions on Commission proposals, formulated by the Secretariat of the ETUC with the help of member organisations, are passed by majority.

There have also been instances where trade unions practised a certain amount of solidarity. For example, the ETUC cancelled its participation in the Community Employment Conference of 1973 because of the invitation by the Council of two non-affiliated ETUC trade unions from Germany and France. Both the German DGB and the French FO/CGT had expressed opposition to the participation of these two non-affiliates and, in turn, the total withdrawal of the ETUC from the Conference could be considered as a gesture of solidarity of British, Scandinavian, Italian and Benelux trade unions towards the German and French affiliates of the ETUC.

In contrast, however, other stands for European unity, such as the various appeals made by representatives of the continental trade unions to the British TUC in 1971-74 for participation in EC committees did not lead to positive results. As Roberts and Liebhaberg point out: [13]

> The refusal of the TUC to send representatives to any meeting of the EEC institutions gave rise to sharp criticism from the other unions since it deprived the ETUC of its full quota of committee delegation members. This situation only changed after British entry into the EEC had been confirmed by the Referendum of June 1975.

The effectiveness of the ETUC as a pressure group

While still largely ineffective in coming to terms with such key issues as industrial democracy and supranationalism of the EC, the ETUC and its two forerunners have been able to deal partially with their main adversary (the employers) in seeking from the EC:

a) Protective measures against the activities of employers' organisations with regard to collective redundancies and the safeguarding of workers' rights in the event of mergers, transfers or amalgamations of firms. Thus it was made more difficult for multinational firms to bias their employment in favour of certain EC countries with weak protection; providing that arbitrary mass dismissals cannot be undertaken without a system of prior consultation and notification.

b) Alleviation of certain social problems arising from the working of the Customs Union (resulting in an increasing number of business mergers and subsequent structural unemployment), the Common Agricultural Policy (affecting employment and vocational training), and the free movement of labour (creating infrastructural problems in the host countries and family problems, especially for the children of migrant workers). This was effected mainly through improvements of the budget, the method of operation and application of the ESF, and through the improvements in social security benefits for migrant workers and members of their families.

c)   Advancement of living and working conditions for workers in the Community, exemplified by the legislation concerning equal pay and equal work conditions for men and women, the principle of the 40-hour week, 4 weeks' annual holiday, and the Commission's proposals on workers' participation.

The term 'partially able' has been chosen deliberately because, as pointed out in chapter 6, it is difficult to isolate accurately a one-to-one causal relationship between the trade unions' demands and the Commission's actions, on the one hand, and the Council's decision on whether or not to pass legislation, on the other. Certainly the Commission's role in promoting social policy harmonisation (both with respect to the Council of Ministers and to the demands of trade unions and employers) and, to a lesser extent, the initiatives taken by some governments to seek certain legislative or executive action by the EC in the social field influenced the outcome of EC social policy, but by what degree is not easy to measure. The task is made more difficult because of the many informal contacts and discussions between Commission officials and European pressure group representatives, on the one hand, and the Commission and CPR or national civil servants, on the other. However, the data collected proved sufficiently conclusive to indicate that both trade unions and the Commission had exercised influence on the three points mentioned above.

The data also seemed to indicate that trade unions responded more to the Commission's proposals rather than calling for 'new' initiatives to be taken. This appeared to be even more true in the case of employers' organisations who generally took a passive stand on social policy demands. Their primary preference seemed to be to respond to suggestions made by either the Commission or the trade unions.

This does not imply that Community pressure groups centre their demands exclusively on Commission proposals. On the contrary, both sides of industry have sought a dialogue directly with the Council of Ministers (Ministers of Social Affairs, Employment and Finance) to air their views and to express their demands on social policy. The various Community Employment Conferences since 1970, the Standing Committee on Employment (established in 1971), the granting of the right of initiative to the ESC (1972) and the foundation of a number of Advisory Committees, are evidence of the pressure and importance Community pressure groups have attached to this dialogue. In many ways, it is a reflection of the high level of consultation practised among employers, trade unions and governments in the national context, and the somewhat fragile position held by the Commission in social affairs with respect to the Council of Ministers.

But while this fragile position is due mainly to the fact that the Commission is only the recommending body in the EC institutional structure, and the Council of Ministers is the decision-making one, the Commission had, in addition, a difficult development in the social policy sector with the Council of Ministers. This was due both to insufficient specific Treaty provisions (aims and timetables), and the attitudes of certain governments, such as the French, who only let the Commission exercise a 'minimum' promotion role in the hard core areas of social security, vocational training, wages and employment. It must also be said that the Council's insistence on a close relationship between the Commission and the CPR has obscured the Commission's activities, diluted the question of competences between the two and given outside observers, such as the Community pressure groups, the impression that the status of the Commission is declining to the point where it is becoming more and more the 'mere' General Secretariat of the Council of Ministers. Moreover, even though the Commission has taken a line in its social policy proposals which seems to be 'closer' to the trade unions than to the employers, [14] and has for a long time tried to cultivate close relations with the European trade union organisations, it suffered another blow in its position vis-à-vis the Council when some of the ETUC affiliates (EFTA wing and CGIL) for political reasons blurred the relationship between the two in 1973-1975. In addition in that period the British TUC did not attend joint meetings with the Commission and instead lobbied the Council of Ministers or the CPR.

Neither development was particularly conducive to trade union pressures for social policy action and legislation at Community level. On the one hand, with the increasing integrative and co-operative attempts of trade unions at the Community level, more co-ordination of policies is necessary on their part. This means that they will have to reach more compromise solutions. Yet, once compromises are reached in the ETUC, the Commission, pursuing Community objectives, rather than the Council or the CPR pursuing national aims,

173

appears to be the most likely partner for the ETUC in safeguarding and promoting trade union interests at the Community level. This was reflected in the position taken by the trade unions of the former ECFTU and EO/WCL.

On the other hand, the Commission, being basically in an inferior position to the Council of Ministers, needs not only the support of trade unions for its proposals, but must also try to capture the support of the employers' organisations in order to bargain effectively with the Council. But in doing so, the Commission may have to accept objections from the employers' organisations on its initial proposal and thus downgrade the proposal by deducting or changing aspects favoured by the trade unions. An example of this is the principle of the 40-hour week and 4 weeks' annual paid holiday which, because of employers' objections, only obtained 'recommendation' status as an EC action and could only be implemented two years later than envisaged by the trade unions and the Commission. Situations like this substantiate the claims of those ETUC affiliates who prefer 'more' lobbying in the Council of Ministers or CPR than in the Commission.

In some instances the Commission is able to obtain the support of both the trade unions and the employers' organisations where they see equal benefits, although for different purposes, arising from a certain proposal of the Commission, and the Commission does not have to change much to the detriment of either side; or where the Commission can contribute towards compromise solutions between the two sides. This was largely the case on proposals concerning the ESF and social security benefits for migrant workers. It was considerably less so on issues relating to social security provisions in general (especially Article 2) and a common vocational training policy, especially on the mutual recognition of diplomas and vocational training certificates. On these latter issues, the Commission was unable to obtain 'enough' support from employers' organisations, but rather faced opposition on 'proposals calling for progressive measures of harmonisation'. On the other hand, while considerably more demanding in their calls for harmonisation on these two issues, trade unions were not ready to exert great pressures either on specific priority actions (leaving aside for the moment such considerations as full and better employment or unemployment compensation) or on timetables for achievement with respect to the Commission or the Council of Ministers. [15] This is an implication we will come back to shortly.

The data presented in chapter 7 suggest that greater progress has been made towards harmonisation of the five social policy issues since mid-1968 than in the period prior to that, and there are indications that this progress is continuing. It is perhaps most marked in the case of the ESF and social security for migrant workers, followed by the issue on equal pay for men and women and, to a lesser extent, by the issues on vocational training and social security provisions in general. Whereas up to 1968 social policy had been essentially thought of as a 'fellow-traveller' with economic integration and the Customs Union, which was supposed to spill over from economic integration more or less spontaneously, much greater emphasis was placed on the independence of social policy and the subsequent need for independent measures by the Council of Ministers since 1968 and especially from 1973 onwards.

While noting that there had been positive results with regard to demands, trade unions still questioned the willingness of governments to relinquish their powers relating to social policy. However, neither the Commission nor the trade unions appear to be in a position where they can introduce significant pressures or sanctions against the Council of Ministers for failing to comply with their wishes. The Commission cannot act as a broker in the absence of majority decision-making on some crucial social policy issues, [16] and the trade unions cannot utilise strikes.

Trade unions cannot maximise their influence at the Community level until such time as collective bargaining is introduced and accepted. Collective bargaining is being moved to this level only very slowly, not least because of substantial objections from the employers' organisations, but also because trade unions themselves foresee difficulties in overcoming existing differences concerning wage and fringe benefit levels in the various member countries. Moreover, as pointed out above, no sufficient industry trade union substructure as yet exists. Thus, in the absence of collective bargaining agreements, it would seem that the main means the trade unions have for exerting pressure to influence EC decisions would be limited to lobbying and publicity. [17]

However, the trade unions have threatened on several occasions either to stop or to withdraw co-operation if their demands are not met [18] and have, in two cases, actually demonstrated that they are willing to carry out their threats. These two occasions were the unsatisfactory handling by the Council of the admittance of certain trade union representatives (mentioned above) to the Standing Committee on Employment and the scheduled Community Employ- ment Conference in 1973. Not only did the trade unions refuse to attend meetings of the SCE between the beginning of 1973 and the end of 1974 (resulting in a suspension of SCE meetings by the

Council), they also refused to attend the 1973 Employment Conference which again resulted in cancellation by the Council.

These two examples demonstrate the potential strength of the ETUC to exert pressure on the Council of Ministers. Moreover, in the two EC directives cited above, intended to harmonise the redundancy laws of the Member States and to establish statutory provisions guaranteeing workers' rights, ETUC pressure has been successfully employed in dealing with employers' organisations or multinational firms through Community legislation. [19] These are encouraging developments which suggest that, contrary to Hoffmann's view, trade unions play an important role in the shaping of EC social policy. [20] However, much more needs to be done on the trade union side to ensure that the proliferation and growth of multinational firms does not adversely affect the interests of their members. Thus, more pressure must be brought to bear on the EC institutions to obtain legislation.

So far neither the ETUC as a whole, nor one of its national affiliates, nor an individual trade union branch have been able to persuade a single multinational firm to negotiate collective agreements covering all its European subsidiaries. Much of the work that the trade unions have so far done in their attempts to control the activities and operations of multinational firms has been in the nature of preparation. The tendency for collective bargaining to decentralise in Western Europe since the late 1960's and for the number of plant-level requirements to increase should encourage rather than hinder the growth of bargaining between multinational firms and representatives of workers from all their subsidiaries. Also encouraging are attempts to expand (broaden and diversify) the subject matter of collective bargaining from the mere content of wage and safety standards to such items as new investment, mergers and acquisitions and production planning. Similarly, increased powers granted to the works councils in a number of countries concerning dismissals, plant closures and profit sharing schemes, are promoting the trade unions' aim for greater control over the activities of multinational firms and employers' organisations; an aim which can also be associated with attempts to either introduce or expand the system of workers' participation.

Yet the bulk of these control measures are performed in different ways and with varying degrees of intensity in different countries. Not only is there a lack of co-ordination among different national trade unions dealing, perhaps, with subsidiaries of the same firm, but there is often even a lack of understanding on either the extent and activities of subsidiaries or the content of the measures introduced by trade unions in other countries. It is only in the metal trade union industry branch that there has been some degree of effective co-ordination and dissemination of information. [21] What is needed, and hopefully the proposed EC Statute for a European Company will help to introduce this, is a co-ordination of these measures, the creation of common structures in order to bargain effectively with firms at their headquarters, and the introduction of common standards of industrial relations for the subsidiaries of such firms.

To some extent the development of industrial relations at Community level has been positively affected by the practice of Community Employment Conferences, especially that of 1976 where European employers and trade union organisations, together with government representatives, worked out guidelines on European economic and social policies. [22] One of the obvious limitations of such conferences, or for that matter of EC legislative and executive action in general, is that not all ETUC affiliates benefit from the output; 14 out of the 31 ETUC affiliates come from non-EC countries. It is still an open question whether similar Employment Conferences at EFTA level, which have recently been started, will either produce similar results to those of the EC conferences, or allow the ETUC to pursue similar aims and objectives at both conference levels.

The creation of the EC has increased the interest of national trade unions and their national federations in the activities of their counter-parts, both in other Member States and in the ETUC. There is a growing desire among ETUC affiliates to exchange information: systems of industrial relations, democratisation of the economy, equal pay for men and women, voluntary or statutory wage guide-lines, vocational training schemes, social security systems, forms of social assistance and job protection, to name some of the most important. But the record of closer contacts among the ETUC affiliates or more intensive involvement is a mixed one. There are instances where this exchange has led to fruitful results. There are other examples where the co-ordination of policies between trade union demands in the national context and trade union demands in the European context have not been so successful. For example, trade unions in the continental countries have taken advice from the British system of shop stewards (shown in chapter 3) in strengthening their system of works' councils. In turn, the British trade unions have been learning from the continental trade unions about systems of workers' participation. There are also indications that certain national trade union confederations have benefitted in pressing their claims at the national level from contacts with colleagues in the ETUC.

177

Against this must be held the part trade unions play in pressing for wages and social benefits at the national level which, if not wholly contradictory, differed in some important aspects from the guidelines pursued by the ETUC. As illustrated in chapter 7, comparing national legislation on social security provisions and especially the changes which have occurred since 1970, seems to lead to both positive and negative findings. On the positive side, for example, we can note that Member States have aligned more closely on family benefits. On the negative side, we find that total benefits as a percentage of national income have greatly widened, as well as sickness benefits and old age pensions. Subsequently there seems to be a discrepancy between the priorities or emphasis certain trade unions place on national objectives and those they place on European objectives — a phenomenon which perhaps explains why the ETUC has not been able to exert enough pressure to overcome the objections of the employers' organisations towards EC legislation on social security provisions such as old age pensions, sickness and family benefits and unemployment compensation and on a common vocational training policy, especially as it concerns the mutual recognition of vocational training certificates.

It must be said in this context that if one were to weigh up the success and failure of the trade unions in obtaining legislation on the five social policy issues (excluding for the moment the two directives on 'job protection' and the recommendation on a 40-hour week, 4 weeks' annual paid holiday) against the success and failure of the employers' organisations in stifling or preventing legislation on these issues, then it might be found that the employers' organisations have only really conceded on one issue, namely legislation concerning the principle of equal pay for men and women. The two other successes of the trade unions (the improvement of the ESF and social security for migrant workers) coincided with the interests of the employers' organisations to advance legislation at Community level.

Thus in those areas where the ETUC succeeds in making its members in each country more quickly aware of events that are taking place elsewhere in Europe and in speeding up the process of common concern, there is no guarantee that members will be equally ready to adapt. As Sorge explains: [23]

> In this search for recipes and explanations across borders, however, no firm conclusions are usually reached. A debate on whether to introduce another country's institutions at home quickly finds two sides at variance, one recommending it because another country benefitted from the institution,

the other opposing it because present and historical
conditions in that country are too different.

Moreover, it is only within the last two years that German trade
unions have been willing to extend trade union rights to migrant
workers of the EC countries; believing earlier that it might either up-
set the German system of industrial relations or the system of
workers' participation. This reservation was one of the reasons
explaining why it took the Council until late 1975 before it adopted a
regulation providing for equality of treatment in the exercise of trade
union rights to cover admission to leading positions in trade union
organisations. [24]

It is probably too short a time since mid-1974 to fully assess the
extent to which trade unions in the ETUC have overcome political
and ideological differences and the extent to which such differences
remain. Too much is still in a state of flux. Important strides have
been made towards overcoming trade union plurality and the conflict
and competition among trade unions, both within and between
countries, have diminished. Also encouraging is the progress made in
the ETUC towards agreement on such key issues as workers'
participation.

While much remains to be done on increasing the effectiveness of
the ETUC in dealing with multinational corporations or employers'
organisations at European level (either on a bilateral basis through the
establishment of collective bargaining agreements or on an EC
legislative basis through the enactment of labour laws) a promising
start has been made. This is signified by the two EC directives on
mass dismissals and workers' rights. It is perhaps in the social policy
sector proper (social security provisions in general) that the need for
increased effectiveness is most urgent. Here the discrepancies seem to
widen rather than to narrow and the question must be raised as to
how trade unions can continue to participate in an organisation
(ETUC) in which some members disproportionately raise their social
benefits to the levels of other members.

There seems to be agreement among most writers on the subject of
European trade unions that the development of multinational
corporations has become an issue of considerable importance to the
ETUC as it provides the ETUC with an opportunity to exercise a
significant influence over the development of the collective bargaining process at the European level. [25] So far, however, we have only
seen the potential for that. Resources, substructure and cohesion
must increase and agreement must be reached on the extent to which
certain channels, such as the Commission, the CPR, the EP and the

ESC, should be used. But while it will take some time before the ETUC will have the strength, competences and effectiveness of national trade union confederations, the speed with which the ETUC will emulate national structures will depend in part on the integrative development of the EC, and in part on the activities of multinational firms and employers' organisations.

Notes

[1]   Roberts and Liebhaberg make a very apt observation when they state:

> The fundamental problem that confronts the ETUC is in essence the same problem that confronts the European Economic Community, namely diversity in the pattern of trade unionism and the diversity of national trade union economic and political interest. Each trade union centre exists in a national culture that is different, each has its own history, traditions, and national interests that differentiate from other national countries.

See Roberts and Liebhaberg, 'The European Trade Union Confederation,' p.272.
    They also provide some useful examples on how the various national trade union organisations differ in size, structure, role, power and objectives. See also Robert Lieber, 'Interest Groups and Political Integration: British Entry into Europe,' in Kimber and Richardson, *Pressure Groups in Britain*, pp 47-8.
[2]   For example, Hine makes such an argument on the shift of power. See David Hine, 'The Labour Movement and Communism in France and Italy,' in Martin Kolinsky and William Patterson, *Social and Political Movements in Western Europe*, Croom Helm, London 1976, pp 195-9.
[3]   See speech by Dr P.J. Hillery, Vice-President of the Commission of the EC, to the Royal Irish Academy, Dublin, 28 April 1975. *Information*: Social Policy, 98/75, Commission of the European Communities, Brussels.
[4]   Political party influences have played a role in the integrative attempts among trade unions, both in the national and in the European contexts. The former can be observed in Italy in the attempts by trade unions to achieve unity between the CGIL and CISL, where the two trade unions were reluctant to abandon formal links with the Communist and Socialist Parties, respectively, and thus

delayed the progress towards trade union unity in Italy. Political party influence also played a role, and continues to play a role in Germany, as shown by the stand taken by the trade unions there with regard to the admittance of the Italian Communist trade union, CGIL, to the ETUC in 1974. The German DGB gave a dissenting vote and continues to be unsympathetic to CGIL participation. The reason for this, as one leading DGB official pointed out in an interview, was the DGB's support for the German Government's policy on Ostpolitik, which had experienced some setbacks. Thus the DGB's position was a reflection of solidarity on the 'tougher' line taken by the SDP German Government by 1974 towards relations with Eastern European countries in general, and to the German Government's growing concern over the spread of Communism in Western Europe, in particular. For details on the influence of political parties on trade union integration in Italy, see Hine, 'The Labour Movement and Communism in France and Italy', p.199.

[5]   The Danish Government intervened in the collective bargaining deadlock situation in March 1975, using Parliamentary enactment of an award by the public arbitrator to effect a two-year settlement. The agreement contained a declaration that wage and salary increases must not exceed those expected under the statutory settlement by Parliament earlier in the year. See *Report on the Development of the Social Situation in the Community in 1975*, p.68.

[6]   See Feld, 'National Economic Interest Groups and Policy Formation in the EEC,' p.407.

[7]   Lieber provides a useful example of the disharmony between economic interests and political or ideological outlooks with regard to British pressure groups, such as the CBI, TUC and the NFU. He finds that these groups were generally opposed, or at best guardedly favourable towards integration throughout a period when British membership of the EC offered economic prospects ranging from breaking even to clear and substantial advantages. 'Evidently these group orientations reflected organisational rather than strictly economic considerations.' See Lieber, 'Interest Groups and Political Integration,' pp 47-8.

[8]   For clarification of the perceptions of the British and Irish trade unions and the different reasons relating to the Danish trade unions and the Italian CGIL, see chapter 3, pp 55-7.

[9]   This point is made by Roberts and Liebhaberg in 'The European Trade Union Confederation,' p.264.

[10]   Examples on some of the differences encountered were presented in chapter 3. For additional examples, see Sorge, 'The Evolution of Industrial Democracy in the Countries of the EEC,'

pp 278-9; and see Hine, 'The Labour Movement and Communism in France and Italy', pp 178-210.

[11]   Some of the main remaining differences over the forms and methods involve: (a) dual board form of management (supervisory and management board) versus unitary management structure; (b) one-third workers' representatives or one-half; (c) the size of a firm (those with 500, 1,000 or 2,000 employees); (d) the selection or election of workers' representatives: should the entire workforce of a firm be eligible to vote or should only trade union members be so entitled; (e) the recruitment of workers' representatives: should works' council members or shop stewards be used; (f) the link between the scope and emphasis of collective bargaining and the nature and content of workers' participation; and (g) the extent of statutory provisions to be used. For further details, see chapter 3, pp 46-8.

[12]   Some of the problems faced by the national trade union federations in representing and co-ordinating conflicting sub-group interests are illustrated in the contributing articles to Barkin's *Worker Militancy and its Consequences*; and Kendall, *The Labour Movement in Europe.*

[13]   See Roberts and Liebhaberg, 'The European Trade Union Confederation,' p.264.

[14]   There was generally a great deal of similarity between the initial proposal submitted by the Commission on the five social policy issues and the demands expressed by trade unions, particularly regarding mass dismissals, workers' rights, the European Trade Union Institute and Joint Committees.

[15]   In general it should be noted that the social security systems in force in the Member States of the EC have, to a large extent, evolved independently in response to the different social and economic conditions of each country. As a result, they vary widely, not only in respect of objectives, organisation and resources, but they are also based on certain different conceptions prevailing, not only between trade unions and employers in general, but also, for example, between the Danish trade unions and the Italian trade unions, as well as between the German and the French employers' organisations. See Bouvard, *Labor Movements*, p.248.

[16]   In contrast to the issues on the ESF and social security benefits for migrant workers, where majority decision-making has been the practice in the Council of Ministers, unanimity has been the rule on the issues of social security provisions in general (especially when based on Article 118) and vocational training.

[17]   This is the conclusion reached by Bouvard, *Labor Movements*, p.71.

[18]   For example, in December 1973: '... the ETUC reminded the governments and the EC institutions that it would not hesitate to call off co-operation with them if its demands receive a rejecting echo.' See 'Europaische Malaise,' *Pressemitteilung* nr.14, Europaischer Gewerkschaftsbund, 19 December 1973.

[19]   In the second half of 1977, the Commission intends to send a report to the Council on the situation of workers affected by individual dismissals, as well as on the problems involved in the protection of workers in the event of bankruptcy of a firm, and on the protection of young people at work. This reflects trade union pressures and advances their demands for further EC legislation aimed at achieving greater security of employment for workers.

[20]   For example, Hoffman argues that trade union activities and the efforts of the Commission are not enough to bring about greater social policy harmonisation. See Hoffmann, Foreword to *Labor Movements* by Bouvard. My own findings, in opposition to Hoffmann's claim, correspond with the findings of Fogarty, *Work and Industrial Relations in the EC*, pp 8-9; Reed in Lawson and Reed, *Social Security in the EC*, p.47; and Schierwater, 'Der Arbeitnehmer und Europa,' pp 317-8.

[21]   The European Metal Trade Unions (EMF) have held some promising discussions with such firms as Philips, Siemens and Citroen covering wage provisions for the nine EC countries. One of the trade union aims was to avoid the possibility of a manufacturer closing plants where labour costs were higher and concentrating production in cheaper labour markets. Another objective was to try to stop companies transferring work from one country to another during strikes. Through these activities the EMF aimed (and still aims) at universal collective bargaining agreements.

[22]   At the end of the meeting Mr Vouel, Chairman of the Council of Ministers, and Mr Haferkamp, Vice-President of the Commission, stressed that: 'It was the first time that the two sides of industry and the governments of the Member States had entered into a collective Community agreement at Community level.' Quoted from *European Communities Trade Union Information* 7/8.

[23]   See Sorge, 'The Evolution of Industrial Democracy,' p.274.

[24]   The respective Regulation no. 312/76 specifies that a worker who is a national of a Member State and who is employed in the territory of another Member State shall enjoy equality of treatment as regards membership of trade unions and the exercise of rights attaching thereto, including the right of eligibility for workers' representative bodies. See *Council Review*, 1975, p.48.

[25]   This point is made in one way or another by Roberts and

183

Liebhaberg, 'The European Trade Union Confederation,' p.269; Barkin, *Worker Militancy and its Consequences*, pp 400-401; Willatt, *Multinational Unions*, p.35; and Sorge, 'The Evolution of Industrial Democracy,' p.274.

Bibliography

Books and articles

Barber, James and Reed, Bruce,. eds, *European Community: Vision and Reality*, Croom Helm, in association with the Open University Press, London, 1973.

Barkin, Solomon, ed. *Worker Militancy and its Consequences 1965-1975*: New Directions in Western Industrial Relations, Praeger Special Studies in International Economics and Development, London, 1975.

Barry-Braunthal, Thomas, 'Multinational Labour: European Workers Unite,' *European Community*, April 1973.

Beever, R. Colin, *Trade Unions and Free Labour Movement in the European Economic Community*, Chatham House, PEP, London, 1969.

Boedler, Hermann, 'Internationale und Supranationale Sozialpolitik,' 2nd ed. *Sozialpolitik in Deutschland* 49, Bundesministerium fur Arbeit und Sozialordnung, Bonn, June 1968.

Bouvard, Marguerite, *Labor Movements in the Common Market Countries: The Formation of a European Pressure Group*, Praeger, New York, 1972.

Braun, Gerald, *Die Rolle der Wirtschaftsverbände im agrarpolitischen Entscheidungsprozess der Europäischen Wirtschaftsgemeinschaft: Eine Analyse der Markt-, Regional- und Agrarstrukturpolitik*, Duncker & Humblot, Berlin, 1972.

Buitner, Harm G., 'Interest Groups and the European Community,' *Internationale Spectator* 7, The Hague, 8 April 1965, pp 597-604.

Caporaso, James A., *Functionalism and Regional Integration: a Logical and Empirical Assessment*, Sage Publications, Beverly Hills, California, 1972.

Carew, Anthony, 'Shop Floor Trade Unionism in Western Europe,' *European Studies* 18, 1974.

Clark, W.H., *The Politics of the Common Market*, Prentice-Hall, Englewood Cliffs, N.J., 1967.

Coates, Ken and Topham, Tony, *The New Unionism: Case for Workers' Control*, Penguin Books, Middlesex, 1974.

Cool, A., 'Die Europäische Organisation des WVA Vertritt die Arbeitnehmer auf Europäischer Ebene,' *Labor* 3/4, May/August

1970.

Coombes, David, *Politics and Bureaucracy in the European Community*, George Allen & Unwin, London, 1970.

Crijns, Leo H.J., 'Collective Bargaining in Nations of the European Economic Community' in *Western European Labor and the American Corporation*, pp 93-8, edited by Alfred Kamin, Bureau of National Affairs, Washington, 1970.

Curzon, Gerard and Curzon, Victoria, eds, *The Multinational Enterprise in a Hostile World*, The Macmillan Press Ltd., London, 1977.

Dahlberg, Kenneth, 'The EEC Commission and the Politics of the Free Movement of Labour,' *Journal of Common Market Studies 6*, June 1968, pp 310-33.

Danaho, Raoul, 'La Politique de l'Emploi en tant que partie intégrante de la Politique Economique: Elements pour une Théorie d'Ensemble de la Politique de l'Emploi,' *Droit Social 5*, June 1969, pp 341-60.

De Grave, Michel J., *Dimension Européenne du Syndicalisme Ouvrier*, Universite Catholique de Louvain, Institut de Sciences Politiques et Sociales, Louvain 1968.

Delperée, A., 'Y a-t-il une Politique Sociale Européenne?' *Revue Belge de Sécurité Sociale*, November-December 1967, pp 1557-72.

De Vree, Johan K., *Political Integration: The Formation of Theory and its Problems*, Mouton & Co., The Hague, 1972.

Downs, Anthony, *Inside Bureaucracy*, Little, Brown & Co., Boston, 1969.

Ekenvall, Asta, *Women in the Nordic Countries*, exhibition arranged by the Nordic Council for International Women's Year, Stockholm, 1976.

Feld, Werner J., 'Diplomatic Behaviour in the European Community: Milieus and Motivations,' *Journal of Common Market Studies 11*, September 1972, pp 18-35.

Feld, Werner J., 'National Economic Interest Groups and Policy Formation in the European Economic Community,' *Political Science Quarterly 81*, 1966, pp 392-411.

Feld, Werner J., *Transnational Business Collaboration among Common Market Countries*, Praeger, New York, 1970.

Fischer, Fritz, *Die Institutionalisierte Vertretung der Verbände in der Europäischen Wirtschaftsgemeinschaft*, Hansischer Gildenverlag, Veroffentlichungen des Instituts fur Internationales Recht an der Universitat Kiel, Hamburg, 1965.

Fischer, Fritz, 'The Development of Interest Groups in the European Economic Community,' *Memoir* presented for the Diploma of the

College of Europe, Bruges, 1963.

Fogarty, Michael P., *Work and Industrial Relations in the European Community*, Chatham House, PEP, European Series 24, London, 1975.

Friedrich, Carl J., *Europe: An Emergent Nation?* Harper & Row, New York, 1969.

Friedrich, Carl J., ed., *Politische Dimensionen der Europäischen Gemeinschaftsbildung*, Westdeutscher Verlag, Cologne, 1968.

Genton, J., 'Der Wirtschafts und Sozialausschuss,' *Europa Informationen des Gustav Stresemann Instituts* 9, 1966.

Gerritse, G., 'La Place des Travailleurs dans une Europe en Mutation,' *Supplement to First Congress of the EO/WCL*, Brussels, 9 May 1969.

Greenstein, Fred I., "A Note on the Ambiguity of Political Socialisation: Definitions, Criticisms and Strategies of Inquiry,' *Journal of Politics* 32, November 1970, pp 969-78.

Hammerich, K. Ewerlog, *L'Union des Industries de la Communauté Européenne dans le Marché Commun.*, Sveriges Industriforbund, Stockholm, 1969.

Heynig, E., 'Problèmes Institutionnels posés par la Mise en Oeuvre d'une Politique Sociale au Niveau Communautaire,' *Revue du Marché Commun*, March 1967.

Hine, David, 'The Labour Movement and Communism in France and Italy,' in *Social and Political Movements in Western Europe*, edited by Martin Kolinsky and William Patterson, Croom Helm, London, 1976, pp 178-210.

Hoffmann, Stanley, Foreword to *Labor Movements in the Common Market Countries*: The Formation of a European Pressure Group, by Marguerite Bouvard, Praeger, New York, 1972.

Jacobs, Erik, *European Trade Unionism*, Croom Helm, London, 1973.

Kendall, Walter, *The Labour Movement in Europe*, Allen Lane, London, 1974.

Kimber, Richard and Richardson, J.J., eds, *Pressure Groups in Britain,* J.M. Dent & Sons, London 1974.

Kulakowski, J., 'Die Zukunft der Europäischen Organisation — Probleme und Aussichten,' *Labor* 3/4, May/August 1970.

Kulakowski, J., 'Les Organisations Syndicales et la Construction de l'Europe,' CFDT/CMT Conference given in Paris at l'Institut des Hautes Etudes de Défense Nationale, 17 March 1973.

Kulakowski, J., 'Der Beitrag der Gewerkschaften zur Europäischen Integration,' *Sozial- und Gesellschaftspolitik in der Europäischen Gemeinschaft*, 1973, pp 39-49

Lappas, Alfons, 'Worker Participation', Financial Times Conference

Department, London, December 1973.

Lawson, Roger and Reed, Bruce, *Social Security in the EC*, Chatham House, PEP, European Series 23, London, 1975.

Leitolf, Andreas, *Das Einwirken der Wirtschaftsverbände auf die Agrarmarktorganisation der EWG*, Nomos Verlagsgesellschaft Schriftenreihe Europaische Wirtschaft, Baden-Baden, 1971.

Levi-Sandri, Lionello, 'Les Difficultes de la Politique Sociale Européenne,' *Speech* given at l'Institut d'Etudes Européennes et Association des Diplômes de l'Institut du Travail de l'Université Libre de Bruxelles, 21 March 1968.

Levi-Sandri, Lionello, 'Social Policy in the Common Market, 1958-1965,' *Community Topics* 22, European Community Information Service, London, July 1966.

Lieber, Robert, *British Politics and European Unity Parties*: Elites and Pressure Groups, University of California Press, Berkeley, 1970.

Macridis, R.C., 'Interest Groups in Comparative Analysis,' *Journal of Politics*, vol.23, no.1, February 1961, pp 25-45.

Malterre, Andre, 'Ein geeintes Europa auch für die leitenden Angestellten,' *Der Europäer*, Deutschland Büro, Essen, 1971, pp 28-9.

Meynaud, Jean and Sidjanski, Dusan, *Les Groupes de Pression dans la Communauté Européenne, 1958-1968*: Theses et Travaux Politiques, Institut d'Etudes Européennes de l'Université Libre de Bruxelles, Editions de l'Institut de Sociologie, Brussels 1971.

Neirinck, J.D., *The EEC on the Eve of the Customs Union*: A supplement and updating of the author's advance paper: 'Social Policy of the EEC Commission.' For presentation at Chicago Loyola University's Business and Law Summer Institute on 'The Supranational Corporation and Western European Labor: Lessons for Americans,' Highland Park, Illinois, July 1968.

Neirinck, J.D., 'Social Policy of the EEC,' in *Western European Labor and the American Corporation*, edited by Alfred Kamin, Bureau of National Affairs, Washington, 1970, pp 21-65.

Neunreither, K.H., 'Wirtschaftsverbände im Prozess der Europäischen Integration,' in *Politische Dimensionen der Europäischen Gemeinschaftsbildung*, edited by Carl J. Friedrich, Westdeutscher Verlag, Cologne, 1968, pp 358-442.

Nielsen, Terkel T., 'Aspects of the EEC Influence of European Groups in the Decision-Making Processes: The Common Agricultural Policy,' *Government and Opposition* 6, Autumn 1971, pp 539-58.

Nielsen, Terkel T., 'European Groups and the Decision-Making Process,' in *European Community: Vision and Reality*, edited by James Barber and Bruce Reed, Croom Helm, in association with the Open University Press, London, 1973, pp.149-57.

Noel, Emile, 'How the European Economic Community's Institutions Work,' *Community Topics* 39, European Community Information Service, London.

Noel, Emile and Etienne, Henri, 'The Permanent Representatives Committee and the "Deepening" of the Communities,' *Government and Opposition* 6, Autumn 1971, pp 422-47.

Ortoli, Francois-Xavier, 'The Construction of Europe: Balance Sheet and Outlook,' *Address* given in Mainz at the 12th Annual Congress of the Association of European Journalists, 13 September 1974. Offprint from *Bulletin of the European Communities 9*, 1974.

Paulus, Daniel, *La Création du Comité Permanente de l'Emploi des Communautés Européennes*, Emile Bruylant, Brussels, 1972.

Pryce, Roy, 'Interest Groups in the Community,' *European Community* 5, May 1968.

Ribas, Jacques Jean, 'Social Security in the European Community,' *Community Topics* 18, European Community Information Service, London.

Rifflet, Raymond, 'After the Hague,' *Journal of Common Market Studies* 8, June 1970, pp 281-90.

Rittstieg, Helmut, *Wirtschaftsverbände und europäische Gemeinschaften*, Ludwig Appel Verlag, Hamburg 1967.

Roberts, B.C. and Liebhaberg, Bruno, 'The European Trade Union Confederation: Influence of Regionalism, Detente and Multinationals,' *British Journal of Industrial Relations*, vol. 14, no.3, November 1976, pp 261-73.

Scheinman, Lawrence, 'Some Preliminary Notes on Bureaucratic Relationships in the European Economic Community,' *International Organisation* 20, Autumn 1966, pp 750-74.

Schierwater, Viktor, 'Der Arbeitnehmer und Europa- Integrations- tendenzen und-Strukturen im Sozialbereich des Gemeinsamen Marktes,' in *Politische Dimensionen der Europäischen Gemeinschaftsbildung*, edited by Carl J. Friedrich, Westdeutscher Verlag, Cologne, 1968, pp 294-357.

Sidjanski, Dusan, 'Pressure Groups and the EEC,' in *The New International Actors in the UN and the EEC*, edited by Carol and Ann Cosgrave and Kenneth Twitchett, vol.1 of Dealings in International Politics, Gen. ed. J.E. Spence, Macmillan, London, 1970, pp 221-41.

Sorge, Arndt, 'The Evolution of Industrial Democracy in the Countries of the European Community,' *British Journal of Industrial Relations*, vol.14, no.3, November 1976, pp 274-94.

Van Praag, Philippe, 'L'Harmonisation et l'Egalisation au Niveau

Européen des Systemes de Securite Sociale,' *Droit Social* 4, April 1968, pp 259-63.

Van Praag, Philippe, 'Trends and Achievements in the Field of Social Policy in the European Communities,' *Bulletin* 1, Louvain University, Labour Law Faculty, Louvain, 1971.

Veldkamp, G.M.J., 'Manpower in Western Europe,' in *Western European Labor and the American Corporation*, edited by Alfred Kamin, Bureau of National Affairs, Washington, 1970, pp 435-38.

Veldkamp, G.M.J., 'Towards Harmonisation of Social Security in the EEC,' in *Western European Labor and the American Corporation*, pp 351-73.

Vetter, Heinz, speech delivered for the Report La CESL face à là Communauté en Transformation: 'L'Europe ... 20 ans après la Proclamation du Plan Schuman,' CESL *Information a la Presse* 75, 1970.

Willatt, Norris, *Multinational Unions*, Financial Times, London, 1974.

Windmuller, John P., 'Realignment in the ICFTU: The Impact of Detente,' *British Journal of Industrial Relations*, vol.14, no.3, November 1976, pp 247-60.

Winslow, Martin, 'The Acquisition-Merger Movement in Western Europe Today,' an Address presented at the International Corporate Symposium on Merging, Acquiring and Selling, Brussels, 8 December 1969.

Zellentin, Gerda, 'Krisen der Europäischen Integration,' *Integration: European Studies Review*, Commission of the European Communities, Brussels, 1970.

Commission of the EC

Arbeitsmarktlage in der Gemeinschaft, Die, Commission of the European Communities, Brussels, 1971.

Background notes, Commission of the European Communities, London, 1976.

2 April	New Proposal for Long Distance Drivers
8 April	The Community's Human Face: Progress Report on the Social Action Programme
4 May	Unemployment Slowing Down
11 May	An EC Strategy for Full Employment and Stability
28 May	The Liberal Professions
4 June	Vocational Training for Women
9 June	Social Fund Applications Approved - 1st Series

12 July   Community Action in the Social Field: Annual Report
          on a Difficult Year
Background reports, Commission of the European Communities,
   London.
20 December 1976   The Community Economy — a Cautious
                    Optimism
8 March 1977   A New Look at Social Security Systems
3 May 1977   Lawyers and the Community
Bulletin of the European Communities, various issues, 1968-1977
Common Agricultural Policy, Commission of the European
   Communities, July 1974.
Common Market and the Common Good, The, Commission of the
   European Communities, n.d., Brussels.
*Comparative Tables of the Social Security Systems in the Member
   States of the European Communities*, eighth edition (situation at
   1 July 1974); general system; Office for Official Publications,
   Luxembourg.
*Employment of Women and the Problems it raises in the Member
   States of the European Community, The,* Office for Official
   Publications of the European Communities, n.d., Luxembourg.
*Employment Trends to 1980 in the Member States of the
   Community*, Commission of the European Communities, Brussels,
   10 May 1976.
Euroforum, weekly series, DG X, Information, Commission of the
   European Communities, Brussels, 1977.
European Communities Trade Union Information, monthly series and
   Special Numbers, Commission of the European Communities,
   Brussels, 1975-Spring 1977.
European Community, various issues, Commission of the European
   Communities, London, 1968-Spring 1977.
European Community Studies, various issues, Commission of the
   European Communities, Brussels, 1973-Spring 1977.
European Documentation, Trade Union Series Periodical 1976/1,
   'The Protection of Workers in Multinational Companies,'
   Commission of the European Communities, Brussels.
European Studies, Trade Union Series, Commission of the European
   Communities, Brussels, 1972.
European Studies, various issues, Commission of the European
   Communities, Brussels, 1968-Spring 1977.
European Studies, Teacher's series, no.17, 1973, Commission of the
   European Communities, Brussels.
Eurostat, general statistics, monthly; various issues, Office for Official
   Publications for the European Communities, 1973-1976.

191

Eurostat, social statistics, various issues, Office for Official Publications for the European Communities, Luxembourg, 1968-1972.

Eurostat News, Office for Official Publications, nos.10-12, 1976.

Evaluation of Vocational Training, The, Report of a Seminar held at the University of Manchester, UK, January 1975, Office for Official Publications, Luxembourg.

General Reports on the Activities of the European Communities, annual, issues from 1967-1976, Brussels.

Indikatoren der Sozialen Sicherheit, Commission of the European Communities, Brussels, 1971.

Industriepolitik der Gemeinschaft, Die, Memorandum der Kommission an den Rat, Brussels, 1970.

Information, brochures showing the principal activities of the various services of the Commission of the European Communities, Commission of the European Communities, Brussels, 1973.

Information, bulletin of the Commission of the European Communities, series 'P', various issues, 1969-1977, Brussels.

Information, Social Policy series, various issues, 1971-1975, Brussels.

Integration: European Studies Review 3/4, Commission of the European Communities, Brussels, 1971.

New European Social Fund, The, Commission of the European Communities, Brussels, 1973.

Official Journal of the European Communities, Special (English) Edition, various issues, 1968-Spring 1977, Brussels.

Outlook for Employment in the European Community to 1980. A report on the first phase of the work of a group of independent experts, DG for Social Affairs, Commission of the European Communities, Brussels, 1976.

Polyvalenz in der Berufsausbildung in den Landern der Gemeinschaft, Die, Commission of the European Communities, Brussels, 1971.

Press Releases, Commission of the European Communities, London.
19 March 1976   Improving the Homes of Handicapped Persons
28 July 1976   Second Allocation from 1976 Social Fund
22 December 1976   Equal Social Security Treatment for Men and Women Proposed
24 January 1977   Social Fund - 3rd Series 1976: 'Extensive Grants to N. Ireland.'
9 March 1977   European Centre for the Development of Vocational Training, Berlin.

Repertoire des organismes communs crees dans le cadre des Communautés Européennes par les Associations Industrielles, Artisanales, Commerciales et de Services des Six Pays;

Associations de Professions Liberales; Organisations Syndicales de Salaries et Groupements de Consommateurs. Services des Publications des Communautés Européennes, 1973.

Repertoire des Organizations Agricoles non Gouvernementales groupées dans le Cadre de la Communauté Economique Européenne. Services des Publications des Communautés Européennes, 1972.

Report on the Development of the Social Situation in the Community, annual, issues from 1963-1977, Office for Official Publications of the European Communities, Luxembourg.

Social Policy A, European Communities Information Service, Washington, April 1975.

Social Security for Migrant Workers, guide no.1, 1975; guide no.2, 1976, Office for Official Publications of the European Communities, Luxembourg.

Studies, Commission of the European Communities.

No.10 Reihe Wettbewerb-Rechtsangleichung, 1970. 'Beitrag zu den Moglichkeiten der Vertretung der Interessen der Arbeitnehmer in der Europäischen Aktiengesellschaft.'

No.20 Reihe Sozialpolitik, 1970. 'Die Finanzierung der Sozialen Sicherheit in der Landwirtschaft.'

No.21 Social Policy Series, 1971. 'The Economic Impact of Social Security.'

Supplement au no.188 de 30 Jours d'Europe. Le Comite Economique et Social, Bureau d'Information de la Communauté Européenne, Paris.

Supplement to Bulletin of the European Communities.

8/75 Employee Participation and Company Structure

3/76 Action Programme in Favour of Migrant Workers and their Families

System of Structural Indicators, DG for Economic and Financial Affairs, Commission of the European Communities, Brussels, June 1975.

Trade Union News from the European Community, monthly and quarterly; issues from 1968-1975, European Communities Press and Information Office, London.

Treaties Establishing the European Communities, Treaties amending these Treaties; documents concerning the accession, Office for Official Publications of the European Communities, Luxembourg, 1973.

Vergleichende Darstellung der Systeme der Sozialen Sicherheit in den Mitgliedstaaten der europäischen Gemeinschaften, auflage 7, Commission of the European Communities, Luxembourg, 1 July 1972.

Vocational Training Information Bulletin no.2, Office for Official
Publications of the European Communities, Luxembourg, October
1974.

Youth Unemployment in the European Community, DG for Social
Affairs, Commission of the European Communities, Brussels,
November 1976.

Zweites Programm für die Mittelfristige Wirtschaftspolitik, Office for
Official Publications of the European Communities, Luxembourg,
May 1969.

Trade Unions

CESL and OE/CMT: *Aide Memoire* de la CESL et de l'OE/CMT
concernant la création d'un Conseil Européen de l'Emploi établi à
l'intention du Conseil des Ministres des Affaires Sociales, May 1970.

CFDT/CMT: *Les Organisations Syndicales et la Construction de
l'Europe*, 1972-1973.

CGT: *Exposé* de Georges Seguy, Sécrétaire-Général de la CGT.
Conference de Presse, Brussels, 25 June 1974.

CGT: *Service de Presse* nos 06/1976; 08/1976; 19/1976; 10/1976;
13/1976.

CGT/CGIL: *Communiqué* on L'Evolution Sociale de la
Communauté en 1971.' 29 June 1972.

CISL: *Rapport sur les Activités*, 1965-1969, Ninth World Congress,
Brussels, July 1969.

Deutscher Gewerkschaftsbund: *Vorschläge zum Sozialen Aktionsprogramm in der Europäischen Gemeinschaft*, Dusseldorf, April
1973.

DGB: *Die Quelle*, monthly publication, 1973-1975.

EBFG: *1ter Kongress: Reden-Beschlüsse-Entschliessungen*, The
Hague, 23-25 April 1969.

EBFG: *Pressemitteilungen* (press releases)
  Nr.77 Memorandum zur Reform des ESF, 10 November 1969.
  Nr.83 Le Conseil respecte les Engagements pris à Luxembourg,
         10 December 1970
  Nr.84 Europäische Aktiengesellschaft, 4 November 1970.
  Nr.85 Industriepolitik in der Gemeinschaft, 4 November 1970.
  Nr.86 Erklärung zur dritten Richtlinie, 4 November 1970.
  Nr.88 Reform des ESF, 17 February 1971.
  Nr.93 Für eine Gemeinschaft des Sozialen Fortschritts:
         Stellungnahme zur Konferenz der Staats und Regierungs-
         chefs, 15 September 1973.

Nr.95 Meinungsaustausch zwischen Regierungen/Kommission/
Arbeitgeber-und Arbeitnehmer-Organisationen, 9 November
1972.

EBFG and EFTA/ICFTU: *Künftige Gewerkschaftliche Zusammenar-
beit in Europa*: Aufzeichnung über einige noch ungelöste Probleme,
Luxembourg, 30 November-1 December 1972.

ECFTU: *Press Release* no.80, 'The European Company,' Brussels,
15 April 1970.

EFA: *Action Program*, n.d.

EGB: *Satzungsvorschlag*, 8/9 February 1973.

EGB: *Vorschläge* des NVV für ein Aktionsporgramm des EGB,
25 June 1973.

EGB: *Erklärung*: Soziales Aktionsprogramm der Europäischen
Gemeinschaft, 7 September 1973.

EGB: *Pressemitteilung* nr.14, 'Europäische Malaise,' 19 December
1973.

EMB: *Statut*, Brussels, 18 February 1971.

EMB: Kurzmeldungen: Gewerkschafts und Arbeitnehmer
Informationen nr.37, June 1971.

EMB: 'Der EMB: Was ist er und was will er?' *Information* 1/71,
September 1971.

EMB: Gesellschafts- und Sozialpolitik Gegenüber Multinationalen
Unternehmen, n.d.

EMF: *Provisional Report on Collective Bargaining in the Engineering
Industries of the European Countries:* situation at the beginning
of November 1973.

EO/IBCG-WVA: 5ten *Tätigkeitsbericht* (1 Teil-2 Teil): 1ter Kongress,
Brussels, 7-9 May 1969.

EO/WCL: *Towards Trade Union Unity on the European Level,*
28 March 1973.

EO/WVA: *Satzungen*, Luxembourg, 18 May 1972.

EO/WVA: 6ter *Tätigkeitsbericht* (1 Teil), 1969-1972: Die
Inswerksetzung der Entscheidungen des 1ter Kongresses, n.d.

EO/WVA: *Tätigkeitsbericht* (2 Teil), 1969-1972, n.d.

EO/WVA: *Für Ein Soziales Europa*, second congress, Luxembourg,
16-19 May 1972.

EO/WVA: *Stellungnahmen*
European Social Fund (OE/EX 478), 9 October 1969
Standing Committee on Employment (OE/RES 27 rev.),
23 October 1969.
Erklärung: Standing Committee on Employment (OE/RES 31),
18 December 1969.
Vorschlag Bezüglich einer Arbeitsmöglichkeitspolitik auf

Europäischen Niveau (OE/RES 26), 12 June 1970.
Betreff des Ständigen Beschäftigungsausschusses (OE/RES 27),
23 October 1970.
Bezug auf das Permanente Komitee für die Arbeitsangelegenheit
(OE/RES 31), December 1970.
Ein Antrag in Bezug auf den ESF (OE/RES 33), 11 March 1971.
Blaudrucks für ein Gemeinschaftliches Sozialprogramm (OE/RES
36), 4-5 November 1971.
Erklärung der Europäischen Organisation des WVA im Hinblick
auf die Europäische Gipfelkonferenz (OE/RES 47), September
1972.
Erklärung im Hinblick auf die Kopenhagener Gipfelkonferenz
(OE/RES 58), 4 December 1973.
ETUC: *Constitution* decided by the Constitutional Assembly,
    Brussels, 8 February 1973; amended by the Copenhagen Congress
    (May 1974) and the London Congress (1976).
ETUC: *First Congress Report*, 8 September 1973.
ETUC: *Objectives* 1976-1979. Approved by the Secondary Statutory
    Congress, London, 22-24 April 1976.
ETUC: *Press Release* no.4, 'Views of the European Trade Union
    Confederation on the Question of a Social Action Programme of
    the EC,' 23 May 1973.
ETUC: *Press Release* no.5, 'Who Represents What at Community
    Level?' 18 June 1973.
ETUC: *Proposal* from the European Commission for the Statutes of
    the European Company, 9 July 1974.
ETUC: *Memorandum*, 'A Social Action Programme of the European
    Community,' October 1973.
ETUC: *Resolution* of the London Congress of the ETUC, 22-24 April
    1976, 'Democratisation of the Economy — Multinational Groups of
    Companies,'
ETUC: *Supplement to Report on Activities*, 1973-75, including
    major declarations
    Resolution on Multinational Corporations
    Statement on International Women's Year, July 1975
    Secure Employment — Guaranteed Income, November 1975
    Statement on the Situation in Spain, February 1976.
    ETUC Demands for Company Law Regulations on Multinational
    Groups of Companies, March 1976
Europa '71. Zwanzigstes Europäisches Gespräch in Recklinghausen
    vom EBFG, K. Brankmann Bund-Verlag, Koln-Deutz, 1971.
IBCG: *Informationsbericht*, Satzungen, First Congress of the IBCG,
    Brussels, 7-9 May 1969.

IBFG: Freie Gewerkschaften in der Europäischen Gemeinschaft, *Sechste Generalversammlung: Tätigkeitsbericht*, 1966-1968. The Hague, 23-25 April 1969.

IBFG-IBCG: *Memorandum* zur Ausarbeitung des Einheitsvertrags der Europäischen Gemeinschaft, Luxembourg, 6-7 March 1969.

ICFTU: *Information Bulletin*, bi-monthly, various issues, 1968-1973, Brussels.

ICFTU: *The Multinational Challenge*, ICFTU World Economic Conference Report no.2, Brussels, September 1971.

Labor, various issues, 1968-1973; Generalsekretariat, Internationaler Bund der Christlichen Gewerkschaften (IBCG), Brussels.

OE/CMT: Documents
Declaration concernant la Malaise Sociale dans la CE (OE/RES 32), 11 March 1971.

Prise de Position de l'OE/CMT concernant les Orientations Préliminaires pour un Programme Social Communautaire (OE/RES 36), 4-5 November 1971.

Problèmes et Conditions de l'Emigration en Europe, Belgrade, 24-26 April 1972.

Résolution concernant le Syndicalism Européen (OE/RES 43), 16-19 May 1972.

Prise de Position de l'OE/CMT sur le Problème d'une Politique Sociale Communautaire (OE/RES 49), October 1972.

Position concernant l'Action Sociale des Communautés Européennes, (OE/RES 56), 13 September 1973.

Prise de Position de l'Organisation Européenne de la CMT concernant le Document: 'Les Enterprises Multinationales et la Réglementation Communautaire.' (OE/RES 59), 7 November 1973.

Communication du Répresentant de l'OE/CMT à la Deuxième Conference sur l'Emigration, Istanbul, 7-10 November 1973.

Program of Action for 1971-1975: Consultative body of the NVV-NKV-CNV, Utrecht, n.d.

Employers' Organisations

CEPFAR: 'European Training and Promotion Centre for Farming and Rural Life,' *Statute*, 1972.

CEPFAR: *Action Program* (CE/73&59), 2 July 1973.

COCCEE: *Einfluss des COCCEE auf die Ausarbeitung des sozialen Aktionsprogrammes*, January 1974.

COCCEE: *Ergebnisprotokol der Generalversammlung von OIC und COCCEE*, 17 and 26 April 1973.

COCCEE: *Progress Report*, 1972-1973.

COCCEE: *Stellungnahme*; Gemeinschaftliche Sozialpolitik,
22 March 1973.

COPA: *Prise de Position* du COPA concernant les Orientations
Preliminaires pour un Programme de Politique Sociale
Communautaire, 25 November 1971.

COPA: *Rules of Procedure of COPA*, 11 May 1973.

COPA: *Stellungnahme:* Zum Programm einer Gemeinsamen Sozialpolitik (CQS 73/9), 22 May 1973.

COPA: *Mitteilung* con COPA im Hinblick auf die Dreier Konferenz
uber die Sozialpolitik in der Gemeinschaft (Pr/73 16 rev.)
20 June 1973.

ELC: *Vermerk:* Beschaftigungskonferenz, 20 March 1971.

ELC: *Elaboration de l'Expose sur l'Evolution de la Situation Sociale
dans la Communauté*, 2 June 1971.

ELC: *Orientations Préliminaires pour un Programme de Politique
Sociale Communautaire*, 19 July 1971.

ELC: *Note* sur les Activites en Matiere de Formation Professionnelle
(Doc. 834/71 CPE 19 — Annexe I), 26 August 1971.

ELC: *Note* du Comite de Liaison d'Employeurs sur le Memorandum
du Gouvernement Italien sur la Politique de l'Emploi dans la
Communaute, 27 September 1971.

ELC: *Avis* concernant le Rapprochement des Legislations des Etats
Membres relatives aux Licenciements Collectifs, 9 October 1973.

ELC: *Press Release*, 'Actions Prioritaires du Programme d'Action
Sociale,' 5 December 1973.

UNICE: Documents:
Activity Reports, 1970 and 1971
Die Industriepolitik der Gemeinschaft, 10 September 1970.
Gipfelkonferenz *Resolution* der UNICE, 27 October 1969.
Information Sheet, November 1974.
Memorandum zur Sozialpolitik in der EWG.
Note sur les Activites de l'UNICE au cours de l'Annee 1970.
Stellungnahme der UNICE zum Vorschlag der Kommission an den
Rat über die Reform des ESF. (Amtsblatt vom 13 October 1969),
26 February 1970.
Stellungnahme der UNICE zum Vorschlag eines Statuts für
Europäische Aktiengesellschaften, 12 May 1971.

UNICE: *Zweites Memorandum* der UNICE zur Sozialpolitik in der
Europäischen Gemeinschaft, 11 November 1973.

UNICE: *Joint Press Release*, Brussels, 4 November 1976, US-EEC
Businessmen's Council Third Annual Meeting, 26-27 October 1976.

UNICE: *Press Releases*, Brussels, 25 November 1976:

Memorandum submitted by UNICE on the Occasion of the
Replacement of the EC.
European Industry's Appeal to Governments.

Others

Agence Europe, various issues, 1968-1977.
Council of Ministers, *Neunzehnter Uberblick* über die Tätigkeiten des
  Rates, General Secretariat of the Council of Ministers of the
  European Communities, Brussels, 1 August 1970-31 December 1971.
Council of Ministers, *Press Release* (Presse 154) Session of Council of
  Social Affairs Ministers, 11-12 December 1973.
Council of Ministers, *Press Release* (Presse 115) Conference on
  Future European Social Policy, 16 December 1974.
Council of Ministers, *Twenty-third Review of the Council's Work*,
  1 January-31 December 1975, Office for Official Publications of
  the European Communities, Luxembourg.
ECSC: *Consultative Committee Year Book*: 3 May 1973, 9 July 1974.
  Office for Official Publications of the European Communities,
  Luxembourg.
ESC: *Annual Report of the Economic and Social Committee*, 1968,
  1973, 1974 and 1975.
ESC: *Bulletin* of the Economic and Social Committee, monthly,
  various issues, 1967-77.
ESC: *General Documentation:*
  The Economic and Social Committee, January 1975 (leaflet)
  The Economic and Social Committee, April 1975
  Directory, November 1975.
ESC: *Opinions and Studies:*
  Study of the Educational and Vocational Training Systems in the
  Member States of the EC, Brussels, 13 August 1973.
  Study on the Situation of Small and Medium-sized Undertakings in
  the European Community, March 1975.
  Study on Progress Report on the Common Agricultural Policy,
  February 1975.
  Opinion on European Union, July 1975.
  Opinion on Regional Policy, March 1976.
  Study on Systems of Education and Vocational Training,
  August 1976.
  Study on Research and Development, November 1976.
Future of Social Policy in the European Communities, The,
  International Committee, National Council of Social Service,

199

London, 24 February 1977.

Economist, The, 9 September 1972.

Hauptergebnisse der Arbeits- und Sozialstatistik 1970, Die
Bundesminister für Arbeit und Sozialordnung, Bonn, 1971.

Information 16, 'Labour Management,' Press and Information Office
of the Government of the Federal Republic of Germany, Bonn,
1974.

Latest from Germany: facts, figures, background; series , 1976-77.
Issued by the Embassy of the Federal Republic of Germany,
London.

Observer, The, 'The Bullock Report,' 23 January 1977.

Sozialpolitik in Deutschland, various issues, 1968-1974, distributed
by Bundesministerium für Arbeit und Sozialordnung,
W. Kohlhammer Verlag, Bonn.

Week, The, 18-22 April 1977, DG for Information and PR,
European Parliament, Strasbourg.

Appendix A

Abbreviations

CEEP	Centre Européen de l'Entreprise Publique (European Centre for Public Enterprises)
CEM/WCL	Commission of the European Organisation for Metallurgy in the EC of the World Confederation of Labour
CEPFAR	Centre Européen pour la Promotion et la Formation en Milieu Agricole et Rural (European Training and Promotion Centre for Farming and Rural Life)
CES	French version of ESC
CESL	French version of ECFTU
CFDT	Confédération Française Démocratique du Travail (French Liberal Trade Union)
CFTC	Confédération Française des Travailleurs Chrétiens
CGIL	Confederazione Generale Italiana del Lavoro (Italian Communist Trade Union)
CGT	Confédération Générale du Travail (French Communist Trade Union)
CGT/FO	Confédération Générale du Travail – Force Ouvrière (French Socialist Trade Union)
CIC	Secrétariat Européenne de la Confédération Internationale des Cadres (International Confederation of Executive Staffs)
CISC	French version of WCL
CISL	Confederazione Italiana Sindacati Lavoratori (Italian Social Democrat Trade Union)
CLE	French version of ELC
CNV	Christelijk Nationaal Vakverbond (Netherlands Protestant Trade Union Federation)

CSC	Confédération des Syndicats Chrétiens de Belgique (Belgian Christian Trade Union)
COCCEE	Committee of Commercial Organisations of the EC
COGECA	General Committee of Agricultural Co-operatives of the EC
COPA	Committee of Professional Agricultural Organisations in the EC
CPR	Committee of Permanent Representatives
DAG	Deutsche Angestellten Gewerkschaft (German Trade Union for Executive Staffs)
DGB	Deutscher Gewerkschaftsbund (German Trade Union Federation)
EAGGF	European Agricultural Guarantee and Guidance Fund
EBFG	German version of ECFTU
EC	European Community
ECFTU	European Confederation of Free Trade Unions
ECSC	European Coal and Steel Community
EFA	European Federation of Agricultural Workers' Unions in the Community
EFTA	European Free Trade Area
EFTA/ICFTU	Regional Organisation of the International Confederation of Free Trade Unions for the EFTA countries
EGB	German version of ETUC
EIB	European Investment Bank
ELC	Employers' Liaison Committee
EMB	German version of EMF
EMF	European Metal Trade Union Federation
EO/WCL	European Organisation of the World Confederation of Labour
EO/WVA	German version of EO/WCL
EOM/WCL	European Organisation for the Metal Trade Union of the World Confederation of Labour
ESB	European Social Budget

ESC	Economic and Social Committee
ESF	European Social Fund
ETUC	European Trade Union Confederation
EUROFIET	Trade Union Committee of Employees, Technicians and Supervisory Staffs
FGTB	Fédération Générale du Travail de Belgique (Belgian Social Democrat Trade Union)
IBCG	German version of IFCTU
IBFG	German version of ICFTU
ICFTU	International Confederation of Free Trade Unions
IFCTU	International Federation of Christian Trade Unions (This organisation ceased to exist under its original name after it joined the WCL in 1969).
LO	Landsorganisationen i Danmark (Danish Federation of Trade Unions)
NKV	Nederlands Katholiek Vakverbond (Netherlands Catholic Trade Union Federation)
NVV	Nederlands Verbond van Vakverenigingen (Netherlands Federation of Trade Unions)
OE/CMT	French version of EO/WCL
SCE	Standing Committee on Employment
TUC	British Trade Union Congress
UACEE	Union of Crafts of the EC
UIL	Unione Italiani del Lavoro (Italian Socialist Trade Union)
UNICE	Union of Industries of the EC
WCL	World Confederation of Labour
WFTU	World Federation of Trade Unions

Appendix B

The different forms of workers' participation

The aim of this Appendix is to give a brief view of the various examples of workers' participation. Only those aspects dealing with the running of concerns will be discussed. No mention or description of the various other aspects (e.g. asset formation, co-existence or works' councils of the purely consultative nature, as in Germany) will be made.

Workers' participation seems to have been confined to those countries with a fairly centralised union organisation which is prepared to collaborate with employers. In those countries where unions are opposed, on political grounds, to their economic structure, little progress towards this goal has been made. Let us therefore consider the experiences of West Germany, the Netherlands and Denmark, as well as Britain, where the recently published Bullock Report will be examined.

A very good in-depth examination of this subject has been undertaken by the Commission, under the guiding influence of Commissioner Gundelach, which was published as Supplement 8/75.

West Germany

The most experienced exponents of workers' participation are perhaps the West Germans who have had legislation in this field since 1951.

a)   The Co-determination Law (Mitbestimmungsgesetz) of 1951;

b)   The Co-determination Amendment Law (Mitbestimmungsergänzungsgesetz) of 1956;

c)   Works Constitution Act (Betriebsverfassungsgesetz) of 1952.

The Co-determination Law of 1951 was instigated for companies within the coal and steel industries and was, in part, the result of allied pressure. In essence this Act and the one of 1956 provide for employee representation on a supervisory board equal to that of the employers. Generally the boards have 11 members, although there are provisions for 15 or 21-member boards; however, the method of selecting these members varies with each Act.

1. 1951: All members are appointed by the General Meeting of Shareholders. Four members are appointed by the shareholders without restriction; one other must be appointed who must be independent of the shareholders and so should represent the public interest. Two members can be nominated by the works' council; two more by the various unions involved (e.g. white or blue-collar); one further member may be nominated with the same regard as the independent for the shareholders. Thus there are two equal blocks who may now nominate a neutral eleventh, fifteenth or twenty-first member for election by the shareholders.

The supervisory board may now appoint members of a second tier management board with a proviso that the labour director must be acceptable to the employees who have the right of veto over his dismissal or enstatement. It is this management board that is responsible for the day-to-day operation of the concern.

2. 1956: This Act deals mainly with concerns which have half their components allied to processes involving coal and steel, and has basically the same provisions as the 1951 Act. However, it has the added provision of the 'electors' assembly', which facilitates the selection of members onto the group's main supervisory board. It was this innovation that was the basis of many later proposals on the extension of workers' participation.

3. 1952: This Act was brought in to cover all industries not included in coal and steel, and therefore not covered by the other Acts. Its basic difference lies in the question of shares on the supervisory boards. The Act provides that only one third of the board members should be employee representatives. They are to be elected by all workers and nominations must be made by employees or the works' councils. There is apparently no union influence regarding the Act, but de facto trade unions do have some influence through their union lists of nominated candidates.

There has been considerable pressure to extend the representation of the employees in such companies. In January 1974 Brandt's Social Democratic Government finally succeeded in a compromise solution to extend participation to 50:50. Unlike the 1952 Act, this scheme was to apply to firms with 2,000 employees as opposed to the 500 previously. The major elements, as well as a profit-sharing plan not discussed here, are:

a) Each side is to elect 10 members to the Board;

b) The employees' representatives should have one junior executive;

c) The Chairman of the Board should be elected from within by a two-thirds majority. This is very important because he has a casting vote in any deadlock.

d) If his decision is still not agreed on by both sides, then there is an arbitration process.

The Netherlands

With the spread of managerial capitalism and the ever-increasing autonomy of the management sector, the Netherlands saw the need for some 'countervailing power'. Under the Law of 1971, all firms meeting certain criteria (i.e. capital of 10 million Dutch Guilders, approx. £1.4 million) a constituted works council and at least 100 employees in the Netherlands have to have an appointed board of directors. Shareholders and employees can now influence new board appointments to the same degree. The method used is termed 'co-option' and consists of a system of nominations by the various groups (i.e. shareholders, works' council and management). However, the nominations must consider the following restrictions:

a) No nominee can be in the service of the company;

b) No nominee can be a member of a trade union involved with the company's existence.

However, an important fact is that the board itself may nominate its own choice but the other groups have the right of veto. Although this system does not allow for equal representation, it does allow for at least a voice to be heard and a modicum of influence to be exerted in the selection of the board.

Denmark

The Danish system, proposed in 1973, is perhaps the most far-reaching in its implications for workers' control and ownership. However, only those aspects affecting control will be discussed here.

Much of the pressure for these proposals came from the Danish LO or trade union body. However, the basic provision of only two representatives to the board is only a basis for further expansion with the introduction of the asset formation aspect of the proposals. Perhaps of even more interest is the notion of the representation of the public interest on the management boards, especially in those companies thought to be important to the Danish economy. As stated in the Commission Supplement 8/75, it is already the case in Danish banks, where a representative is appointed by the State.

Like the West German and Dutch systems, the Danes also have a two-tier board system with the supervisory board appointing a management board. However, the board of directors has close links with the management board and this is a two-way exchange. Another twist is that in a few companies the shareholders still maintain their influence over the company via a shareholders' committee, which has the power to hire and fire the directors.

Perhaps it would be worthwhile to look at Norway as well, which has had a form of co-determination since January 1973. It applies to firms with 200 and more employees. Within these companies a 'democratic factory council' must be constituted. This council consists of at least 12 members, one third of whom are elected by the employees. In turn it can elect at least 2 members to the board of the company. The Council must be consulted on several important issues, e.g. rationalisation or reorganisation, before a final board decision is made.

United Kingdom

The UK has been very suspicious of co-determination and until the Labour Government's announcement of 1975, legislating for it in 1976-77, very little has been attempted to effect it voluntarily.

The Labour Government appointed a Commission, chaired by Lord Bullock, to investigate the best system to be adopted, which produced its Report in January 1977. The suggestions in this Report will now be examined.

Perhaps the most striking difference of the Bullock recommendations is the absence of a two-tier board system. The main suggestion is that existing boards will be used as a framework for workers' participation at board level. Companies with more than 2,000 employees will have to adopt equal numbers of workers' and shareholders' representatives, together with a quota of independents, to provide a balance (e.g. bankers, accountants). These latter independent professionals will be paid a fee for their services. The workers' representatives will be chosen through union machinery. The overall arrangement has been termed the $2x + y$ formula, with x's representing the workers and shareholders and y representing the co-opted professionals.

As the size of the undertaking increases, so do the number of directors: — 2,000-1,000 will have $2(4) + 3$; over 2,500 will have $2(7) + 5$. The question of a Chairman remains the same no matter what the size of the company, and initially he should come from the shareholders' representatives because of past experience. However, as the workers' representatives gain experience, the choice could be made on a meritocratic basis in the future. The unions have managed to obtain some degree of influence over the whole question of co-determination. Their argument is that they represent some 80 per cent of the workers in the larger industrial firms and as co-determination seems to be directed towards these companies, so they want their position maintained. The influence mainly involves the election process. They have sole discretion in selecting their quota of directors to the board — the method suggested was that the shop stewards could act as an electoral college and do the selecting among themselves. However, only union members may vote in the elections for directors; but all workers have a vote on the question of the general principles involved in co-determination. In this case there must be an absolute majority of the workforce in favour in order for co-determination to be adopted.

There was disagreement on the subject of the Bullock Commission and a group of members wanted the more European ideas, e.g. two-tier boards, universal elections for worker-members, to be recommended. They thought that the unions had too great an influence without the backing of all workers. Perhaps the eagerness for co-determination can be seen by the inclusion of a provision for ballots to determine whether co-determination, once adopted, is such a good thing after five years. If there is a one-third minority that want it stopped, then the principle can be discarded.

On the other hand, the establishment of an Industrial Democracy Commission as an information and aid service for workers' participation would indicate some acceptance of the ideas involved. This body would also act as an arbitrator on disagreements between the various factions on the boards or those wishing to seek positions on the boards.